T0323888

'Drawing on literature, research, scripture and ancient tradition and philosophy, Peter takes us on a journey that deepens our understanding and embodiment of beauty. He urges us to see how beauty comes into being in relationship, and shows us in practical and elegant ways how we can bring beauty into our own relationships as coaches and leaders – for the transformation of those with whom we work, for our own agency and for a better world.'

Dr Hilary Lines, *Executive and Systemic Team Coach, Leadership Consultant, Supervisor and Author; Founder, Touchpoint Leadership Ltd*

'Amid an ego-centric world caught up in its own dysfunctional digitized distraction, Professor Peter Hawkins provides a clarion call, a deep coherent call to action in leadership and beyond. Bringing his vast leadership experience and polymath mind to bear on the vitally important – yet seldom explored in leadership circles – soul-virtue of beauty Hawkins discloses, indeed activates, a transformation in leadership consciousness that might just save our humanity from the meta-crisis of its own making. Beautifully written and researched, *Beauty in Leadership and Coaching* is a wise and urgent text. This is a must-read for future-fit leaders and practitioners interested in shifting from ego-centric to life-centric living and leading.'

Giles Hutchins, *Leadership Coach and Author of* Leading by Nature *(2022) and* Nature Works *(2024)*

'John Keats described the loss of awe at a rainbow as reducing it to "the dull catalogue of common things". Our capacity for wonder, for feeling small against the beauty and majesty of the cosmos, is what makes us fully human. Here is a reminder of what it means to rediscover the beauty that resides within and around us – and what we need to do to sustain it.'

Professor David Clutterbuck, *Special Ambassador European Coaching and Mentoring Council*

'*Beauty in Leadership and Coaching* is Hawkins' opus magnus. The book ranges across a vast territory of human history and human ideas, identifying the challenges humanity faces in a globalised industrial age, before offering insights on ways we can create a more sustainable consciousness, which connects people with each other and with the only planet humanity will ever call home. If you are seeking a guidebook for seeing and experiencing the world around us in ways we have forgotten, this is it.'

Professor Jonathan Passmore, *Henley Business School and EZRA Coaching*

'This astounding book is dedicated to nurturing highly-skilled, beautiful leaders and coaches – and it does this with grace and profound depth – but it does more than that. It is an education in being human. It has the power to nurture the beautiful in all of us. Peter Hawkins offers us here the great harvest of his life – as brilliant teacher, psychotherapist, systems thinker, world-class leader, and humble gardener. His vast reading and erudition are met on every page by his empathy and humanness. Open this book anywhere and you'll find yourself enlightened by insights you didn't know you knew, vistas of the beautiful, the good, and the true that will enliven your work and your life. Once you've read it, I promise, you'll be thankful.'

Elias Amidon, *Spiritual Director (Pir) of the Sufi Way,*
Author, International Spiritual Teacher
and Ecologist

'I am delighted to endorse *Beauty in Leadership and Coaching* by Prof. Peter Hawkins, a luminary systemic thinker whose new book tackles global challenges through the lens of evolved consciousness. His insightful analysis of how our narrowed perceptions have led to today's crises is both compelling and enlightening. Peter advocates for a systemic change in leadership and coaching, promoting a connection to beauty, truth, and goodness. This book is essential for anyone seeking accessible and soulful wisdom to navigate and lead through these incredibly complex times.'

Dr Catherine Carr, *Co-author of* High Performance
Team Coaching *and* 50 Tips for Terrific Teams

'As I read this beautiful book, I let out a sigh of relief many times and felt deep gratitude for this personal, impassioned plea to us all to reconnect with our purpose and fall in love again with the wider world around us, laying out a path to heal the split between the human and more-than-human world, to be in service of, and have reverence for, life. It is a book full of wisdom, poetry, helpful practice, apposite quotes and stories – It is a gift.'

Eve Turner, *Multi-award-winning Author, Researcher, Master*
Executive Coach and Supervisor, Co-founder of the Climate Coaching
Alliance, Founder of the Global Supervisors' Network, Former Chair,
APECS (Association for Professional Executive Coaching
and Supervision)

'Peter stands on the shoulders of philosophical giants and gives us a beautiful synthesis of centuries of wisdom on Beauty, Grace and Truth. Awakened in me a thirst to seek Beauty in all aspects of life. Peter eloquently challenges the orthodox coaching boundaries and aligns with my Gestalt principles which encourages us to engage deeply with our coachees with love and Beauty. To move from being an empathetic observer to a "fully embodied participant.'''

John Leary-Joyce, *Founder and CEO of the Academy of Executive Coaching and Leading Gestalt Coach and Author*

'This ground breaking book addresses the many inter-connected challenges of our time, and how crucial it is for coaches and leaders to pave the way in shifting human consciousness. Peter Hawkins provides practical ways leaders and coaches can work together to bring new ways of thinking, perceiving, doing, and being. I encourage all leaders and coaches to read it.'

Dr Marshall Goldsmith *is the Thinkers50 #1 Executive Coach and New York Times Bestselling Author of* The Earned Life, Triggers, *and* What Got You Here Won't Get You There

'Hawkins invites leaders and coaches to embrace a radical transformation in consciousness, recognizing themselves as a part of a global family and integral to the broader ecological framework. Using beauty as a guide, he weaves a mixture of storytelling, philosophical depth, and poetics to lead readers through a thought-provoking journey, advocating for a more expansive sense of self that allows us to live in our world in a way that is "future-fit" rather than finding ourselves trapped in old narratives and ways of thinking that inhibits the new emerging. Provocative and powerful – a must read! Great writing, compelling read, so needed.'

Pam McLean, *Founder and ex CEO of the Hudson Coaching School California*

'Peter Hawkins has seen all the seasons across the leadership and coaching industries over many decades. This book expresses his deep insight and profound appreciation of beauty, with a capital B, that is to be found at the heart of this work. Highly recommended!'

Dr Marc Kahn, *Chief Strategy & Sustainability Officer, Investec Plc*

'Peter's book offers a refreshing holistic approach to systemic coaching, emphasizing not only the functional aspects of leadership but also the significant roles of ethics and aesthetics. This blend makes his work a unique and invaluable contribution to the field. Peter's accumulated wisdom is in it!'

Dr Frank Quante, *CEO Fraport Bulgaria*

'In an era where leadership is as much about beauty and consciousness as it is about decision-making, *Beauty in Leadership and Coaching* emerges as a timely masterpiece, intricately weaving the complexities of modern challenges with the transformative power of coaching. With a keen understanding of the evolving landscape of work, Peter eloquently argues that leadership in the new world is not merely a scientific endeavor but an art form enriched by deep, systemic human connections. Each chapter, invites you, the reader to reflect on not just the role of beauty in leadership, but its essentiality in fostering meaningful relationships and ethical practices in an increasingly transient world. For anyone looking to navigate the complexities of modern leadership with grace and systemic insight, *Beauty in Leadership and Coaching* is an indispensable guide. It doesn't just educate; it inspires a much-needed transformation in our perception of the roles of beauty, love, and truth in our professional lives. This book is a call to action for all who aspire to lead, coach, and create with beauty at the forefront of their endeavours.'

Jan Sipsma, *Head of Strategy and People GHD*

'With his new focus on Beauty, based on what he calls inter-poiesis, Peter Hawkins shapes a new paradigm for leadership and coaching that only can exist as a co-created endeavour and a perpetual becoming. This book is for readers who are aware of a world suffering from a shortage of our love.'

Reinhard Stelter, PhD, *Professor of Coaching Psychology at the University of Copenhagen*

Beauty in Leadership and Coaching

Written by best-selling author and global thought leader Peter Hawkins, *Beauty in Leadership and Coaching* explores how leaders and coaches can contribute to the urgent task to transform human consciousness to address the great interconnected challenges of our times.

Building on a growing interest in ecologically conscious leadership and coaching, as well as the role that poetry, story and beauty can play to transform our work, this book creates a space for both inspiration and reflection, moving beyond seeing the climate crisis and the other major global challenges as a problem to be solved towards an attitude of learning and partnering with the human and the more-than-human world.

Globally and transculturally inclusive, this book will appeal to leaders, coaches, organizational development consultants and managers throughout the world, who aspire to grow and develop in their practice and make a greater contribution to the challenges we now face.

Peter Hawkins, PhD, is Founder and Chairman of Renewal Associates and Emeritus Professor of Leadership at Henley Business School. He is a leading consultant, writer and researcher in organizational transformation, leadership and leadership development and an international thought leader and best-selling author in systemic coaching, systemic team coaching and leadership teams.

Beauty in Leadership and Coaching

And Its Role in Transforming Human Consciousness

Peter Hawkins

Routledge
Taylor & Francis Group

LONDON AND NEW YORK

Designed cover image: Getty Images

First published 2025
by Routledge
4 Park Square, Milton Park, Abingdon, Oxon OX14 4RN

and by Routledge
605 Third Avenue, New York, NY 10158

Routledge is an imprint of the Taylor & Francis Group, an informa business

British Library Cataloguing-in-Publication Data
A catalogue record for this book is available from the British Library

Library of Congress Cataloging-in-Publication Data
Names: Hawkins, Peter, 1950– author.
Title: Beauty in leadership and coaching : and its role in transforming
  human consciousness / Peter Hawkins.
Identifiers: LCCN 2024032730 (print) | LCCN 2024032731 (ebook) |
  ISBN 9781032394145 (hardback) | ISBN 9781032394138 (paperback) |
  ISBN 9781003349600 (ebook)
Subjects: LCSH: Leadership—Philosophy. | Executive coaching—Philosophy.
Classification: LCC HM1261 .H394 2025 (print) | LCC HM1261 (ebook) |
  DDC 303.3/4—dc23/eng/20240730
LC record available at https://lccn.loc.gov/2024032730
LC ebook record available at https://lccn.loc.gov/2024032731

ISBN: 978-1-032-39414-5 (hbk)
ISBN: 978-1-032-39413-8 (pbk)
ISBN: 978-1-003-34960-0 (ebk)

DOI: 10.4324/9781003349600

Typeset in Times New Roman
by Apex CoVantage, LLC

To all those who are working at the leading edge
to help evolve human consciousness.

Contents

Acknowledgements

A bow of enormous gratitude to my contemporary teachers in Beauty: Elias Amidon, Judy Ryde, Piero Ferrucci, François Cheng, John O'Donohue.

And to my teachers – the poets and philosophers of the past whose teachings are ever-living: Jesus, Mevlana Rumi, William Blake, Lao Tsu, Samuel Taylor Coleridge, Hafiz, William Shakespeare, Rilke, Dante, Plotinus, Rabindranath Tagore, Hazrat Inayat Khan.

I am indebted beyond measure to both groups for greatly enriching my life, work and writing.

A big thank you to those who have made writing the book possible: Anna Wilson, for copyediting and checking references and permissions; Jo Ellis, Julie Jeffery and Natalie Bearman for keeping my work organized and at bay while I was writing. Also, to many people who have read and commented on early drafts of the chapters including Peter Binns, Malcolm Parlett, Jeremey Young Elias Amidon and others. Your feedback has been of great value to maturing the book.

To my children and grandchildren, and to Judy who is my soul companion on so many levels, you all will always have an important place in my heart, and I hope one day my children and grandchildren will all read this book written from my heart.

Welcome

Welcome to this book and thank you for beginning to read it. Without you, this book would not exist. Readers co-create books in the same way the listeners co-create a talk and the audience a play. Without the encouragement of previous readers, I would lack sufficient courage to embark on such an awe-full challenge of undertaking the endeavour to write a book on Beauty and the challenges of our current world. Without courage, the book would be a terrible act of hubris, rather than coming from a courageous heart, for it is in our heart that courage resides, but it is a muscle we cannot build alone.

Before you begin reading, please let me ask: How many times have you checked your phone or computer for messages, posts on X, emails or other notifications in the last 24 hours? Please write your answer down. Now ask yourself: In the last 24 hours, how many moments of beauty, awe or wonder have you engaged in – moments that went beyond seeing, hearing, touching, smelling or tasting something pleasing; moments that awakened a depth response within you? Please write down both the number and what these moments were.

Now compare the two numbers. Unless you are fortunate to be reading this book on holiday or on retreat, for most of us, the first number will be much greater than the second. Is this ratio or balance one that you want to have or need to have in your life? If not, please write down what you would like the ratio to be between these two numbers.

If you have a felt hunger to engage more with beauty, awe and wonder, then this book is for you. It is fundamentally a book of healing, at all levels: from the personal, making whole our relationship with our self; through the relational, in how we engage with others, including our loved ones, families, colleagues, teams, organizations and communities; to how we engage with the 'more-than-human' world that surrounds us and flows through us. Throughout this book, I have used the term 'more-than-human', which I learnt from David Abram (1996), to counteract how when we talk about 'nature', 'the environment' and 'the ecology', we make the larger world we are nested within something 'other', something separate from us, rather than a world we are inextricably part of and totally dependent upon, and which in turn is part of us and flows through us, with every

DOI: 10.4324/9781003349600-1

breath we breathe, through everything that flows through the windows of our senses and the food and drink that sustains our living. The exploration of how we heal the destructive split between the human and the more-than-human world at large is at the heart of this book, as I believe this split is at the root of the great challenges that our Earth is currently facing.

Those of you who have read one or more of my earlier books may be surprised by the nature of this one. It is unapologetically more philosophical, poetic and spiritual than my earlier, more practical books, although many of those also had a number of passages which were both spiritual and philosophical. The reason for this turn is that the change now required in our much-challenged world is bigger and more complex than can be responded to with just more knowledge, skill and technique, drawn from what are increasingly narrow, siloed fields of study. As I argue in this book, the world's major challenges are all products of collective human action, which have arisen from the human ways of thinking and being, deeply rooted in the now globally dominant hegemony of modernist ways of perceiving and thinking about the world. Without a change in our fundamental ontologies and epistemologies (ways of conceiving of the nature of our being and ways of knowing the world), in the words of Gregory Bateson (1972), 'we do not have a snowball in hell's chance' of addressing the global challenges ranging from climate emergency, pollution and loss of biodiversity to growing global inequality, mass migration and increasing mental illness. (These are all outlined in Chapter 1.)

James Hillman (2001: 265) points out:

> below the ecological crisis lies the deeper crisis of love, that our love has left the world. That the world is loveless results directly from the repression of beauty, its beauty and our sensitivity to beauty. For love to return to the world, beauty must first return, else we love the world only as moral duty.

Our love has turned inward and become narcissism, which Hillman (2001) suggests is a 'beauty disorder'. So writing and reading this book is not a dilettante aesthetic diversion but an urgent medicine for the fatal illness of our times and a clarion call for a new depth engagement to the wider world beyond our self.

The book is also somewhat autobiographical and personal. All books, and indeed research papers, are autobiographical, as what authors write is always filtered through the specifics of their life, culture and context. However, in most writing, this is hidden, whereas in this book, I have chosen the path of greater transparency. Also, my hope is that being clear about my own engagement will provide an easier access, for you the reader, to what are quite complex and challenging ideas, foreign to much of the current ways of thinking we in the white Western world have nearly all been schooled in.

The 'white Western world' is another term I use in this book. It is a term that is both limited and problematic, but I use it to describe the dominant way of thinking that developed in the European world, which became turbo-charged by the three 'Cs' of the Industrial Revolution – coal, capitalism and colonization – and then took root in the countries taken by force and settled by the European expansionists, particularly in the Americas, Africa, Asia and Australasia. Its growth into becoming the dominant global hegemony has been furthered by economic and cultural colonization through Western global companies, such as Disney, McDonald's, Apple, Microsoft, Amazon and Netflix, and indeed some talk of the 'Disneyfication of the world', to describe this phenomenon. In using it, I want not only to recognize this historical process, in both its light and dark aspects, but also to recognize that there are many other human cultural traditions and ways of living in the world, which have longer, richer and deeper roots, including those of many indigenous communities. Throughout this book, I have included learnings from indigenous communities, as well as from pre-modernity thinkers and writers, who can help us see the limited and dangerous lenses through which we, the dominant peoples of this planet, have come to view the world.

I have also, throughout the book, often written Beauty with a capital B, where I have wanted to distinguish Beauty not just as an object of human perception but also as an archetype and active process in life in its own right. Beauty as a subjectivity, not relegated to being just an adjective of our objects. I have applied the same convention to a few of Beauty's partners that are archetypes with their own power, such as Truth, Goodness and Grace.

This book, however, is situated beyond the personal and beyond the philosophical, in the current global challenges of our time. We will explore these challenges in Chapter 1 and how these are not only all interconnected but also symptoms of a much deeper challenge – that of our human consciousness, which is the cause of these challenges, and thus not fit for addressing and resolving them.

In Chapter 2, I trace the origins of the consciousness of modernity and its descent into left-brain, atomized, linear, rational and individualized ways of thinking and acting. Then in Chapter 3, I map out a possible return journey and how Beauty can be the guide on this quest. In Chapter 4, I link this return journey to the world's urgent need for new leadership at all levels – in our governments, communities and organizations – and how this requires a new paradigm for both leadership and coaching.

Part 2 is a deeper exploration of 'Awakening to Beauty' in its many guises. Each chapter shows different stages and aspects of this journey: how Beauty opens the door to Love (Chapter 5); how she can introduce us to her two sisters in the family of 'verities': Truth (Chapter 6) and Goodness (Chapter 7). From Goodness, we explore the important role of Ethics (Chapter 8) and how the ethics that are so needed in the world are an ethics that goes way beyond the human-centric ethics of the past and are expanded to embrace the whole living planet. An ethics that has an ecological aesthetics at its heart.

The exploration of aesthetics takes us into Chapter 9, to 'The Beauty of Death and Transience', to find Beauty not just in the budding and blooming of a flower but also in the falling of its petals, the forming of its seed heads and the releasing of its seeds to the wind. A beauty that transcends the duality of life and death. Then in Chapter 10, on Beauty and Grace, we explore four aspects of Grace: gifting, gratitude and graceful and aesthetic grace.

Having awakened to Beauty in so many ways, in Part 3, we focus on 'Doing the Beautiful', first in the 'Art of Leadership' (Chapter 11) and then in the 'Art of Coaching' (Chapter 12). These practices are then more deeply developed in Chapter 13 on the 'Beauty of the Space Between and the Marriage of Opposites' and how we can move beyond dualistic, oppositional ways of thinking and relating to discover the triangulating and coming-together of opposites to co-create and give birth to that which is new. Then we move to 'Co-creating Beauty', through relating and conversing poetically (Chapter 14): co-creating a dialogue of inter-poiesis so we can discover, relationally and inter-subjectively, new ways of knowing and co-creating through a new poetic language that emerges between us.

We end with 'Becoming the Beautiful' (Chapter 15) – how to take the teachings of this book into your life, leadership and coaching and how you can, as Mevlana Rumi entreats us, 'Let the beauty you love be the beauty you do', for this book describes just a few of the 'hundreds of ways you can kneel and kiss the earth' (Amidon, 2011).

Thomas Traherne, the 17th-century English metaphysical poet, tells the story of Amasis, sometimes described as the last great Pharaoh of Egypt, who asked the wise men of Greece what was the most beautiful thing in the world. Their answer came back as follows:

> The World. The world certainly being so beautiful that nothing visible is capable of more. Were we to see it only once, the first appearance would amaze us. But being daily seen, we observe it not.
>
> (Traherne, 1908)

Our awe has become blunted and dulled, our joy and delight in embodied and sensuous participation in this beautiful world has diminished, and our ability to love and be loved has also declined.

This book is a guidebook for seeing and experiencing the world around us in ways we have forgotten. On this journey, we will be assisted by multiple guides and hear from many different voices more important than mine. But even more important than their individual voices is the Beauty of the spaces between them and the new harmony they can co-create (see Chapter 13). My hope is that by interweaving voices from different perspectives, cultures and human history, we can discover a deeper pattern that connects – one that is needed to face the great challenges of our times.

My hope is that rather than fall in love with the many quotes that are scattered through this book, you will fall in love with what they are collectively pointing to and that this love will make a difference in your life and what you do in the world. Certainly, as I have written this book over the last three years, I have discovered more Beauty in every aspect of the world around me, and my love for life in all its many forms has greatly deepened. My hope is that reading this book will have the same benefit for you.

In Chapter 5, I quote Andreas Weber (2017: xiv) saying: 'the earth is currently suffering from a shortage of our love'. My hope is that this book will help you fall in love again with the wider world around you, and that in doing so, you will discover how the wider ecology has been loving you in so many ways that you and I have stopped noticing.

Part 1

The challenges of our times and what is required in the transformation of human consciousness

Chapter 1

The great challenges of our time

Introduction

Never in known history has humanity been so challenged and so interconnected.

In this opening chapter, I will provide a brief overview of the great challenges of our current times. I will then explore how these challenges are not problems that can be solved by techno-scientific solutions or by governments acting alone or in parallel to each other – for these challenges are, by their very nature, global and interdependent. Nor can they be solved by the human thinking that has created them and of which they can be seen as both symptoms and unintended consequences. These challenges are also the price the world is now having to pay for the great benefits the privileged world has received from the industrial, scientific and technological development of the last 300 years.

The great leap forward – or is it?

It is 1969. I sit with my mother, watching on television the first human beings to leave our earthbound existence and land on the moon. As he leaves his space capsule, Neil Armstrong utters the famous words: 'One small step for man, one giant leap for mankind'. Shortly afterwards, like many explorers and colonialists before him, he proudly plants and salutes his country's flag. As I watch the television, I become aware of our own family's great leap forward. I look around our house and reflect that, 15 years earlier, within my own memory, we had no television, no fridge, no washing machine or tumble drier, no stereo, no central heating, no car, no foreign holidays. In 1969, my brother, like many of our cousins, has gone to university, and I will shortly follow. Like many, we will be the first generation in our family to do so. We are experiencing our own 'great leap forward' – in the words of Harold Macmillan, the UK Prime Minister from 1957 to 1963, 'we have never had it so good'.

We are riding the wave of exponential growth that started two to three hundred years previously in the white Western world, with the coming-together of three major revolutionary forces. We could call the period the Age of Science,

DOI: 10.4324/9781003349600-3

or the Age of Carbon, or the Age of Capital. All would be correct but only show one side of the pyramid that these three forces rapidly built together. In our history books, it was called the Industrial Revolution, and I studied how rapidly the United Kingdom moved from a predominantly agricultural and trading economy to an industrial economy.

This was made possible by accessing vast amounts of carbon-based energy from the earth beneath us – first in the form of coal, then later in the form of gas and oil. This fueled the Iron and Steam Ages and the ability to produce and transport goods using newly invented machines – steam pumps, ships and trains, then later, motor cars and airplanes. Mills that previously ground wheat and corn into flour, and used local wind and water energy, were replaced by large, mechanized and carbon-fueled factories – what the poet William Blake (1968a) termed 'Satanic Mills' – producing manufactured goods.

Thousands of people left the countryside to find new employment in the factories of the newly industrialized and rapidly expanding cities. To build the factories, grow the cities, create the new forms of transport – first by canals and ships, then by trains – took large amounts of up-front investment of speculative money. Shareholder capitalism was born to meet this challenge. Fortunes were quickly won and lost, as people invested in each of the possible next 'leaps forward' in new products, new forms of production and transport and new markets.

The marriage of capital, carbon and scientific ingenuity was a three-way 'marriage made in heaven' – or so it seemed. None of the three could have been so successful without the others. The approach gradually became globally dominant, and even the Marxist-based revolutions in Russia and China gave way to a form of state capitalism, financing rapid carbon mining and industrialization across the USSR and China – the latter of which led to the starvation and death of many Chinese people living in the countryside.

The Industrial Age moved from steam to electricity, from mechanical machines to computers, from trains to planes and from post and telephones to instant digital communication, networked around the World Wide Web. This, in turn, is developing into the internet of things, where our phones, televisions, cars, heating systems and so on can all 'talk' to each other.

The age of exponential and unlimited growth was fueled by the dream that, with unlimited energy, we can command and control at the flick of a switch and the turn of a dial and that with the constant invention of labour-saving devices and medical breakthroughs, everybody would soon be living long, healthy lives of serviced leisure, with unlimited choice and opportunity. A small percentage of the human population still lives this dream, and millions more still believe in it. In *Abundance*, Diamandis and Kotler (2014) present a world that is getting better and better; and Fukuyama (2020) confidently writes about the end of history, as we humans have succeeded and arrived.

If we zoom the lens of our perspective further out and look at these 300 years not just as an aberration but also as having their roots much deeper in human history and evolution, we can see them as the result of long-developed human ingenuity that carbon, capitalism, colonization and science had helped greatly to accelerate. So let us step back and look through a long-time lens at ourselves as a species.

We human beings have always been good at solving problems – you could even say we are addicted to problem-solving. After a day's work, we might travel home with our brains immersed in a sudoku, Nerdle, Wordle, crosswords or other puzzles. We like, or even crave, puzzles that have neat solutions, that provide a sense of completion and achievement.

We human beings are good at adapting to different ecological niches. Over our relatively short time on this planet (far less than 1% of the Earth's existence), different human groups have found ways of thriving not just on the wide-open savanna of Africa but also in dense tropical forests of the Amazon, Indonesia and Central Africa; in the high, cold mountain valleys of the Himalayas; the arid deserts of the Sahara, Mongolia and Utah; the Arctic tundra; and many places in between.

We human beings have become successful at extracting and exploiting the many gifts and resources our planet has to offer – from hunting, trapping, fishing or corralling nearly all our fellow species of the land, sea and air for our food, use and enjoyment; to commandeering the precious, thin layer of topsoil so it produces greater amounts of human food; to mining the deep mineral resources in the rocks beneath us for weapons, fuel, shelter and adornment.

We humans have become good at exponential growth in expanding the size of our species. Between 1830 and 1930, we doubled the world's population from 1 billion to 2 billion. Between 1930 and 2023, we have quadrupled the human population from 2 billion to 8 billion. We have become super-clever at reducing child mortality and keeping humans alive for longer while at the same time creating mass extinction in so many other life-forms right across our biosphere.

We humans are the first species to have created its own geological age – the 'Anthropocene' – where most other animals are dependent on us for their survival. And we are the first species to fundamentally change the atmosphere, the hydrosphere and the lithosphere, all at the same time.

So if you believe in 'materialistic neo-Darwinian' notions of the 'selfish gene' and survival of the fittest, there is only one winner – it is us!

And we are not finished yet. Harari (2016), in his brilliant book *Homo Deus,* shows how the most privileged beneficiaries of human successful exploitation of this Earth, not satisfied with winning this competition, want to conquer space (live on Mars for starters!). Their next goal is to conquer death, through a mixture of extending life expectancy, replacing failing organs with intelligent implants, using plastic surgery to preserve the image of eternal youth and cryogenics so we are ready for resurrection.

In our hubris and rush to win every competition, we have failed to see our own willful blindness, as we bought the lie that we were playing a zero-sum game of winners and losers. 'Everyone taught us it was all about winning, so what do we do now?' we cry.

We have discovered the footprint of our enemy, the one predator that humans still have left but failed to recognize: the footprint is our own.

Nobody taught us that win-lose always turns into lose-lose, or as Gregory Bateson (1972: 457) said:

> It is now empirically clear that Darwinian evolutionary theory contained a very great error in its identification of the unit of survival under natural selection. The unit which was believed to be crucial and around which the theory was set up was either the breeding individual or the family line or the sub-species or some similar homogeneous set of conspecifics. Now I suggest that the last hundred years have demonstrated empirically that if an organism or aggregate of organisms sets to work with a focus on its own survival and thinks that that is the way to select its adaptive moves, its 'progress' ends up with a destroyed environment. If the organism ends up destroying its environment, it has in fact destroyed itself. And we may very easily see this process carried to its ultimate *reductio ad absurdum* in the next twenty years. The unit of survival is not the breeding organism, or the family line, or the society.

But are we learning? Yes, we are beginning to see the bitter litany of ecological damage that we have wrought out of our solipsistic selfishness. Are we capable of responding? Or does our very survival, and that of life on our now human-dependent planet, require a new way of thinking, learning and being?

The great challenges

Many people find that listening to, or reading, the 'dreadful' litany of challenges we humans have created in this beautiful world we inhabit creates dread, overwhelms, depresses, shames or even leads them to despair. This, in turn, can lead them to willful blindness or denial and diminish their ability to respond (see Whybrow et al., 2023). However, if we are collectively to find ways of responding to the crisis and the challenges of our times, we need to face these challenges with our eyes wide open and listen not only to what the science is telling us but also to what nature and the whole ecology is screaming at us. As Amson-Bradshaw (2019) says:

> The scale of the threats to the biosphere and all its lifeforms – including Humanity – is in fact so great that it is difficult to grasp for even well informed experts . . . what political or economic system, or leadership, is prepared to handle the predicted disasters, or even capable of such action?

1   Climate emergency

Currently this is the most talked-about challenge, but the talking and action by governments, scientists and the media is both too little and quite late: we have known about greenhouse gasses and the warming of our planet for decades, and we are still changing far too slowly.

The planet's average surface temperature has risen about 1.8 degrees Fahrenheit (1.01 degrees Celsius) since 1880 (NASA, 2022a), a change driven largely by increased carbon dioxide (CO_2) emissions into the atmosphere. Most of the warming has occurred in the past 40 years, with the seven most recent years being the warmest. 2016 and 2020 are the warmest years on record (NASA, 2022b). The Paris and Glasgow UN Climate Change Conferences agreed we needed to stay below 1.5% Celsius temperature rise from preindustrial levels, but currently, we are on track for a rise of approximately 3% by the turn of the century. To avoid a catastrophic climate crisis, we need, at the very least, to halve carbon emissions by 2030 and get to zero emissions by 2050 – but hardly any countries are currently implementing realistic plans for achieving this.

2   Pollution

We generate around 300 million tonnes of plastic waste each year, 60% of which ends up in our natural environment or landfill. Plastic pollution is currently one of the biggest problems affecting the marine environment, with an estimated 8 million tonnes of plastic entering the ocean annually. Roughly 40% of the ocean's surface is now covered in plastic debris, and if our plastic consumption continues, it is estimated that by 2050, there will be more plastic than fish in the ocean.

Since the beginning of the Industrial Revolution, the acidity of surface ocean waters has increased by about 30% (NOAA, 2022). This increase is the result of humans emitting more CO_2 into the atmosphere and, hence, more CO_2 being absorbed into the ocean. The ocean has absorbed between 20% and 30% of total anthropogenic CO_2 emissions in recent decades (7.2 billion to 10.8 billion metric tonnes per year) (NASA, 2022b). At the same time, the oceans are getting to the limits of what they can absorb.

3   Loss of biodiversity

Kolbert (2015) showed how 'One-third of corals, freshwater molluscs, sharks, and rays, one-fourth of all mammals, one-fifth of all reptiles, and one-sixth of all birds are heading towards extinction'. In less than 50 years, the population of mammals, birds, amphibians and fish has dropped by a staggering 68% (Polman and Winston, 2021: 14). We are in the sixth mass extinction – around 200 species become extinct every single day – and 1 million are on a path to extinction (United Nations, 2019). Whole branches of the tree of life are being broken off or burnt.

4   Soil erosion

One of the most critical ecological elements is fertile topsoil, which provides the home for billions of small and micro, organisms and the basis for the growth of plants and trees. I enjoy taking people down to the compost heaps in my garden, asking them to hold in their hands the black-gold of rich compost and then telling them that there are more organisms held in their hands than people living on this Earth (Wilson, 2018).

The world grows 95% of its food in the uppermost layer of soil, making topsoil the most important component of the human food system. The World Wide Fund for Nature (WWF) has estimated that due to conventional farming practices, nearly half of the most productive soil in the world has disappeared in the last 150 years (WWF, 2022). Each year, an estimated 24 billion tonnes of fertile soil are lost due to erosion. That's 3 tonnes lost every year for every person on the planet (Global Agriculture, 2022). Cosier (2019) has shown how this will drastically affect crop yields and contribute to nutrient pollution, dead zones and further erosion. She also shows how in the US, soil on cropland is eroding ten times faster than it can be replenished (Cosier, 2019). Maria-Helena Semedo of the UN's Food and Agriculture Organization suggests that if we continue to degrade the soil at the rate we are doing now, the world could run out of topsoil in about 60 years (Cosier, 2019).

5   Widening inequality

In 1960, the average CEO earned 20 times more than the average worker in their company. Today, they earn 271 times more than the average worker. The growing gap between rich and poor has become even greater in the last ten years, when the richest 1% of the population has captured around half of the new global wealth. Since 2020, this same 1% has amassed nearly two-thirds of the $42 trillion in newly created wealth, nearly twice as much money as gained by the remaining 99%. Currently, in 2023, the collective wealth of the world's super-rich is increasing by $2.7 billion a day (Bucher, 2023). As Ghandhi so aptly put it, 'Earth provides enough to satisfy every man's need but not any man's greed' (quoted in Gupta, 2015).

This wealth is allowing the super-rich to fund and control media and political parties and acquire enormous power and influence in the world, whether that be in so-called Western 'democracies', the growing economies of countries like Brazil and India or in the state capitalism of Russia and China. The super-rich predominantly want politics of low tax, government subsidies of innovation and employment and smaller state provision of social benefit and services. Bucher (2023) calculates that in the next five years, the world's governments are planning spending cuts of $7.8 trillion dollars. Increasing inequality in wealth is creating even greater inequality in power. This, in turn, is leading to further extraction and exploitation of natural resources.

6 Migration

The number of human migrants has been growing steadily. According to the United Nations, in 2020, migrants made up 3.5% of the global population, compared to 2.8% in 2000 and 2.3% in 1980 (https://www.un.org/en/global-issues/migration). However, it is predicted that this will now grow exponentially, due to both growing inequality and climate-change-induced floods, storms, forest fires and droughts. These are all increasing each year and are already making people homeless and hungry and furthering ecological migration.

In this century, 'An estimated one to three billion people will become climate refugees' (Polman and Winston, 2021: 14). Already, many countries are putting up barriers to stop people trying to enter their countries – people fleeing their own countries because of poverty, climate change, oppression or warfare – and there is a lack of international cooperation to address this growing challenge. Climate-driven migration is also giving rise to increasingly authoritarian governments – as attested by, for example, the recent coups in sub-Saharan Africa.

7 Increasing mental distress

'Stress is the global health epidemic of the 21st century' (WHO, 2023) – with more people on antidepressants than any other form of medical treatment and many leaders at all levels reporting stress and burnout. The Gallup Global Emotions Report 2023 showed that 40% of people reported feeling stressed and another 41% a lot of worry. The World Health Authority 2023 report on mental health found that 21% of adults are experiencing at least one mental illness, with 5.44% experiencing severe mental illness. The predominant mental health problem worldwide is depression, followed by anxiety, but 55% of mental health issues remain untreated. Depressive disorders also contribute to the likelihood of suicide as well as heart disease; hence, they have both a direct and an indirect impact on length and quality of life.

Over 12.1 million adults (4.8%) have reported serious thoughts of suicide, and in 2020, there were 93,300 overdose deaths in the USA alone (NSS Behavioural Health, 2023). We are in the first century where more young people between 18 and 40 are dying from suicide than from all wars and murder put together. The enemy is within.

So why, when the human species is getting richer, healthier and more resourced, is mental illness becoming more prevalent and happiness not increasing? In the book I wrote with my wife (Hawkins and Ryde, 2020), we suggested that there are four main factors that go some way to explaining this.

- Psychological overload: the sheer amount of fragmented data and images we are processing every day is overwhelming our ability to integrate what we absorb.

- The conscious or unconscious registering of ecological devastation: in a number of countries, eco-anxiety is now recognized as a prevalent form of mental distress.
- The fragmentation of the psychological containers in and through which we psychologically process our experience and form our sense of meaning. By these, we meant the breakup of families, the dispersal of extended families, the loss of communities – with shared beliefs, rituals and collective caring – the loss of the regularity and shape of the working week and the rituals marking the rhythms and seasons of the year.
- Human-centrism and living in what we have termed 'the Age of More': an addicted society that is searching for happiness in ways that can never be satiated.

To these, I would add the increasing narrowing of human consciousness, resulting in being imprisoned in the left-hemisphere neo-cortex of the brain, from whose narrow windows we can no longer see the beauty or experience the love of the wider world. We will explore this in greater length in the next chapter.

8 Human prejudice, mistrust and lack of collaboration

All these seven aforementioned global challenges require international and other forms of global collaboration. However, the superpowers of USA (and NATO), Russia and China are returning to growing their military arsenals, including their nuclear weapons. The United Nations Climate Change Conferences struggle

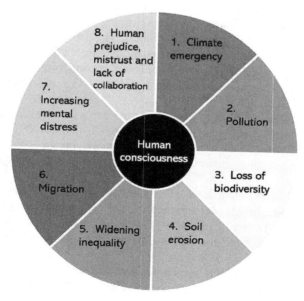

Figure 1.1 The eight interconnected global challenges

to address how the 'Global North', which has created the vast majority of the greenhouse gases that are causing the climate crisis, will compensate the countries in the 'Global South', who are often the first to suffer the devastation of climate change. Racism, sexism and elitism are still major blocks to achieving the levels of collaboration needed to address the great challenges of our times.

The underlying deeper challenge

All these major challenges are interconnected. Each challenge affects and increases the scale of the other challenges; none of them can be solved alone. Yet different academic disciplines focus on different challenges. There is a lack of interdisciplinary and systemic thinking and awareness that studies the interdependencies and causal loops between these challenges and ways they build and accelerate each other, each feeding the soil in which the others grow, seemingly out of control and often unnoticed.

All these challenges are not just interconnected and feeding on each other. They are symptoms of a failure of human consciousness to evolve fast enough to develop the wisdom necessary to respond to the world that we – and our human ways of thinking, being and doing – have created. As Einstein is reputed to have said, 'You cannot solve a problem with the same form of thinking that created it'.

Gregory Bateson was one of the first to recognize that the ecological crisis was a crisis rooted in human epistemology – that is, our ways of perceiving, conceiving and knowing about the world we are part of. As I quoted earlier, Bateson showed how the unit of survival is never the individual, community or species and how 'The unit of survival is organism plus environment. We are learning by bitter experience that the organism that destroys its environment destroys itself' (Bateson, 2000: 491).

We have to move from just fighting to save this species or that to working with the preservation and development of living ecologies, from thinking of the environment as a thing to seeing that it is a complex web of connections and from seeing it as other to experiencing it as part of us. There is no self, no nature, only 'nature-self'. Neither can exist without the other. The organism that destroys its ecological niche destroys itself.

The human species has created the 'Anthropocene' with a greatly degraded topsoil and a biosphere where we, *Homo sapiens*, have, in our extractive and exploitative greed and omnipotence, greatly reduced the biodiversity and driven thousands of wild species to extinction and where the majority of other mammalian species are now entirely dependent on humans for their existence. Surrounding the biosphere is an atmosphere filled with human-generated pollution, carbon, nitrogen and methane. On our current trajectory, we are on course for a 3- to 5-degree rise in temperature, causing large rises in sea levels and causing many parts of the world to become uninhabitable. We could run out of topsoil for growing our vegetables within 60 years and possibly see the extinction of our pollinating bees and insects even sooner.

Within this biosphere is the social sphere of human relationships, which are greatly polluted by racism, sexism, sectarianism and all forms of 'othering'; by gross economic and social inequality that has accelerated exponentially in the last 40 years; and by increases in mental illness, distress and loss of shared meaning and purpose.

Gus Speth, who was a senior US lawyer and presidential advisor, professor of law at Georgetown University Law Centre (where he taught environmental and constitutional law) and then later a dean at Yale University, sums this up very clearly:

> I used to think the top environment challenges were biodiversity loss, eco-system collapse and climate change. I thought that with thirty years of good science we could address these problems. But I was wrong. The top environmental problems are selfishness greed and apathy . . . and to deal with that we need a cultural and spiritual transformation and we (lawyers) and scientists do not know how to do that.
>
> (Speth, 2023)

Technology and the scientific thinking that created the modern industrial world – and in its wake created the ecological devastation – will not by itself reverse the destruction. As Donna Meadows, one of the pioneers who, very early on, pointed to the limits to growth and the dangers of ignoring them, wrote: 'If you want to really restructure a system so that we can have a peaceful, just, or sustainable world – that means changing the paradigm in our heads' (Meadows, 1991: 59). Only with a massive transformation of human consciousness can we address the greatest challenges our species has ever faced. As James Baldwin, the great black American writer, said, 'It is very difficult to ask people to give up the assumptions by which they have always lived, and yet that is the demand the world has got to make now of everybody' (Baldwin and Mead, 1971).

Traditionally, paradigm shifts in human thinking, as defined by Kuhn (1970), have taken centuries to develop, take root and then spread across the globe. The current ecological crisis and climate emergency will not afford us that length of time. There is an urgent need to articulate the necessary shift in consciousness towards a new paradigm and to create many interconnected pathways and practices through which it can be collectively actualized and evolved.

Iain McGilchrist (2022), in his website introduction to his book *The Matter with Things*, writes:

> I believe that we are engaged in committing suicide: intellectual suicide, moral suicide and physical suicide. If there is anything as important as stopping us poisoning our seas and destroying our forests, it is stopping us poisoning our minds and destroying our souls.

Our dominant value – sometimes I fear our only value – has, very clearly, become that of power. This aligns us with a brain system, that of the left hemisphere, the raison d'être of which is to control and manipulate the world. But not to understand it: ... [which is] the raison d'être of our – more intelligent, in every sense – right hemisphere. Unfortunately, the left hemisphere, knowing less, thinks it knows more. It is a good servant, but a ruinous – a peremptory – master. And the predictable outcome of assuming the role of master is the devastation of all that is important to us – or should be important, if we really know what we are about. Even if we could, by some miracle, reverse the course on which we are set, unless we change our way of thinking, of being in the world – the way that is destroying us as we speak – it would all be in vain.

Conclusion

In this chapter, I have posed the question: Has my lifetime been part of 'a great leap forward for mankind' or an increasing acceleration towards the edge of a cliff of devastating destruction? In my privileged lifetime, there have been many great benefits for those in privileged countries, including longer life expectancy, improved diet and health, knowledge at the click of a button, many labour-saving machines and devices, and ease of travel.

We have grown up in a world that has been infused by what is popularly called the 'American dream' (which is not limited to the USA but found in all parts of Europe, the European diaspora and countries colonized by force or culture). A dream that, at its extreme, is one of rampant individualism: emigrating, colonizing, exploiting and extracting to build its personal good life, defended by guns, security firms, armies, nuclear weapons and pervasive surveillance. This dream is part of the wider dream of modernity – a dream of perpetual growth and development of global human wealth and prosperity.

In this chapter, we have shown how this so-called development has come at a huge and growing cost: one that has not been carried by the privileged but by the exploited; not owned by humans but borne by other sentient creatures; and not just by living creatures but also by the wider biosphere, the living ecology of the earth, the waters and the air.

The price of privilege of today's generations has come at the cost of mortgaging the future. That price will be visited upon our daughters and sons for many future generations and not just our human descendants but also that will live on this Earth we call home, long after we have departed.

Chapter 2

The gradual shrinking and imprisonment of human consciousness

Introduction

The great Sufi poet, Mevlana Jalaludin Rumi, in the *Mathnawi* (1977) asks us: 'Why in the plenitude of God's Universe have you chosen to fall asleep in such a small dark prison?' Many years later, this was echoed by the English mystical poet William Blake (1968b): 'If the doors of perception were cleansed, everything would appear as it is, infinite. For we have closed ourselves up, 'til we see all through the narrow chinks of our own cavern'.

Both poets point to how we humans have shrunk our consciousness, from being conjoined with the world around us, and we have retreated from being embodied, to being in our brains. Iain McGilchrist has gone further and shown how we have become more and more imprisoned in the left hemisphere neo-cortex of our brains and how we 'Have reached the point where there is an urgent need to transform both how we think of the world and what we make of ourselves' (McGilchrist, 2021: 3).

In this chapter, we will explore the descent of human thinking and being – particularly that of white Western modernist thinking – which over the last few hundred years has gradually become the globally dominant and all-pervasive hegemony of the world.

As we have grown exponentially – the number of our species, our life expectancy and our global dominance of the world around us – we have at the same time shrunk our consciousness. We have gradually moved away from being embodied, participatory beings, living in a state of interdependence with our wider human communities, embedded in and inextricably dependent on our local ecology. We have moved away from a state where consciousness and mind were not located within the individual but flowed through the community and the wider nature that sustained them.

In this chapter, we will look at the history of this descent, this shrinking, before looking in Chapter 3 at how, with Beauty as our guide, we can begin to make the return journey to a fuller way of perceiving, being and doing.

DOI: 10.4324/9781003349600-4

The rise of modernity and the narrowing of human consciousness

The term 'modernity' is highly contested and is understood in many different ways (for instance, Machado de Oliveira, 2021; Eisenstadt, 2017; Featherstone et al., 1995; Toulmin, 1990; Tarnas, 1991). But through my reading of different writers from varied disciplines, I can discern a collective pattern. Many writings point to the birth of modernity in the scientific paradigms of the 16th century. Some point to the birth and gradual global spread of the Industrial Revolution. Others follow the philosophical and epistemological roots back through the Islamic and European Christian Renaissance to Greek Platonic and Aristotelian ways of construing the world and how it became framed within the dominant monotheistic religions of Judaism, Christianity and Islam. Some go further back to our transition from hunter-gathers to an agrarian economy of farming and domestication of livestock, enabled by the building of reservoirs and canals, which massively increased the amount of farmable land.

Here, I offer my own historical narrative underlying the different approaches to modernity, returning to my first academic discipline of being a cultural historian but recognizing that this is a view based on hindsight and written through the lens of today's way of thinking and making sense of the world.

The move from hunter-gatherer to agrarian farming: domesticating nature

The first agrarian, or Neolithic, revolution started over 11,000 years ago in the Holocene geological period. Humans devised ways of damming and canalizing rivers to increase the areas of farmable land and develop crops, of which barley, which they could grow at scale, was probably the first. Granaries for storage were needed, and this required a less nomadic lifestyle than that of the hunter-gatherer. With more food, the population expanded and communities developed specialized workers and more advanced tools. Now farmers could raise their economic standard (note not necessarily the *quality* of their life or, indeed, their overall nutrition) by growing excess crops and herding livestock, which they could use to trade with those who, having been liberated from focussing on growing their own food, could now focus on crafts, trade or knowledge.

Peter Reason (1994: 27) writes about how this, and the later changes that followed in its wake, led to a loss of a sense of participation:

Original participation honours humanity's embeddedness in the wholeness, the seamless web of the world. It allows us to resonate with being, to experience our presence in the world, to encounter directly other presences in the world and presence of the world as a whole . . . the human capacity for directly encountering the presence of the world, and the imagery that cascades from this, is prior to language, categories and concepts, and is the bedrock experiential knowing on which all else is built.

The growth of urban city states

Early city development can be found in the great irrigated agricultural river valleys of the Tigris, Euphrates and Nile in Africa, the Yangtze and Yellow River (or Huang He) in China and the Indus in what is now called India. Only with the great enlargement of farmed areas was it possible to move beyond subsistence farming – that is, growing just enough for the needs of one's own family and community. This, in turn, was enabled by managing the rivers to extend irrigated, farmable land. An exception to this is the development of the earliest-known city in the Americas, Huaricanga of the Norte Chico civilization, which was enabled by new methods of harvesting large amounts of fish from the sea.

The development of an abstracted language

In earlier indigenous communities, spoken language was naturally onomatopoeic – that is, the sound would echo the event or being it referred to. It was a human representation of the language of the 'more-than-human' world. Early writing in both China and Egypt was cuneiform and, like spoken language, echoed the world around it, this time in complex stylized pictures. It was not until the 2nd millennium BCE that Semitic and Greek cultures created the first 'alphabet' – the ordering of language with alpha followed by beta – a scripted, more abstracted language. This was then developed and adapted by many of the peoples in the eastern Mediterranean.

With the emergence of urban centres, language, writing and measurement became conscripted for the use of trade. Words and measures were no longer metaphorically poetic – carrying an echo of what they retell or compare to. Language no longer has the world dwelling within it nor does it belong to the wider natural world. It has become abstracted – from the Latin *abstractus*, meaning drawn away from, from the verb *abstrahere*, meaning to drag away, detach, pull away, divert. From then on, village, town and city-dwellers started to become indigenous orphans, their language and way of thinking detached from the sensuous world that we inhabit.

Sending God upstairs

As far as we can tell from archaeological explorations, all hunter-gather communities were basically animist – that is, they saw all of nature, not just humans or animals, as having interiority and subjectivity. Animism comes from the Latin *anima*, meaning having breath or spirit life. Only much later did Europeans lose a felt-sense of an *anima mundi* – a living, breathing world – and limit the concept of *anima* to animals. Even the beliefs of the early city and agrarian civilizations, as well as the beliefs that grew out of the great transformations of the Axial Age (Abram, 1996; Armstrong, 2006), were animated religions. Many early cultures and religions saw breath as flowing through all life – animating everything that lives.

The breath, which in Hebrew is called *ruach*, was that which continuously created life and substance, as in the Hebrew book of Job 33:4: 'The Spirit of God hath made me, and the breath of the Almighty hath given me life'. In Greek, breath was *pneuma*, which was also the spirit or soul of a being. This is echoed in the Christian Bible in the breath of God, the Holy Spirit. In Hinduism, the Sanskrit word for breath is *prana*, the vital force of life, which could be eternal, living beyond our human corporeal form.

Only with the spread of monotheism, and particularly abstracted Platonic forms of monotheism, was God sent upstairs and seen as wholly separate from creation. The splitting off of God and ascribing all transcendence and sacredness to Him (sic) made creation and nature as only imminent, material and desacralized (Abram, 1996). Gradually, humans would become the only creature that, being made in the image of God, would have mind and value; everything else was without mind and, therefore, exploitable.

As Gregory Bateson (1972: 468) pointed out:

> If you put God outside and set him vis-à-vis his creation and if you have the idea that you are created in his image, you will logically and naturally see yourself as outside and against the things around you. And as you arrogate all mind to yourself, you will see the world around you as mindless and therefore as not entitled to moral or ethical consideration. The environment will be yours to exploit. . . . If this is your estimate of your relation to nature and you have an advanced technology, your likelihood of survival will be that of a snowball in hell. You will die either of the toxic by-products of your own hate, or, simply, of over population and over-grazing.

The splitting of the mind from the body

The early 17th-century philosopher René Descartes (2001) infamously said: 'Cogito, ergo sum' – 'I think, therefore, I am', thereby reducing humans to being a *res cogitans* (a thinking thing) surrounded by a material world, or *res extensa*, created by God. Thus, Descartes created the 'Cartesian split' between mind and body. The mind was located in the human brain; all other creatures and forms of life were part of *res extensa* and, therefore, without mind, thinking or feeling.

Even our own human bodies could be seen as part of *res extensa* and, therefore, devoid of mind. Our whole identity retreated from the external world to the internal and from the body to the brain.

This philosophical creation of a mind-body dualism has had lasting consequences, as it became a core part of the beliefs of both science and modernity. Even today, if you ask people where the mind is, they nearly always point to their heads.

Jullien and Lloyd (2002), in their paper 'Did Philosophers have to Become Fixated on Truth?', contrasted: 'Philosophers who set out to explain the world and provide an exhaustive and accurate representation of it, and the Chinese sages who sought to find ways of living in harmony and congruence with the world'. The philosopher lived in his ivory tower, both internally and externally, objectifying the world; while the sage lived in wild nature, studying and learning from the world and echoing it in poetry, calligraphy and metaphor. Truth in the West became abstracted, literalized and universalized. This led to Western views of superiority, assuming the right to dominate and evangelistically educate the rest of the world.

The growth of science and scientism

Stephen Toulmin (1990) shows how, in the 17th century, a vision arose that would captivate the Western imagination for the next 300 years: the vision of what Toulmin terms a 'Cosmopolis', a society as rationally ordered as the Newtonian view of nature. While fuelling extraordinary advances in all fields of human endeavour, this vision perpetuated a hidden, yet persistent, agenda: the drive to fully know, understand and control the world around us, based on the delusion that nature and society could be fitted into precise and manageable rational categories.

From the 17th century onwards, science developed what came to be known as the 'scientific method of empiricism'. The emphasis was on researcher objectivity and value neutrality and the production of repeatable experiments, often under laboratory conditions. It is doubtful that the early scientists imagined that this would become a dominant, epistemological way of experiencing the world: a way of knowing the world by studying separate objects, frozen in time and separated from context, with whom there is supposedly no emotional or two-way communicative engagement between what is studied and the person studying.

Emotion and engagement were excommunicated from serious scientific study. The world, viewed through the microscope of empiricism, became inanimate matter, devoid of life and spirit, devoid of meaning, other than that which we humans give to it. Very quickly this way of seeing the world extended to seeing the Earth as a resource for humans to exploit. This then extended to all non-human forms of life – plants, trees, fish and other animals – and then beyond that to include all non-white European people. The last of these led to the slave trade and to the ethnic cleansing of indigenous people from many newly colonized parts of the world in the 17th, 18th and 19th centuries.

Science has brought vast amounts of new understanding of the world we live in and great material, power and benefit to human beings. But science has also played a growing role in the rise of secularism and human arrogance and has itself assumed the role and trappings of religion. Scientism has become the arbiter of truth, establishing its own dogmas and laws and decrying those seen as heretics.

In nature, there are no straight lines, no fixed borders. These only exist in the taxonomies of scientists and the borders created by colonizers, creating states and nations.

We have arrived at what McGilchrist (2021) describes as an extreme left-brain neo-cortex way of experiencing the world.

Industrialization, urbanization and utility

The Industrial Age, which began in the new United Kingdom in the 18th century and then spread across Western Europe and the countries colonized by European adventurers and armies, was built on the 'three Cs': colonization, capital and carbon. It was the capital accumulated from colonization, slavery and colonial trade that financed the extraction of carbon from the Earth – first coal and later oil and gas.

Economic capitalism is seen by some historians as starting with the British East India Company (Tirthankar, 2012; Dalrymple, 2019), financed by earlier piracy and slavery and creating a new form of economic and cultural colonization, supported by partnering with powerful local leaders and backed up by military force when necessary. The Portuguese and Dutch also had their own East India companies.

Many benefits and opportunities have been opened up for humans, especially the privileged, from carbon-based energy, industrialization and travel – but at enormous cost, both to our ecology and the narrowing of our ways of engaging with the world.

Soon, carbon was driving the machinery of the factories, manufacturing clothes from imported cotton, cigarettes from tobacco, chocolate from cocoa beans, sugar from the slave plantations and many other goods imported from the colonies. Excess coal, iron and manufactured goods could then be exported through the Navy-protected sea routes.

As countries industrialized, there followed massive migration from the countryside to the new cities. The embodied community life – living in partnership with the surrounding ecology – was replaced by long hours spent down coal or mineral mines or working in often unhealthy factories, living far from nature.

In his autobiographical poem 'The Prelude', Wordsworth (1850) contrasts the confining urban industrial cities with the unfettered participation in the natural world, as he wanders through the beautiful hills and valleys and along the shores of the lakes and rivers of the English Lake District:

escaped
From the vast city, where I long had pined

A discontented sojourner: now free,
Free as a bird to settle where I will . . .
I breathe again!

Wordsworth mourns the loss of his childhood, dwelling in an animated landscape, with its two-way flow between the living, breathing world we inhabit and our own felt, embodied, living, breathing being. He captures this beautifully in another poem (Wordsworth, 1798) written earlier, *Tintern Abbey*, in the beautiful Wye Valley:

a sense sublime
Of something far more deeply interfused,
Whose dwelling is the light of setting suns,
And the round ocean and the living air,
And the blue sky, and in the mind of man;
A motion and a spirit, that impels
All thinking things, all objects of all thought,
And rolls through all things

This echoes the sentiment of his close friend and fellow poet Samuel Taylor Coleridge, who wrote in his poem 'The Aeolian Harp' (1794) of 'the one Life within us and abroad'.

Wordsworth is not just mourning a personal loss but also the loss of a whole generation that was leaving the countryside to become factory workers in the growing, industrialized cities. The UK was one of the first countries to experience this mass migration and urbanization, necessary to feed the hungry factories of mass production, but it has now been echoed in most countries. According to the World Bank (2023):

Today, some 56% of the world's population – 4.4 billion inhabitants – live in cities. This trend is expected to continue, with the urban population more than doubling its current size by 2050, at which point nearly 7 out of 10 people will live in cities.

At the time of Wordsworth, only 2% of the world's population lived in cities, which was less than 2 million people, a smaller global urban population than that of Houston, Texas, today and only one-fifteenth the size of one of China's mega cities. Whereas previously, most humans were indigenous – embedded in a community, which itself was embedded in a familiar landscape. Increasingly, much of the world's population has become indigenous orphans, with communities scattered and meeting 'online' and our only engagement with the wilderness being through celluloid.

In the wake of industrialization came an ethic of 'utility', most clearly expressed by Jeremy Bentham and James Mill in the early 19th century (see also

Chapter 8 on ethics and aesthetics). Now value – not just of material objects but also of living beings – was 'measured' by what use they could be put to, what they produced and how they would benefit humans, particularly those who were white Western Europeans. The Good (see Chapter 6) became that which created 'the greatest happiness for the greatest number'. Everything, and every being, was there to service human happiness!

Retreat from embodiment

As we have explored earlier, participatory consciousness was, by its very nature, embodied consciousness. We experienced the world not just through our senses but through our whole bodies. As David Abram (2011: 143) writes:

> The world we inhabit . . . Is a sensitive sphere suspended in the solar wind, a round field of sentience, sustained by the relationships between the myriad lives and sensibilities that compose it. We come to know more of this sphere not by detaching ourselves from our felt experience, but by inhabiting or bodily experience, all the more richly and wakefully, feeling our way into deeper contact with other experiencing bodies, and hence with the wild, intercorporeal life of the Earth itself.

From farming and walking in the hills, industrialized humans were first sitting at the mechanized looms or at the clerk's desk and, within the next 100–200 years, after the third Industrial Revolution, at the computer (Schwab, 2016).

Our life has become sedentary. Like many, I spend far too many hours sitting in front of a computer screen, not even feeling the weight of words in the tree-based paper of a book but watching words move past on a screen. Dialogue increasingly happens between my own and other talking heads, in small boxes on a screen. Psychologists since the time of Mehrabian (1972) have shown that only a small percentage of communication lies in words themselves and a very large percentage (up to 93%) lies in contextual and non-verbal communication.

The growing control and dominance of the left-hemisphere neo-cortex

Iain McGilchrist has spent most of his life in a quest to understand how the parts of the human brain all work differentially, first as a consultant psychiatrist, then as a neuropsychology researcher and for the last 14 years assembling the best scientific data from around the world to write *The Matter with Things* (McGilchrist, 2021), his brilliant *magnum opus*.

By reviewing a great many studies of people who have had brain lesions in one of the two hemispheres, as well as people who have split-brain or callosal syndrome, McGilchrist explores at great length the different ways in which the left-hemisphere neo-cortex and the right-hemisphere neo-cortex perceive and conceive the world. Here is one of his briefer accounts of 'each hemisphere's vision of reality' (McGilchrist, 2021: 31–32, bold added):

> the left hemisphere view, is of a world composed of static, isolated, fragmentary elements that can be manipulated easily, are decontextualised, abstracted, detached, disembodied, mechanical, relatively uncomplicated by issues of **beauty and morality** (except in a consequentialist sense) and relatively untroubled by the complexity of empathy, emotion and human significance. They are put together, like brick on brick to build a wall, so as to reach conclusions that are taken to be unimpeachable. It is an inanimate universe – and a bureaucrat's dream. There is an excess of confidence and a lack of insight. This world is useful for purposes of manipulation, but is not a helpful guide to understanding the nature of what it encounters. Its use is local and for the short term.
>
> In the other (the right hemisphere version), as in the world the map represents, and in the world revealed to us by physics, by poetry, and simply by the business of living, things are almost infinitely more complex. Nothing is clearly the same as anything else. All is flowing and changing, provisional, and complexly interconnected with everything else. Nothing is ever static, detached from our awareness of it, or disembodied; and everything needs to be understood in context, where, if it is not to be denatured, it must remain implicit. Here, wholes are different from the sum of the parts, and **beauty and morality**, along with empathy and emotional depth, help us to intuit meaning that lies beyond the banality of the familiar and everyday. It is an animate universe – and a bureaucrat's nightmare. This is a world from which we cannot detach ourselves, since we are part of it and affect it by our relationship with it. The overall timbre is sober and tentative. The world is truer to what is, but is harder to comprehend and to express in language, and less useful for practical issues that are local and short term. On the other hand, for a broader or longer-term understanding the right hemisphere is essential.
>
> These two ways of seeing the world are each vital to our survival. We need to simplify and stand apart to manipulate things, to deal with the necessities of life, and to build the foundations of a civilisation. But to live in it, we also need to belong to the world and to understand the complexity of what it is we are dealing with. This division of attention works to our advantage when we use both. However, it is a handicap – in fact, it is a catastrophe – when we use only one.

At a time when artificial intelligence (AI) is beginning to replace many of the routine tasks that our left hemispheres would have originally done (such as memorizing facts, calculations, codifying, indexing, routine manual jobs) and thus free us up to focus on right-hemisphere ways of engaging with the world, we are becoming increasingly 'digitalized' and left-hemisphere dominated in our ways of thinking. Instead of us teaching computers to think like humans, we could argue that computers are increasingly teaching us how to think like machines. Our education has become more specialized, segregated and siloed – focussing on what can be measured and examined, the amassing of atomized facts and calculations that can be either deemed right or wrong. We have arrived at what McGilchrist (2021) describes as an extreme left-brain neo-cortex way of experiencing the world. The left hemisphere is a great servant but a disastrous master (McGilchrist, 2009).

Fragmentation and the growth of specialization

Another great teacher and mentor who has opened my eyes to understanding the epistemological descent has been David Bohm (1994: 3–6), who states:

> one of the obvious things wrong with thought is fragmentation. Thought is breaking things up into bits which should not be broken up . . . and at the same time, we are trying to establish unity where there isn't any . . . thus we have false division and false unification. Thought is always doing a great deal, but it tends to say that it hasn't done anything, this is just telling you the way things are . . . that 'you' are inside there, deciding what to with the information. But I want to say that you don't decide what to do with the information. The information takes over. It runs you. Thought runs you. Thought, however gives the false information that you are running it, that you are the one who controls thought, whereas actually thought is the one which controls each one of us. Until thought is understood – better yet, more than understood, perceived – it will actually control us; but it will create the impression that it is our servant, that it is just doing what we want it to do.

Bohm (1994: 6) saw our ways of thinking as creating unhelpful divisions and fragmentation. 'Thought is creating divisions out of itself and then saying they are there naturally . . . thought divides itself from feeling, from the body'. Like Bateson, Bohm explains how, in order to understand and analyse the world, we need to apply analytic scissors to the seamless web of existence; but we then forget that the divisions have been created by the scissors of our mind, and we believe the cuts exist in the world around us.

This fragmentation of knowledge has increasingly become institutionalized by the growth of specialization. The great physicist Erwin Schrödinger was concerned about this as far back as 1951, when he gave a series of lectures at Cambridge University, which later became his book *Science & Humanism* (1951).

> It seems plain and self-evident, yet it needs to be said: the isolated knowledge obtained by a group of specialists in a narrow field has in itself no value whatsoever, but only in its synthesis with all the rest of knowledge and only inasmuch as it really contributes in this synthesis toward answering the demand, 'Who are we?'

Another great thinker, Arnold Toynbee, was concerned by the growing specializations of academic disciplines:

> Specialisation . . . leaves critical questions not only unanswered but unasked. And they will remain unasked if the microscopic approach is not supplemented by a panoramic one. Without a combination of the two, there can be no stereoscopic vision.
>
> (Toynbee, 1961: 633–634)

There is a telling joke that the definition of a top specialist is someone who knows more, and more, and more about less, and less, and less, until they know everything about nothing.

Loss of depth

The post-war Christian theologian Paul Tillich, whose books played a key role in helping me with my theological struggles as a teenager, showed how religion has become a vehicle for this descent and in so doing lost its key role in helping us experience wonder, awe, depth and meaning in our world. Tillich (1958: 29) wrote: 'when man has deprived himself of the dimension of depth and the symbols of expressing it, he then becomes a part of the horizontal plane. He loses his self that becomes a thing among things'. Tillich (1958: 29) goes on to say:

> the loss of the dimensions of depth is caused by the relation of man to his world and to himself in our period, the period in which nature is being subjected scientifically and technically to the control of man. In this period, life in the 'dimension of depth' is replaced by life in the horizontal dimension. The driving forces of the industrial society of which we are a part go ahead horizontally and not vertically . . . he transforms everything he encounters into a tool: and in doing so he himself becomes a tool. But if he asks, a tool for what, there is no answer.

Later Tillich (1958: 78) adds:

> The first step toward the nonreligion of the Western World was made by religion itself. When it defended its great symbols, not as symbols, but as literal stories, it had already lost the battle . . . if the symbol of the Fall of Man, which points to the tragic estrangement of man and his world from their true being is transferred to the horizontal plane, it becomes a story of a human couple a few thousand years ago in what is now present-day Iraq. One of the most profound psychological descriptions of the general human predicament becomes an absurdity on the horizontal plane.

A contemporary of Tillich was the great poet T.S. Eliot, who wrote in 'Choruses from "The Rock"' (1963: 161):

> Where is the wisdom we have lost in knowledge?
> Where is the knowledge we have lost in information?

Literalized and objectified study and language cannot portray or capture the beauty of the world or help us see through the horizontal to the world of depth and meaning. For this, we need to rediscover a different vision and the language of metaphor, poetry and myth; we will explore this in much greater depth in Chapter 14.

The split between the human and the more-than-human world.

In his trilogy of novels, *The Dark Materials*, Philip Pulman (2018) weaves a great fable of our times, in which humans are born attached to their animal daemon – or spirit being – which accompanies, guides and protects them. It is the evil splitting of humans from their daemon that causes the loss of spirit, and we witness the gradual domination by the 'Magisterium', the controlling centralized political power. In this, we can see a symbol of the dangerous split between humans and the 'more-than-human' world and the enormous cost for the fullness of life and being for humans and disastrous consequences for the rest of life on our planet.

In the 1960s and 1970s, Bateson was one of the first powerful voices to speak about the developing ecological crisis facing our planet. Earlier than most other commentators, he showed how our current environmental crisis is rooted in our epistemological mindset – that is, how we generate knowledge of the world we inhabit. If we look at how Bateson describes our collective human epistemological errors, we can reflect on how many of these are present in our own behaviour and belief systems and those of the people we work with:

> The ideas that dominate our civilization at the present time date in their most virulent form from the industrial revolution . . . [and] may be summarized as follows:
>
> 1. it's us against the environment;
> 2. it's us against other men;
> 3. it's the individual that matters;
> 4. we can have unilateral control over the environment and must strive for that control;
> 5. we live in an infinitely expanding 'frontier';
> 6. economic determinism is common sense;
> 7. technology will do it for us.
>
> (Bateson, 1972: 468)

McGilchrist (2021: 1310) echoes these concerns:

> we are experiencing a crisis in meaning. Not coincidentally, far more of us than ever before . . . live divorced from Nature, alienated from the structures and traditions of a stable society, and indifferent to the divine. These three elements have always been what has provided us with an overarching sense of belonging.

He goes on to say (McGilchrist, 2021: 1310):

> each of these divorces has come about very swiftly in a mere 250 to 300 years – the twinkling of an eye in relation to the age of humanity and they have each come about because of an excess of hubris. Nature has become mere resource; divine Maya superstition; and the unruly complexity of life can, we believe, be simply rationalised, ironed out, and subjected to our conscious control, by technology, by bureaucracy and where necessary by law. We know far more, we think, than people of other ages and cultures; indeed we pretty much know it all. However, I suggest no people that ever lived has understood so little.

The ecology is often spoken about as 'the environment' – that which is beyond us, out there. Then it becomes an objective problem for humans, filled with hubris, to solve. The ecology is not out there and cannot be objectified. It is also in us and flows through us, and we influence the environment at the same time it is shaping us. It is in the air we breathe through our nostrils and lungs and absorbed into our bloodstream; it is in the food we eat and which becomes part of us; in the water we absorb and which makes up 60% of our physical being and 73% of our heart and brain (Mitchell et al., 1945).

The ecology is us. To move from *ego*-centric to *eco*-centric thinking, doing and being, we need not only to develop our systemic awareness (see Chapter 4) but to undo centuries of human encultured thinking; to overcome the 'illusion of separation' (Hutchins, 2014); and to stop drawing boundaries and divisions with straight lines in the wrong places. We need to expand out from our left-hemisphere neo-cortex ways of viewing the world to include right-brain and embodied sensing and sensuous knowing. For this, we need a new lifetime curriculum – or perhaps I should say a curriculum that has always been there, provided by life, but that humans with 'singled-eyed vision' have stopped seeing. As William Blake (1968c) prayed, 'May God us keep From Single vision & Newton's sleep'.

Blake (1968c) showed how we need a 'fourfold vision'. Single vision is just seeing atomized data. Twofold vision is seeing the pattern that connects the data; in threefold vision, we sense this pattern in how it resonates and moves within us (and others) in an emotional, connected and embodied way. Finally, in what Blake calls fourfold vision, there is the world of imagination, a world where we directly and holistically perceive the interconnections and the oneness of being.

Bateson was very influenced by Blake, and in his levels of learning (Bateson, 1972), he describes 'Level III learning' as when experience is no longer punctuated by the 'I'. Taoism captures another aspect of this fourfold vision when it talks about *Wu-Wei* – 'effortless effort'. Many spiritual teachers show pathways to 'non-duality', where opposites dissolve: opposites such as self and other, internal and external, immanent and transcendent, human and nature (see Chapter 13).

However, this state of consciousness is beyond words that define; it is best understood through the language of poetry, which points beyond itself and provides hints of the ineffable not only through the words but also through its rhythms, music and silences (see Chapter 14). For as William Blake (1968d) writes in 'Eternity', one of his short quatrains:

> He who binds to himself a joy
> Does the winged life destroy
> He who kisses the joy as it flies
> Lives in eternity's sunrise.

Conclusion: we are all in this together

During the Covid-19 pandemic in 2020–2021, the phrase 'We are all in this together' was used by many political leaders. Sadly, their actions rarely matched their words. This is true not just for one global pandemic but also for each of the major global crises we addressed in Chapter 1, which are all interdependent.

> So long as the smaller systems are enclosed within the larger, and so long as all are connected by complex patterns of interdependency, as we know they are, then whatever affects one system will affect the others.
>
> (Berry, 1983: 46)

McGilchrist (2021: 1312) writes: 'I was, and I'm now still more, fearful that unless we radically change the path we are pursuing we cannot survive – certainly as a civilization, and perhaps as a species'. To which I might add, perhaps as a living Earth. We and our ecology are accelerating further and faster into crisis, while our consciousness, which is the root cause and driver of the crisis, is asleep in the small dark prison we have created for ourselves over the last 300–500 years.

We urgently need to find the pathway to a new human consciousness and the return journey to experiencing ourselves as part of one interconnected global family and an inextricable part of the wider ecology.

In the next chapter, we will start to chart a possible return path, and I will show how Beauty can be a valuable and essential guide on this journey.

Chapter 3

The return journey and the role of Beauty

Introduction

In the last chapter, we charted the history of the narrowing of human consciousness, from intimate participation in the wider world around us right through to imprisonment in left-hemisphere neo-cortex ways of fragmenting what we perceive and seeing the world as problems to be solved.

In this chapter, I will outline a possible return path out of this 'small dark prison', taking us beyond the flat, fragmented world of modernity: a journey that is essential in healing the split between the human and the 'more-than-human' world. For without this healing, we will be unable to address the great challenges of our time as outlined in Chapter 1.

Without a guide, it is hard to find a way out of the labyrinthine prison of our constructed mind that we humans have created. Cassirer (1977: 22) wrote:

> Unless we succeed in finding a clue of Ariadne to lead us out of this labyrinth, we can have no real insight into the general character of human culture; we shall remain lost in a mass of disconnected and disintegrated data, which seem to lack all conceptual unity.

Ariadne was the Greek mythological woman who held the 'clue' or ball of wool to help her lover, Theseus, find his way out of Daedalus' labyrinth once he had killed the Minotaur.

Before we begin to chart this journey, I will explain why I have chosen Beauty as the guide for this journey or perhaps why Beauty has chosen to guide me. Later in the chapter, I will explore what Beauty is and why it makes such an important contribution to each stage of our return journey.

Why beauty?

Many people, when told that I am writing a book on Beauty, have asked: 'Why Beauty?' This morning, as I sat in the garden eating breakfast with my wife, we

DOI: 10.4324/9781003349600-5

were blessed with a visit from a beautiful Comma butterfly (*Polygonia c-album*), which sat on the chair opposite us, warming its speckled orange leaf-cut wings in the morning sunshine. I, too, asked the question: Why Beauty? Why are you, little butterfly, so beautiful?

So one answer to why I am writing this book is that Beauty keeps appearing, engaging me and knocking on the door of my heart. Another answer is that in 2019, I was asked by the International Coaching Federation in Italy to give a talk in the Italian National Botanical Gardens in Padua on 'Beauty in Coaching'. In terms of seduction, they had hit the jackpot! Three hearts appearing together – combining my love for plants and flowers, my love for Italian culture and language and my love for the poetry of Dante, who was connected with Padua and is buried nearby.

I sought a coach who could help me deliver the opening stanzas of Dante's 'Divina Commedia' in barely passable Italian, and I read and reflected widely on what Beauty could offer to both 21st-century leaders and their coaches. Sadly, Covid-19 intervened, and my talk was delivered virtually and less beautifully. But the quest was uninterruptible, and this book is just one of the subsequent turns on this perpetual journey.

We are at the beginning of our return journey and, like Dante at the beginning of the 'Divina Commedia', the journey often starts in the middle of our lives, when we experience ourselves drowning 'in medias res' (in the middle of things), the thousand things that we believe are demanding our attention, when we are caught up in so much complexity and busyness that we have become lost. We have lost a sense of purpose, we are no longer in touch with what our life is about, and life feels barren, no longer fecund and fertile.

Dante opens his amazing poem journey with these words. I invite you first to read them out loud in Italian, even if you do not understand that language, as the music of the words is so much more beautiful in Dante's own language.

Nel mezzo del cammin di nostra vita
mi ritrovai per una selva oscura,
ché la diritta via era smarrita.

Ahi quanto a dir qual era è cosa dura
esta selva selvaggia e aspra e forte
che nel pensier rinova la paura!

(Alighieri, 1301–1314a)

In English:

Midway upon the journey of our life
I found myself within a forest dark,
For the straightforward pathway had been lost.

Ah me! how hard a thing it is to say
What was this forest savage, rough, and stern,
Which in the very thought renews the fear.

I do not believe we are going to avoid the current headlong race into ecological destruction on our fragile planet by logical realization of what we are doing to the world around us. Nor by so-called 'enlightened self-interest'. Nor by duty or moral aught, leading to good intentions – for, as in the old saying, 'The road to hell is paved with good intentions', which I have more recently translated into *The coaching road to hell is paved with insight and action plans that never get enacted*.

Good intentions are made by the left-hemisphere neo-cortex of the individual, but true change is always embodied and enacted. The evidence is all around us in the combination of the ever-worsening data from science and our own experience of extreme weather conditions, destructive pollution, mass migration, gross inequality and political instability. Our human responses are a worrying mixture of willful blindness, good intentions that fail to get enacted, blaming others, a blind faith that either techno-science or God will save us and small – but inadequate and too-slow – changes in behaviour.

Like Dante, we need to open our eyes and face the 'inferno' that our own sins or inadequacies have created on this planet. This is the journey that we travel on by watching the news, listening to science (as Greta Thunberg entreats us to do), feeling the grief at the extinction of so many species through human ecocide. We should note that Dante's mentor and guide on his journey is the Roman poet Virgil, who had learnt from the mythic journey and tribulations of Ulysses (or Odysseus in the original Homeric Greek). But Virgil can only take Dante part of the way – the journey from being lost in the fearful dark forest, through learning from the inferno, where we have to face our sins and shadow, and purgatory, where we learn patience, to the gates of Paradiso, or heaven. To journey further, his guiding star is the beauty of Beatrice, the muse who made him a poet, the girl who opened up unquenchable love in his heart and whose very name echoes with other words such as 'beautiful', 'the beatific' and 'beatitudes' – with their scent of bliss and blessedness.

The first step on our current return journey out of the imprisonment of our human consciousness, as McGilchrist (2021) convincingly shows, is to put the right-hemisphere neo-cortex back in charge and let the left-hemisphere neo-cortex do what it is best at doing in service of the greater whole. But this is not sufficient by itself and is just step one.

We then need to awaken to 'whole intelligence' (Parlett, 2015), connecting all aspects not only of the 'triune brain' in our skulls but also of our heart and gut brains. We need to realize that our knowing – and all change and transformation – is embodied, informed by and reflected on, but not carried out by, the analytic intelligence of the narrow mind. We need to realize that relationships are more fundamental than relata, as the Italian physicist Rovelli (2017: 115–116) shows:

> In the world described by quantum mechanics there is no reality except in the relations between physical systems. It isn't things that enter into relations but, rather, relations that ground the notion of 'thing'. The world of quantum mechanics is not a world of objects: it is a world of events. Things are built by the happenings of elementary events. . . . A stone is a vibration of quanta that maintains its structure for a while, just as a marine wave maintains its identity for a while before melting again into the sea. . . . We, like waves and like all objects, are a flux of events; we are processes, for a brief time monotonous.

The next step is to realize that the mind is not a thinking thing – a *'res cogitans'* as Descartes (1637) labelled it – but a living process. We do not have a mind, but we participate in 'circuits of mind' (Bateson, 1972, 1979, 1991). Maturana and Varela (1980, 2008) built on the thinking of Bateson to develop what has come to be known as the Santiago theory or the theory of auto-poiesis. Capra and Luisi (2014: 257) summarize their work:

> Mind is not a thing but a process – the process of cognition, which is identified with the process of life. The brain is a specific structure through which this process operates. The relationship between mind and brain, therefore, is one between process and structure. Moreover, the brain is not the only structure through which the process of cognition operates. The entire structure of the organism participates in the process of cognition, whether or not the organism has a brain or a nervous system.

So how do we connect these different concepts of mind? Capra and Luisi (2014) offer a reflection on different types of neuroscience. The first is what Francisco Varela (1991) described as the 'neuro-reductionists', who attempt to reduce consciousness to neural mechanisms. The famous molecular biologist Francis Crick (1994: 3) espoused this approach when he wrote:

> You, your joys and your sorrows, your memories and your ambitions, your sense of personal identity and free will, are in fact no more than the behaviour of a vast assembly of nerve cells and their associated molecules. As Lewis Carroll's Alice might have phrased it: 'You're nothing but a pack of neurons'.

The second group espouses *functionalism* and is very popular among both cognitive scientists and philosophers such as Daniel Dennett (1991). They build on the notions of writers like Ryle (1967) and Koestler (1967), who believe 'that mental states are defined by their "functional organization" – that is, by the patterns of causal relations in the nervous system' (Capra and Luisi, 2014: 263). Mental states are not just patterns of neural connections but create wholes, or holons, which are also created by the function they serve.

The third 'small but growing group' (Capra and Luisi, 2014: 263) are the *neurophenomenologists*. They build on rigorous phenomenological examination of subjective and inter-subjective lived experience and how this is paralleled in neural pathways and patterns. They also embrace complexity theory in order to avoid the reductionism of 'linear cause and effect' explanations. I would include Iain McGilchrist (2009, 2021) in this group.

I would describe the first group as 'scientific materialists', who only acknowledge what can be objectively observed and empirically proven. The second group I see as 'system thinkers' but only the third group as 'systemic thinkers' (see Hawkins, 2015, 2021a and 2022; and Chapter 4). Sloman and Fernbach (2017) have argued that mind is not just dialogic but also collective and that much of what we know is not inside our brains but collectively held between us and our communities and our living and material environment. I have argued in a number of my books and articles that we need to move from IQ to what I have termed 'We Q' – or collective intelligence, which is more than the sum of individual intelligence – and that wisdom is found in the dialogue and connections between people and the world they inhabit.

In Hawkins and Ryde (2020: 82), I argued that mind was experienced through the interconnections between body, brain and relationships and that the mind was:

embedded not just in the relational field of interpersonal relationships, but also in the wider social field of family, community and ethnic culture. Then further out we see the mind as embedded in the co-evolutionary processes of *Homo sapiens*' inter-relationship with their environmental niche.

We need to realize that 'we are Earthlings first, humans second' (Rowe, 2006: 21) – that our species membership is a secondary characteristic. The environment is not something 'out there': we are inextricably part of the wider ecology, and it is part of us. It flows through our lungs, our guts and every fiber of our being: we need to find a new participatory consciousness.

To fully heal the split between the human and more-than-human world, we need to fall in love with the beauty of the world around us. For in each of these steps, Beauty has an important role to play. But before we explore these, let us step back and ask what Beauty really is.

What is Beauty?

There are many books written on Beauty from the perspective of the philosophy of aesthetics. Roger Scruton (2011) provides a useful summary of many of these from a white Western modernist perspective. They tell us about beauty, as analysed through the left-hemisphere neo-cortex; how to measure, judge, categorize and assess beauty. What they don't show is how to awaken to Beauty, engage and relate with and through Beauty, do the Beautiful and be the Beautiful. The aesthetics of living and connecting, rather than the aesthetics of objects and spectators.

Beauty has been a much-debated word and concept for thousands of years, and the creation of art in painting, music and sculpted objects goes back much further and has been found in the dwellings of the very earliest *Homo sapiens*, over 3 million years ago. Engagement with art and aesthetics seem to be core to all the great variety of human cultures. But ways of defining Beauty have been as varied as the array of artefacts each culture offers us.

Some people divide the world into things that are in themselves beautiful and those that are ugly, while others say that 'beauty is in the eye of the beholder'. If Beauty resided in an object, then everyone who encountered it would find it beautiful, which is never the case. If Beauty was in the eye of the beholder, then the beholder would see everything they beheld as beautiful, which is also never the case.

Beauty lies not in the viewed or the viewer but in the viewing, not in the musical score or the listener but the playing and hearing that co-create each other. Beauty is always relational, co-created by the eye and what it sees, the ear and what it hears, the touch, taste and smell and what they are awakened by and awakened to.

In the next section, we shall discover greater depths of Beauty, but for now, let me offer this tentative definition:

Beauty arises in the relationship between a harmonious emergence of life, which opens in the heart and imagination of a receptive being a greater depth and significance to the occurrence.

Beauty is not a fixed bond between an object and a perceiver, for this co-creation of Beauty is forever changing. What I sense as beautiful today may not seem beautiful tomorrow, when my mood, the light and that which I perceive may have changed, for what I see as beautiful is not a fixed object but the different vibrations of light reflecting off its surfaces. The perfume I smell is not fixed but a play of sensations in my nostrils as the scent enters my body. Every moment of beauty is fresh, newly arising, co-created by the occurrence, the perceiver and the context, and all three are evolving through the connection.

I would suggest that it is helpful to distinguish between three levels of Beauty that, though they build on each other, are also distinct; the higher order of Beauty cannot be reduced into the lower orders of Beauty or understood by them.

Level one: beauty that pleases the senses

A landscape that is pleasing to the eye; a beautifully presented plate of food or glass of wine that pleases the eyes and nose and, later, the palate; a charming and harmonious piece of music that pleases the ear. This level of Beauty requires little of the receiver, other than to be present, and often is soon forgotten. It creates a feeling of pleasantness, of enjoyment, of charm; but its touch is like that of a masseuse, making you feel relaxed and nurtured, but not loved.

Level two: beauty that delights

Here, I use 'delight' in the sense that William Blake did, when he wrote in 'The Marriage of Heaven and Hell' (Blake, 1968b):

> Energy is the only life, and is from the Body; and Reason is the bound or outward circumference of Energy. Energy is eternal delight.

Delight – for Beauty is light and lights us up. The receiver has an energetic physical response. Robert Bly, the American poet and writer, said in his workshops that I attended in the 1980s: 'listen for where the story enters your body, and you enter the story'. When you stand in front of a beautiful painting in an art gallery or read a great novel, metaphorically, you are not only in the art gallery but also in the picture; you may be in your chair reading but also living inside the novel.

Level three: beauty as a two-way relationship between participatory subjects

This goes further than level two, as here, we move beyond being the passive receiver to become a participating subject. Energy flows in both directions between two different but deeply connected presences. Beauty from beyond us awakens beauty within us, and from this loving relationship, this co-creation, a new beauty is born.

François Cheng (2009: 105) shows how:

> Beauty is precisely of a threefold nature. . . . The work of beauty, always arising from a between, is a third thing that, springing from the interaction of the two, allows the two to surpass themselves. If there is transcendence, it lies in this super surpassing.

We will explore Beauty in the space between and the marriage of opposites much more fully in Chapter 13.

The journey of our senses

There is another way we can consider how Beauty progressively opens our emotions. For many years, I have taught the seven basic sentic states, or emotional rhythms, that are universally recognizable and necessary for a flourishing human life. This is based on the pioneering work of Manfred Clynes (1977), who articulated the seven bodily rhythms as Anger, Hatred (perhaps better termed 'gut determination'), Grief, Love, Eros (poly-sensual excitement), Joy and Awe.

It is *love* that opens our hearts and our desires for a fuller life. It opens more fully all six of our embodied senses – touch, taste, smell, sound, sight and movement – into fuller sensuous engagement, the *eros* of life. Through sensuous eros, we find *joy* – delight in listening to music, seeing a beautiful vista, tasting a sumptuous meal, sharing love with others and the world in so many ways. As the joy grows, we open in *awe* at the wondrous depth, breadth and richness of life and a thankfulness for being so alive (see more on this in Chapter 10).

Beauty is a sympathetic co-arising, where in one moment, two beings that were formerly separate participate one with another. The Beauty of reconnection, of coming-together, reunion, a moment of wonderous oneness.

John Ruskin, the 19th-century English writer on art and artists, wrote: 'The degree of beauty we can see, in visible things, depends on the love we can bear them' (Ruskin, 1894: 230). He also showed how Beauty does not reside in the thing itself but in its 'felicity' to its surrounding context.

When I first went to university, the painting I took with me and hung over my desk was a reproduction of a Van Gogh painting of a tree in vibrant, vivid blossom, exfoliating and exuding glorious life. Van Gogh was the emotionally stormy antithesis of the measured and cerebral Ruskin. He wrote in his letters about the work of portraying the beauty of cypress trees in the South of France.

> Until now, I have not been able to do them as I feel them; the emotions that come over me in the face of nature can be so intense that I lose consciousness, and the result is a fortnight in which I cannot do any work.
>
> (Van Gogh, 1997: 481)

It is not the cypress tree that he is trying to paint but rather, how the vitality of this particular tree, in this context and light, show up inside his being: a portrayal of the sympathetic co-arising. His advice in his letter to his brother Theo was to 'Find things beautiful as much as you can, most people find too little beautiful' (Van Gogh, 1997).

In another letter, Van Gogh (1997: 470) wrote:

> If one carries on working quietly, beautiful subjects come of their own accord. Believe me, it is of the upmost importance to immerse oneself in reality, without any preconceived ideas, without any Parisian prejudice.

To see, hear and sense Beauty, we have to be quiet, open, receptive to what comes – ready to be taken, and entered into, by the beauty and vibrancy of the life beyond our life.

Beauty cannot be owned and is not collectable – as Sir William Hamilton discovered when Emma Hamilton left him in Naples for the sea captain, Horatio Nelson, and as Ruskin himself found out when his young wife, Effie Gray, ran away to live with the young, emotional and embodied, but impoverished, painter John Everett Millais. Beauty is an inherent and natural aspect of creation. Andreas Weber (2017: 214) writes how about laughter and happiness:

> arises from the joy of experiencing that beauty has its own power to exist. That it asserts itself. That it sustains. That it greets me. That it recognizes me. That I recognize it also. That I am able to see into its eyes, into the eyes of the water lilies . . . into the curious eyes of the ducks, into the calm eye of the lake itself, which welcomingly opens its watery mirror to the hesitant heavens.

Weber (2017: 215) goes on to say that this 'happiness does not belong to me alone, but to the world'.

Beauty is a loving form of symbiogenesis (Margulis, 1998) – a coming-together in co-natality (Spinoza, 1954), each giving birth to something in and trough the other. Van Gogh is breathing new life into the cypress tree at the same moment the tree and its surrounding wheat field is breathing new life into Van Gogh. They are jointly giving birth to something new. Together, Van Gogh and the tree gave birth to a painting that still inspires and ignites Beauty for generations of viewers.

Vincent Van Gogh has died, and the cypress tree may also now have died, both tree and man buried and feeding the earth, from which new life grows. However, the child of their co-natality, the work of art, lives on and arrests the passer-by in the gallery, who stops and is awakened to a fresh first-time experience that opens a spring of life within them. The way a work of art can continue to create fresh relationships in this manner is captured by William Shakespeare (1609) in his famous Sonnet 18, 'Shall I Compare Thee to a Summer's Day?' Shakespeare describes how nature is forever changing, but the poem gives lasting form to a moment of transient beauty. The sonnet ends:

> So long as men can breathe or eyes can see,
> So long lives this, and this gives life to thee.

My studies of Beauty have been guided by the great poets, whose writing came out of a deeply experienced engagement with wider life, and by spiritual teachers who 'walk in beauty'. This is echoed in the words of a Navajo prayer 'Walking in Beauty':

> In beauty I walk
> With beauty before me I walk

With beauty behind me I walk
With beauty above me I walk
With beauty around me I walk
It has become beauty again.

To learn the paths of Beauty, find a being who walks in Beauty and walk with them. This need not necessarily be a human being: you could track a deer, not as prey but as a teacher; or like Blake; or my wife and I breakfasting in the garden, metaphorically kiss a butterfly as it flies.

The poets who have been my teachers on the path of Beauty range from great Islamic Sufi poets and teachers (Ibn Al-Arabi, Saadi, Mevlana Jalaludin Rumi and Hafiz) to European poets (Dante, Blake, Wordsworth, Coleridge, Keats, Rilke and, more contemporaneous, John O'Donohue) to the Chinese, particularly from the Taoist tradition of the Tang dynasty period, but also François Cheng. Their teachings sprinkle this book with illumination and provide depth, as well as open realms way beyond my own capacity.

As we will explore in Chapter 14, poetry is the language of Beauty, for it bypasses the left-hemisphere neo-cortex and conveys much more than words, through its rhythms, rhymes and patterns.

Let us first listen – not just with our ears and neo-cortex but with our whole, embodied, richly experienced being – to John O'Donohue, an Irish Celtic Christian, who was born after me and sadly died young, though his teachings live on.

The human soul is hungry for beauty: we seek it everywhere – in landscape, music art, clothes, furniture, gardening, companionship, love, religion, and in ourselves.
When we experience the beautiful there is a sense of homecoming.
We feel most alive in the presence of the Beautiful for it meets the needs of our soul.
In the experience of beauty we awaken and surrender in the same act.
(O'Donohue, 2003: 2)

Now let us listen in the same way to François Cheng, who as I write is still very much alive in his nineties, as he meditates on 'The Way of Beauty' (Cheng, 2009; page number after each quote).

All beauty collaborates precisely with the uniqueness of the moment. True beauty could not be a perpetually fixed state. (15)
In the midst of the tragic human condition, it is, in fact, from beauty that we draw meaning and pleasure. (23)
true beauty is that which follows the course of the Way [the Tao], the irresistible progress toward open life – in other words, a principle of life that keeps its whole promise open. (23)

beauty is something that is virtually there, eternally there. It is a desire that burst forth from within beings, or Being, like an inexhaustible fountain. (24)

Beauty is always about becoming, an advent, if not to say an epiphany, and more concretely, 'an appearance'. (69)

Beauty implies interconnection, interaction, an encounter between the elements that constitute an occurrence of beauty, between the beauty present and the gaze that beholds it.

(69)

Beauty as a guide on the return journey of human consciousness

Human consciousness has become lost in a terrifying fragmented world of unrelated 'things'; connections have broken down. We can only sense what we can grasp and utilize with our left-hemisphere neo-cortex brain and only partake in what gives us immediate gratification.

Like Dante, we have a long journey to take on the path of return, the path to the fuller realization of Paradise (*Paradiso*). Beauty can start by helping us recognize that our left-hemisphere consciousness has the tendency to reduce all that we sense and perceive to its utility for us human beings – how it will feed us, be useful as a tool, or as fuel, or adornment of ourselves or our homes. Our Modernist consciousness tries to imprison Beauty in separate, collectable objects for self-benefit. To overcome this, we need to return to the perspective of the right brain, where we can experience Beauty in pattern, connections and harmony within contexts.

Now we can begin to realize that Beauty is neither residing in special objects, out there in the world, nor just 'in the eye of the beholder'. We can move beyond this false dualism and realize that all beauty – and indeed all life and all evolution – is co-created between elements, species, organisms and their contexts.

Beauty awakens us from imprisonment in our subjective solipsism to a world beyond us; it also teaches us that it cannot be captured, objectified, frozen in time. It only lives and thrives in living relationships. Here again, the words of William Blake's poem 'Eternity' (Blake, 1968d) say it so beautifully:

He who binds to himself a joy
Does the winged life destroy.
He who kisses the joy as it flies
Lives in eternity's sunrise

However, these words are only beautiful if they move beyond being collected and pinned in some anthology or website of 'great quotes' to being breathed, said aloud, felt in our bodies. In 'Auguries of Innocence', William Blake (1968e) wrote:

> To see a World in a Grain of Sand
> And a Heaven in a Wild Flower,
> Hold Infinity in the palm of your hand
> And Eternity in an hour

For many, this may sound like an unreachable place, reserved only for enlightened mystics, but it is also every person's birthright; it is within us, waiting to be uncovered. Many of us have had glimpses of this: when we feel through our bodies that we are conjoined with the sea we swim in, the mountain air we breathe or the woods we wander through. There is no separation. The sea is swimming me, the air is breathing me, and the woods are growing me.

Beauty is a participatory act. It is more than a spectacle that can entertain and please a passive audience. It is appreciated through the senses but also moves beyond them to awaken feelings and experiences in our bodies and our souls. Beauty gives birth to beauty. The beauty we perceive conceives beauty within us. The beauty we give birth to is perceived by others and gives birth to new beauty within them. François Cheng (2009) describes this in his wonderful meditations on beauty, where he meditates on the role of art:

> Art . . . draws its essence from the beauty contained in nature. . . . The purpose of artistic beauty in its highest state is more than aesthetic pleasure; its function is to give life. (p. 93)
>
> From this encounter, if it is deep enough, something else arises, a revelation, a transfiguration, like a painting by Cezanne born of encounter between the painter and the Sainte-Victoire Mountain.
>
> (p. 69)

Cheng (2009: 26) expands on his reflections on the paintings of Cézanne:

> For Cézanne, beauty results from encounters on all levels. On the level of represented nature, it is the encounter between the hidden and the revealed, between the moving and the fixed; on the level of the artistic act, it's encounter between brush strokes, between the colours applied. And beyond all this, there is this decisive encounter of the human spirit and the landscape at a privileged moment, with something trembling, embracing, unfinished in that interval, as if the artist has made himself the repository or host, awaiting the coming of some visitor who knows how to inhabit what is captured, offered.

Terry Tempest Williams (2009) writes: 'Finding beauty in a broken world is creating beauty in the world we find'. Our role is not just to search out beauty but be inspired by beauty to create beauty, do the beautiful and be the beautiful. Beauty takes us into relationships and then further, for Beauty opens the door to falling in love. (We shall explore this more fully in the next chapter.) As Arne Naess (1987 and Naess and Rothenberg, 2011) shows us in his inspirational writings on 'Deep Ecology', we humans care naturally for what we see as part of our circle of care – our kith and kin. We are capable even of sacrificing our own lives for the sake of our children and loved ones. We humans are also capable of great self-sacrifice for what we hold sacred. This arises not from religious intellectual belief but because such 'saintly' beings experience their God in all that is coming into being.

Naess (1987) argues that we must expand our self-realization to include an ecological self, where the boundaries between self and others – human beings and wider nature – dissolve, and we care for the ecology because it is our kith and kin. It is our mother, Gaia, who continually nurtures us and gives us life. Plants and earth and other animals are our brothers and sisters, as Saint Francis of Assisi taught and lived. Where I live, the flowers and vegetables we plant are our children to be looked after; the insects, birds, rabbits, deer, badgers, foxes and squirrels are our guests to be welcomed, and we are their guests.

The great Sufi teacher, Hazrat Inayat Khan (1926), gave us the trinity of Love, Harmony and Beauty. Through Beauty, we experience Harmony in what we hear, see and taste. Through Beauty, we are opened to Love. Through Love, we experience greater Beauty.

A more recent teacher, also originally from India, was Satish Kumar, who was a Jain monk at 9 years of age and a follower of Gandhi from his teenage years. After a worldwide pilgrimage for peace to the then four 'nuclear capitals of the world' (those that had atomic bombs: Moscow, Paris, London and Washington), he settled in the UK. He has given us the trinity of 'Soil, Society and Soul' (Kumar, 2013). Our being, or soul, is birthed out of a relationship and within society, which in turn is birthed from soil. From soil, we are birthed; in society, we are formed and learn; and to soil, we return – earth to earth, ashes to ashes, dust to dust, as is said in many Christian funerals. Like this present book, Kumar (2023a, 2023b) advocates: 'Radical Love: as a process for taking humanity from separation to connection with the Earth, each other, and ourselves'.

Conclusion

Ram Dass, the 20th-century American spiritual teacher, taught how 'We're all just walking each other home'. In this chapter, we have explored the possible journey home, from our imprisonment in the small dark prison of a flat, fragmented world to living an embodied, sensuous life in intimate participation with the wider nature that surrounds us, flows through us and gives life and meaning, both depth and breadth.

In the next section, we will explore Beauty's partners, all of whom have an important role to play on this journey of return. These partners include Love

(Chapter 5), Truth (6), Goodness (7), Art and Ethics (8), Death and Transience (9) and Grace (10). I will show how each of these partners with Beauty and how each partnership contributes to an important aspect of this return journey.

But let me end with some impassioned words from Arundhati Roy (2002: 34), writing about what had been lost in the Westernization of India and its acquisition of the nuclear bomb:

there is beauty yet in this brutal, damaged world of ours. Hidden, fierce, immense. Beauty that is uniquely ours and beauty that we have received with grace from others, enhanced, re-invented and made our own. We have to seek it out, nurture it, love it.

Chapter 4

Reimagining leadership and coaching

Introduction

So far in this book, we have explored the challenges now facing our planet and all life that it supports; how we cannot, as a species, respond to these great challenges without a fundamental shift in consciousness; and how Beauty might act as an important guide on this quest. Some of you may enjoy these high-altitude meta-reflections, while others may suffer from vertigo and have a need to get back to more solid ground. You may well be questioning what all this has to do with leadership and coaching. So before I go deeper into the many aspects of Beauty, let us explore the urgent need to reimagine both leadership and coaching.

First, we will look at how our ways of conceiving and defining leadership are part of humanity's inability to respond adequately to the challenges of our time and at the urgent need for a new leadership paradigm based on relationality rather than individualism, empathy and engagement rather than decisive directive control; and purpose and partnership rather than power.

Then we will explore how coaching needs to radically transform its purpose and role to help co-create, enable and support this new leadership that the world so desperately needs.

The old leadership paradigm

In 1840, Thomas Carlyle gave a series of lectures on heroism, later published as *On Heroes, Hero-Worship, & the Heroic in History* (1841), in which he states:

> Universal History, the history of what man has accomplished in this world, is at bottom the History of the Great Men who have worked here. They were the leaders of men, these great ones; the modellers, patterns, and in a wide sense creators, of whatsoever the general mass of men contrived to do or to attain; all things that we see standing accomplished in the world are properly the outer material result, the practical realisation and embodiment, of thoughts

DOI: 10.4324/9781003349600-6

that dwelt in the Great Men sent into the world: the soul of the whole world's history, it may justly be considered, were the history of these.

(Carlyle, 1841: 1–2)

This gave birth to the 'great man' theory of history and leadership. Despite Tolstoy's (1869) great critique of this theory, which he shows magnificently in his novel *War and Peace*, Carlyle's theory became a dominant influence of leadership thinking in the 20th century and is still having dangerous consequences in our current times. There are shelves full of biographies and hagiographies (as well as many films) of modern heroic leaders – in the fields of politics, business and sport – such as Churchill, Kennedy, Jack Welch, Bill Gates, Elon Musk, Alex Ferguson, to mention just a few, and much news coverages of their personalities and lives.

Leadership does not reside in leaders. For too long, we have confused the two terms, 'leader' and 'leadership', and many of the 'leadership development programmes' around the world are misnamed, as in truth they are 'leader development programmes', developing individual leaders rather than effective collective leadership (Hawkins, 2017a).

The leadership development industry has become massive, with the website futuremarketinsights.com reporting that economically, in 2022, the industry's revenue was $67,311 million and was growing at over 10% a year; and they estimate that by 2032, it would be $179,916 million. Yet in 2012, Professor Barbara Kellerman from Harvard University wrote:

Leaders of every sort are in disrepute; we don't have much better an idea of how to grow good leaders, or of how to stop or at least slow bad leaders, than we did a hundred or even a thousand years ago . . . **the leadership industry has not in any major, meaningful, measurable way improved the human condition**.

(Kellerman, 2012: xiv)

We may well question if much has changed in the last ten years. There has been a move to decrease the studying of past case studies of great heroic leaders and to spend time on personal and individual development. But the dominant paradigm is still human-centric, individualistic leader development, rather than leadership development that develops collective leadership that can partner with their followers, stakeholders and communities to address the urgent challenges of our times.

The new conception of leadership

If we look at the purpose of leadership at any depth, we discover that its role is first to sense and make sense of the changing world and the context in which the organization they lead exists and then to continually realign the organization, including its focus, priorities, connections, teams and people, to best respond to the changing needs of the coming times.

Collective leadership

I have argued elsewhere (Hawkins, 2017, 2021, 2022) that with the complexity of the current world and the rapid speed of change in the wider context, this task is way beyond the capability of even the best possible CEO and that the age of the heroic CEO is gone. If the only point of integration in an organization is an individual CEO, and others just manage their particular function, the organization is not sustainable in the long term. One global HR director, quoted in our 2017 research report (Hawkins, 2017a), said:

> Leadership is becoming less about being the smartest in the room and much more about how we collaborate, work with diverse stakeholders, inspire and bring the best out of others. Being more inclusive and collaborative. It's about developing our ability to be curious; our ability to explore new approaches, new perspectives, engage different stakeholders and viewpoints, and empathise with diverse perspectives.

I have argued for the need to develop collective leadership, where leadership teams function at more than the sum of their parts; I have shown the ways this can be developed (Hawkins, 2021) and examples of this in practice (Hawkins, 2022). The role of the leader is not only to ensure that this happens in their own team but also to develop the right culture, processes and support for this to happen across the organization, so the organization matures into a 'Team of Teams' that is more than the sum of its parts (Hawkins and Carr, forthcoming; McChrystal et al., 2015).

Relational leadership

Collective leadership and leadership teams are only one key aspect of the new leadership paradigm. Even more fundamental is the understanding that 'Relationship and interconnectedness are the underlying realities of life and existence' (Kumar, 2023b). All we know, all we feel and all we do is through relationship. All aspects of leadership are relational.

Only in more recent years have we seen a growing study of the role and contribution of followership in effective leadership (Kellerman, 2008; Rennaker, 2022). For a leader with no followers is merely a voice crying in the wilderness, from which leadership does not emerge. This has led to a greater focus on the relationship between leaders and followers, rather than on the personality, attributes and competencies of the leader or of the followers. This in turn has led to understanding some of the key attributes of the relational connection – such as engagement, dialogue, trust, partnership and a joint purpose.

1   Engagement

Engagement is different from both informing and communicating. *Informing* is one-way communication, normally about factual information. *Communication* involves two-way participation, which may be questions and answers or consultation. *Engagement* requires involving others in joint exploration and active participation, and here, the leader needs skills in how to hold space and how to facilitate and orchestrate full participation.

2   Dialogue

This I cover much more fully in Chapter 13 on ways to move from oppositional debate to generative and creative dialogue. Many team meetings become full of people reporting back and exchanging pre-cooked thinking or stuck in 'either-or' debates. Facilitating generative dialogue that co-creates fresh thinking, which nobody knew before they came together, is also a key leadership skill.

3   Trust

Every year, the Edelman Trust Barometer shows that public trust in leaders, be they politicians or business leaders, is diminishing, as the public regularly receives a diet of news stories of politicians who lie and cover up and business leaders who seem to be meeting their personal needs rather than serving the needs of the organization. Edelman shows how diminishing trust undermines the very social fabric of our countries (Edelman, 2023).

Good leaders create trust by following through on their commitments, doing what they promise, treating others with respect and in the way they would like to be treated and through the congruence of what they say and how they say it. This leadership behaviour is core to creating 'authentic congruence' (see Chapter 7) and 'Psychological Safety' (Edmondson, 2019), where team members and stakeholders feel confident to speak up without fear of being humiliated or criticized.

4   Inclusiveness

Trust is also built by leaders and collective leadership having an inclusive approach, one that treats everyone equally, whatever their age, gender, race, ability, sexual orientation or other differences. This does not mean they treat everyone the same; how they engage with different people will always be different, as it will arise inter-subjectively out of the relationship and its purpose.

5   Partnership

For leaders to be successful in the 21st century, they need to develop the capacity to work in partnership at many different levels. The leader needs to be able to partner with all their team members for the team to develop from being a team of leaders to a collective leadership team that is more than the sum of its parts (Hawkins, 2021). Then they need to ensure their team can partner with teams above it and beneath it, as well as upstream and downstream from them in the value chain. Furthermore, leaders need to be able to transform every stakeholder group – suppliers, customers, employees, investors, the communities they are part of and the wider ecology – into partners, rather than a person, group or system for whom they are trying to get it right.

The essence of partnership is working as equals, looking at what the partnership can achieve together that neither partner can achieve by themself. This involves developing the capacity for triangulated thinking and being (see Chapter 13). For partnerships to be transformative rather than transactional and formed through negotiation, they need to be purpose-led; and it is to this we will now turn.

The trinity of purposive leadership

Creating collective leadership that can engage, dialogue and partner not only with followers but also with external stakeholders and communities is an important foundation, but it is not sufficient in reimagining leadership that is future-fit for the mid-21st century. We must remember that a leader with lots of committed followers does not create leadership; rather, this leads to celebrity stalking, idolization, dependency and the Twittersphere (or should we now say Xsphere?). The current world has many celebrities with thousands or millions of followers; this demonstrates a hunger in followers but does not lead to leadership.

Therefore, we need to define leadership as being jointly co-created in a triangle of leaders, followers and a joint purpose (see Figure 4.1). In my research, practice and writings on leadership teams, I have shown how it is the purpose that creates the team, not the team members who create the purpose (Hawkins, 2021a, 2021b). If there was not a preexisting purpose, the team would not have been formed. The purpose is present before the team members arrive, but it is constantly changing as the wider context and needs of stakeholders evolve. The team has to constantly rediscover its emerging, evolving purpose through processes such as environmental scanning, continual dialogue with their stakeholders and future foresight. The same is true for an organization, partnership, country, family, marriage or any size of collective human entity.

A collective purpose is very different from a 'mission', which is a term born out of miliary strategy and then adopted and used in evangelism, exploration, exploitation and colonization. Missions are grown out of individual or collective

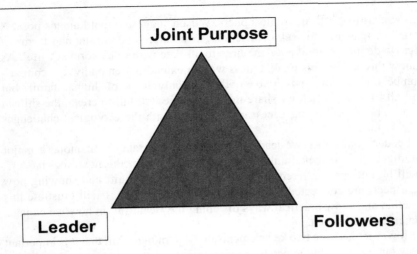

Figure 4.1 The triangle of leadership

ambition and will to power. Christopher Columbus and NASA had missions, as did their royal and governmental backers. I have worked with many companies whose mission was to become the pre-eminent leader in their sector. The Royal Bank of Scotland, before its spectacular and extremely costly collapse, had a mission to be the largest bank in the world. Mission is about control, power and dominance, fuelled by individual and collective egoism.

Purpose is quite different. It is grown out of service and an inquiry that is 'future-back and outside-in', discovering what I, and we, can uniquely do that the world of tomorrow needs. I would go further than just suggesting that leadership is co-created by the triangle of leader, followers and a 'shared purpose'; I would propose that Purpose is the prime originator. It is Purpose that calls forth a new response from the relationship of collective leadership and their followers.

Some might argue that we could do away with followership, see everyone as leaders and just have co-created leadership. In some circumstances, this is valid, but where there is greater complexity, there is a need for individuals and leadership teams to put aside their individual voice and focus on the collective, external and future emerging needs and then to focus on creating engagement and alignment in addressing these needs. The leader is not better or necessarily more important than followers but has a different and wider responsibility and focus.

Eco-systemic leadership

The term 'biophilia' was first used by Eric Fromm (1964) and then popularized by Edward O. Wilson in his book *Biophilia* (1984), although its roots can be seen in the writings of Goethe, Owen Barfield, Naess, as well as many pre-Modernist poets and philosophers. Wilson suggested that humans possess an innate tendency to seek connections with nature and non-human forms of life. He defined biophilia as 'the urge to affiliate with other forms of life'. As I show throughout this book, unless we can extend our empathy and compassion beyond our kith and kin to embrace not only the whole human family but also all life with which we share this planet, we will fail to create the shift in feeling, being and doing necessary to engage with the ecological challenges we now face.

Leaders and collective leadership have to undertake a metanoia, a major paradigm shift in their thinking, doing and being. In the next six chapters, I will be outlining different aspects of this paradigm shift and showing how the aspects are connected by Beauty. In the final section, I will illustrate this in action and show practical ways of 'doing the Beautiful' in how we engage, relate, lead and coach.

However, there are two key elements of the paradigm shift that it is important to lay out here: the difference between atomistic, system and systemic thinking and eco-systemic awareness and the move from human-centric to eco-centric and biophilic ways of being.

The difference between linear and atomistic, system and systemic thinking and eco-systemic awareness

Linear and atomistic thinking is what Blake described as 'Newton's single-eyed vision'. The scientific revolution and the development of the 'empirical method' produced an approach to challenges by breaking them down into their constituent parts by using a lens of building blocks and billiard balls, creating linear cause-and-effect analysis – an atomistic world and a world of subjects and objects. This has brought many benefits to humans, from electronic communication and appliances, to computers, to AI and the 'internets of knowledge and things'. But as we saw in Chapter 2, when it becomes the dominant way of perceiving the world, it shrinks the Beauty and fullness of life.

Influenced by quantum physics and new understandings of time and space, 'systems thinking' was developed in the mid-20th century and was defined by Capra (1996: 27) as follows: 'to study an integrated whole and the essential properties which arise from the relationships between the parts, rather than look at the parts'.

From this systemic perspective, we look at a bicycle not as a compilation of saddle, frame, wheels, tyres, pedals, chain and handlebars, but we look at how the parts interrelate to create a vehicle that can stay upright and move along if the system also contains a cyclist!

Also, from this perspective, we look at a team as an entity rather than the sum of the team members – and ask, 'What can the team do together that they could not do working in parallel?'

Nested systemic thinking

> It is never enough to focus on just one level of system. To understand the human individual, we need to understand the sub-systems that comprise the individual; these could be the physical organs, that are necessary for their physical well-being, or the many roles and sub-personalities that are integral to their way of being in the world.
>
> (Hawkins, 2023b)

We also need to look at the systemic the individual is nested within and shaped by – their family of origin, their current family, the team and organization they work within, the national, local and ethnic culture they are part of. As Wendell Berry (1983: 46), the great American farmer philosopher, shows, we all live within 'a system of nested systems: the individual human within the family, within the community, within agriculture, within nature'.

Thus, we think about the bicycle as part of the system of bicycles, which are part of a transport system, which includes cars, buses, pedestrians, crossroads, traffic lights, flows and stops. These in turn are part of a human community, which requires journeys, which are part of a more-than-human ecology that provides all the resources for roads and all forms of transport.

From this lens, we study teams in the way they are nested within organizational systems, including the following:

- organizational structure – how the team is part of a division, which is part of a business, which is part of group company
- organizational processes, such as production flow, communication, the value change from raw materials, through suppliers, production distribution, to customers and beyond
- stakeholder communities, customers, suppliers, investors, employees, communities in which the organization operates
- the political, economic, social, technological, cultural and legal systems in which the team and the wider organization operate
- the ecological biosphere in which all the aforementioned examples takes place and upon which it is totally dependent.

Systemic thinking focusses on the patterns, relationships and interdependency between systems. This leads to three important notions:

a. **Interdependency** – Every system is dependent on the sub-systems within it and the systems it is nested within.
b. **Co-creation** – The species is shaped by its environmental niche and also changes and shapes this same niche. This is the constant, ever-changing, dynamic dance that is happening at all systemic levels.

c. **Creativity and innovation** Happens both through '*auto-poiesis*' (the self-organizing of the relations and connections within an organism or system) and '*onto-poiesis*' (the co-creation between any organism or system and its wider context or niche). Evolution and change do not happen within closed systems but rather, at the interface between systems and between nested systemic levels.

The bicycle system (including the rider) is changed by the transport system in which it is functioning – the surface of the road, the density of other traffic and so on. And at the same time, it is changing the transport system of which it is part – shaped and shaper.

The team is shaped by the organizational system it is part of and the stakeholder systems with which it interacts, but it is also changing the organization and the stakeholders. However, systems thinking can still keep us trapped within a materialistic and mechanized way of seeing the world. As Peter Senge and colleagues wrote in their book *Presence* (2005):

> our normal way of thinking cheats us. It leads us to think of wholes as made-up of many parts, the way a car is made-up of wheels, a chassis and a train. In this way of thinking the whole is assembled from the parts and depends upon them to work effectively, if a part is broken, it must be repaired or replaced, but living systems are different. . . . The basic problem with [organizations] is that they have not yet become aware of themselves as living.

To understand living systems, we need to move beyond systemic thinking to eco-systemic awareness (Senge et al., 2005; Senge, 2008; Hawkins, 2015, 2020, 2021a, 2021d; Hutchins and Storm, 2019).

Systemic awareness

In systems thinking, we can still be restricted within a limited observer perspective, of static objects within objects, systems within systems, like Russian dolls.

> Nature does not show us any isolated building-blocks, but rather appears as a complex web of relationships between the various parts of a unified whole.
> (Capra, quoted in Hutchins and Storm, 2019: 106)

Ingold (2011: 117) goes further:

> in a world that is truly open there are no objects as such . . . no such boundaries, no insides or outsides, only comings and goings. Such productive movements may generate formations, swellings, growths, protuberances and occurrences, that are not objects.

This is a world not of static being but a meshwork of becoming, where we need verbs rather than nouns, for everything that we classify with nouns is in the process of changing, not by itself but in entwined transformation with others – a relational world that is never static. In the meshwork world, 'lives are not closed in entities that could be enumerated or added up; they are open-ended processes whose most outstanding characteristic is that they carry on' (Ingold, 2011: 11).

There are three fundamental shifts required to move from *systems thinking and nested system thinking* to *systemic awareness:*

a. from studying systems as things to seeing the patterns that dance and flow between and through the many nested systemic levels
b. from left-hemisphere neo-cortex thinking to whole-brain and embodied awareness
c. from believing you can view systems 'objectively' to realizing you are part of everything you study and they are part of you

Systemic awareness requires intuitive as well as analytic thinking, both artistic and scientific craft. It needs sensuous, embodied knowing, not just propositional knowledge, and leads beyond 'knowing about' to 'knowing with and through'.

Systemic awareness involves the holographic notion that the dynamic within one systemic level is mirrored in the systemic levels that are nested within it. So an individual never turns up for coaching alone because the dynamics of their family (both of origin and current); the patterns, language constructions and mindsets of their culture; the organizational dynamics of places they might work and/or live in; the conflicts in the human drama; and the dynamics of the relationship between the human and the more-than-human world all arrive holographically within them and are played out between them and the coach.

In the inter-subjective world (Stolorow and Atwood, 1992) and a meshwork world (Ingold, 2011 and 2015), we can never make categorical statements or judgments about another person or group; we can only say: 'This is how I experienced them, through our relationship in this context, at this time'. In truth, we can only know and describe the relational 'becoming' of another, in and through our inter-subjective relationship. Statements we make about their objectified 'being' are always just a partial snapshot of a frozen moment in time, where the photographer is hiding while, at the same time, co-creating the event and controlling and cropping the frame.

Revisioning coaching

When I was working in post-apartheid South Africa, in the late 1990s and early years of this century, I was asked to help one large region develop a coaching culture that would connect the government, schools, hospitals and the wider population. I brought together the people who had developed the draft strategy with 60 stakeholders, including senior leaders, middle leaders and front-line team leaders, with people from hospitals, schools and taxpayers. I asked some people to step into the role of future generations and some to give voice to the wider ecology. After each section of the draft strategy was read out, I facilitated a pause and invited stakeholder feedback. I will never forget the young, tall, black front-line team leader, who stood up and said:

> *It sounds like the people with the big offices, big cars and big pay checks, now get the big coaches and that coaching is very expensive personal development for the already highly privileged.*

His challenge hit me in the stomach. I began to ask myself if that was what I was spending my life doing, providing expensive personal development for the already highly privileged? Was it what I should be doing? I set out to address the challenge of how coaching could deliver real value beyond the individual (Hawkins, 2015, 2020, 2021a, 2021b, 2022; Hawkins and Turner, 2020; Whybrow et al., 2023).

At the same time, I was addressing the challenge of how coaching could make its most significant contribution to the global need to transform human consciousness. The urgency of the global challenges means that it is unlikely we have the time to shift human consciousness one person at a time, so we have to shift the collective culture and connections, not just the individuals. If the coaching industry is to be of real service to helping create future-fit leadership, it needs to transform itself.

I developed seven major ways of transforming, which I consider are essential for coaching to step up to 'what it could uniquely do that the world of tomorrow needs'. Some have considered these heretical and against the fundamental principles of coaching, while many have welcomed and adopted them and felt liberated from the previous narrow coaching confines. Some, if still not all, are increasingly being adopted in the teaching and practice of coaching.

1 Seeing the coachee as your coaching partner and the coaching as co-created

Traditionally, coaching has been 'client-centric', where the client is seen as the coachee. Coaches have been trained to be on the 'client's agenda' and to start coaching relationships and coaching sessions by asking the 'client' what they want from coaching. Coaching is seen as done solely by the coach; the relationship is that of a supplier and customer, with the customer being asked to rate their customer satisfaction with their coach supplier.

In the new coaching paradigm, we recognize that the relationship is that of a partnership, where both coach and coachee are working together to arrive at new understanding and new ways of being and doing, which neither could have arrived at by themselves. Like all good partnerships, it should achieve more than the sum of its parts (see earlier and Chapter 12.)

2   Seeing the client as all the stakeholders that the coachee's life and work serves

Once the coach and coachee are shoulder-to-shoulder, working in co-creative partnership, then together, they can focus not on what the coachee wants from the coaching but what is necessary to enable the coachee to co-create greater beneficial value with, and for, all their stakeholders, including their colleagues, team, those they report to, the other parts of the organization, customers, suppliers, investors, their professional community, their geographical community and the wider ecology.

3   Bringing the stakeholder's voice into the coaching room

To focus on what is necessary to co-create greater beneficial value for all the coachee's stakeholders requires bringing their voice into the coaching room, at the beginning, middle and end of each session and of the whole coaching relationship. From the first session, we can ask: 'Who does your life and work serve?' Then, 'Who else? Who beyond your team, your function, your organization, the human world, the present?' to ensure a perspective that is as wide as possible is in the room. Then we can ask: 'If these stakeholders were in the room, what would they be saying is the work that you and I need to be doing together in the coaching?' At the end of a session, or in reviewing the coaching relationship, we can ask: 'If your stakeholders had been listening to our coaching, what would they have appreciated about the work we have done together, and what would their challenge be to us?'

The coachee can experiment in standing in the shoes of different stakeholders and imaginatively speaking from their perspective.

This approach can also be assisted by inviting stakeholders live into the coaching, to explore what is needed from the coaching for wider benefit to be created (see Turner and Hawkins, 2016; Hawkins and Turner, 2020; and Chapter 12 of this book).

4   Attending to the wider ecology from the very first meeting

In working with ecological and climate conscious coaching over the last ten years, I have discovered that if you do not address the ecological dimensions of the coachee's world in the first coaching meeting, it becomes harder and harder to mention or address (Whybrow et al., 2023). In many presentations, I have been met with challenges from traditional coaches, saying, 'It is not our job to bring the ecology into the coaching room'. On some occasions, I have replied by asking whether their clients eat and breathe. And when they retort, 'Of course, they do', I point out, 'Then the ecology is already in the room. You are just not paying attention to it'.

5   Jointly working at the learning edge, rather than believing that either the coach or the coachee has the answer

Traditionally, coaching has taught that it is the coachee who has the answer and that the job of the coach is just to help them find and access the answer that they already know. But after 45 years of coaching, this is not my experience or that of the many hundreds of coaches I have supervised. The most valuable coaching work is carried out at what I have termed 'the learning edge', where neither coach nor coachee have the answer, but both are aware of the challenges and questions that urgently need a response. This is where a coach needs the personal patience and emotional strength to resist premature 'solutions', as well as many skills in collaborative inquiry, where the coach and coachee can together discover a new response of which neither were previously aware. We will explore these skills throughout this book and how this collaborative inquiry can be guided and deepened by Beauty. Practical examples and vignettes are included in Chapters 12, Chapters 13 and Chapters 14.

6   Coaching connections, not problems

In traditional coaching, the coachee would arrive at coaching with a semi-prepared agenda of problems they wanted to address, and these would be explored one at a time – problems like 'my difficult boss', 'the conflict between two of my team members', 'this demanding customer' and 'How do I sought these all out?'

Problem-centric coaching is by nature atomistic, non-systemic, and is in search of solutions. In the new paradigm, the role of coaching is to widen the perspective and see the so-called problem in, and as a symptom of, its wider context. You cannot solve a problem that you are not in some way part of, or connected to, so the first work of the coach is to reframe the problem as a challenge for the coachee. When the coachee says, 'I want to talk about my terrible boss', or about a 'difficult team member', the coach replies: 'So we need to explore your challenge in relating to your boss or managing your team member'. Here, we are locating the challenges in a relationship or connection of which the coachee is a part and the only part that can change here in the coaching room. But as we have repeatedly discovered, if this part changes, so will the relationship.

7   Moving beyond insight and action plans to focussing on embodied change in the room

In the early days of developing *Coaching Supervision* (Hawkins and Smith, 2006 and 2013), we discovered through our research (Hawkins and Schwenk, 2006) that the most frequent challenge brought by coaches to supervision was that despite a 'good' coaching session, which had an 'aha moment' and ended with a new 'action plan', the coachee had returned to the next session reporting that nothing had changed and that the action plan had not been carried out. The coach would then often blame the coachee – they 'lacked the courage or the commitment' – rather than ask what they, as coach, needed to do differently in their coaching style to transform this oft- repeated pattern. From this recognition, I developed the phrases: 'The coaching road to hell is paved with "aha" moments and action plans that never get enacted'; and 'If the change does not happen in the coaching room, it is unlikely to happen back in the workplace'.

Insight and commitments are often made with the neo-cortex part of the brain. But change is always embodied, so for coaching to be effective, it cannot end with action plans and good intentions but needs to move these into embodied change, live in the coaching room. We have developed the approach of the 'fast-forward rehearsal' (Hawkins and Smith, 2013) in which, when the coachee creates an action plan to have a very different conversation with their boss next Wednesday, the coach says: 'Let's rehearse next Wednesday right now. Show me [not tell me] how you are going to start that conversation'. Now we begin to move from cerebral good intentions to embodied change in the room.

How Beauty takes us further

In this book, we will take these two new paradigms for leadership and coaching deeper and broader, with Beauty as our guide. Both crafts have been, to a large degree, captured by scientific, atomistic, mechanistic, left-brain ways of viewing the world – from Taylor's (1911) framework of scientific management, through theories of leadership traits and the development of competencies frameworks for both leaders and coaches, to hundreds of books of leadership and coaching tools and methods. Both leadership and coaching can also be seen as art forms, where the instrument that is being used is ourself and the artistry we can spend a lifetime learning and perfecting. Ursula Le Guin (2015) writes in her preface to her late poems:

> Science describes accurately from outside, poetry describes accurately from inside. Science explicates, poetry implicates. Both celebrate what they describe. We need the languages of both science and poetry to save us from merely stockpiling endless 'information' that fails to inform our ignorance or our irresponsibility.

In this book, we will rebalance the worlds of leadership and coaching by hearing more from the poets, the artists and the musicians of life than from the scientists – although the post-modern scientists of quantum physics, the new biology and understanding of evolution and the neuroscientists will have an accompanying voice throughout. Our aim is to find a new marriage of 'poetic objectivity' (Weber, 2019) and 'scientific subjectivity' (Heisenberg, 1971) that illuminates our beautiful world from inside and out.

Conclusion

All of the earlier approaches in the new paradigms for leadership and coaching can be done from a cerebral and technical consciousness. But as we will explore throughout this book, this will not, by itself, achieve the embodied shift in consciousness and the ways of being needed from leaders and coaches for human beings to live on this Earth in a way that is 'future-fit'.

The transformation needs to go way beyond skills, methods and concepts and become a practice that involves not just all parts of the brain but also the knowing of the heart and the gut and the awareness of the whole embodied, relational being. This is where Beauty has such an important part to play, as it transcends left-brain analytic thinking and goals of efficiency and utility and moves us into deeper relational awareness of the feelings and the heart.

Through the next six chapters, we will explore how to practice these new paradigms and develop a number of new capacities in our core being: the capacity to love the people we work with and the work we do together; the capacity to be aesthetically ethical, always in search of the truth and transparency and in service of the collective good and justice; the capacity to embrace death as a natural part of life, not its opposite; and the capacity to be graceful and express gratitude. Only then can we return, in Chapters 11–14, to consider the art of leadership and coaching informed by these capacities and, in Chapter 15, to consider these as a way of living.

Part 2

Awakening to Beauty

Introduction to Part 2

We are now ready for the next stage of our journey. We have looked the intercon-nected challenges of our troubled world fully in the eye and discovered how they are a product of the shrinking of human consciousness, through the scientific, industrial and technological revolutions into the age of the Anthropocene, with great benefits for the privileged minority but enormous costs for the majority of humanity and even bigger costs for the ecology of the Earth. We have looked at how traditional approaches to leadership and coaching have been part of the problem, not part of the remedy, and at the paradigmatic changes necessary in both for them to become wellsprings for the urgently needed shift in human consciousness.

We have introduced how Beauty can be our essential guide on this journey, as she awakens us from our solipsistic narcissism to the amazing world beyond our grasp or control; she opens all our senses to fall in love with a rich relational and embodied world of colours, sounds, smells, tastes and movements. In the following chapters, we will go deeper to explore different aspects and vistas that are opened by Beauty, starting with her sisters, Truth and Good. This naturally leads us to explore Ethics, informed by aesthetics and an ecological ethics that reconnects us to a co-creative relationship with the wider world. To go deeper on this journey, we need to find a new relationship with death and transience, beyond fear, control and clinging to life, as well as discover grace, gracefulness and gratitude and an aesthetic intelligence that can deepen and broaden our lead-ership and coaching.

Only after this journey will we be ready to look, in Part 3, at how the arts of leadership and coaching can practically transform to become the much-needed servants of the required transformation in human consciousness.

DOI: 10.4324/9781003349600-7

Chapter 5

Beauty and love

Introduction

The first partner of Beauty we will explore is Love, for as I have shown in Chapter 3, Beauty opens the door for Love to flow. Beauty awakens us, excites desire and draws us – and all living organisms – into relationship with what previously was 'other'. Having shown how life is primarily relational, we will now explore how Beauty and Love are the currents of connection.

As Andreas Weber (2017: 3) writes:

> it could be that the planet is not actually suffering from either environmental crisis or an economic one. Instead, it could be that the earth is currently suffering from a shortage of our love.

And that only by:

> relearning to understand our existence as a practice of love will we grasp the overwhelming human dilemmas that we face . . . and find the means to deal with them differently than we have thus far.
>
> (Weber, 2017: xiv)

Barcelona's great 20th-century architect, Antoni Gaudí, wrote that to be a great architect, first, you needed love, then technique. The same is true for both leaders and coaches; but in nearly all the trainings for both groups, there is no training on learning to love our work, love the people we work with, their (and our) customers and stakeholders, the communities and wider world around us and the Beauty that life gives us every moment of every day.

We will begin with a trip back to the world of Socrates and Plato to explore the teachings of the female philosopher Diotima on the stages of Love. Like many mystical teachings that have come down to us through Plato, this is somewhat masculinized, individualistic and anthropocentric, so we will explore stories of other journeys of Love and then discover how eco-systemic and evolutionary

DOI: 10.4324/9781003349600-8

love are at the heart of evolving creation. We will then apply this, with examples to how Love is central for both leadership and coaching.

Diotima and the systemic levels of love

Imagine you have been transported to Athens in 414 BC, the birthplace of modern European civilization and philosophy and where the roots of modernity lie, although philosophy has earlier roots in such places as China, India, Egypt, Persia and Africa. You are taken to the house of Agathon, who is hosting an all-male dinner party for his philosopher friends. After much eating and drinking, the guests decide to hold a speech contest, in which each of them delivers a lecture in praise of Eros, the god of love. Each man pontificates on the difference between lower and higher love, ending with Agathon himself, who shows how love is at the heart of what brings people together in collaboration, social gatherings and celebrations.

But then Socrates takes the floor. Instead of competing with the previous speakers, he turns to the teachings of Diotima, a great female prophet and philosopher from whom he learned about love. Due to male hegemony, we talk about 'platonic love', but we should really call it 'Diotimic love', honouring its feminine origins. For according to Socrates and Plato, it is Diotima who first outlined the journey of the maturation of human love, as it opens from the particular and the material to embrace greater systemic breadth and depth.

Diotima tells us that love, *eros*, is the child of poverty and resource. From a realization of our 'poverty', we feel our incompleteness and a hunger to search and reach beyond ourselves. From our 'resource', we develop the creativity to keep travelling to the learning edge to discover more in the world around us, opening up new capacities within us, new depth and breadth.

Diotima describes the following stages on this journey of love.

First: Love for a particular body. The journey of adult love starts when we fall in love with another and are overcome with its physical beauty. We feel our own incompleteness and long to possess the other. The beloved is imbued with all we feel we lack and long for. Different bodies attract different individuals.

Second: Love for all bodies. We recognize the physical features that we are attracted to and understand that many bodies can have the same beauty. We start to see beauty in many bodies and learn to love the differences.

Third: Love for souls. Physical features become less important and spiritual and moral beauty trigger love. In this step, we fall in love with beautiful minds and the beauty of people's 'being'.

Fourth: Love for community. Love for the practices, customs or foundations that were developed by the people with beautiful souls.

Fifth: Love for knowledge. We turn our love to all kinds of knowledge, and we love that there is knowledge and learning to acquire everywhere.

Sixth: Love for love itself. Here, we see Beauty in its archetypal form and love the beauty of love itself. Every beautiful thing is beautiful because it radiates archetypal beauty. The lover now apprehends beauty everywhere and reflects the beauty they experience in their own being and creating.

Socrates, in his recounting of Diotima's teaching, explains that love is a means to 'know the very essence of beauty' (211c-d). In the 'Symposium', Plato (1970b) reports Socrates saying: 'I . . . understand nothing but that love matters' (177e).

Erotic love is seen not just as physical sexual desire but as a broader force that drives us to attain the unattainable. Beauty cannot be possessed, yet humans instinctively long to do so. In our yearning for Beauty, we attempt to come as close to it as possible by creating Beauty ourselves.

All forms of beautiful arts can be viewed as examples of the creation of Beauty enabled by *eros*. When we read a novel or poem, see a great painting or hear a moving piece of music, we may be inspired by its beauty to create our own art – literary, visual or musical. *Eros* enables us to transform ourselves in the light of our beloved's beautiful qualities, with the goal of reaching *kalon*, or Beauty, ourselves. In Plato's view, only eros can provide this driving desire.

Love, said Diotima, must not be confused with the object of love. Love itself is perfectly beautiful and perfectly good. If Love desires but does not try and possess beautiful and good things, then Love cannot, as most people think, be a god; it can only be the child of poverty and resource – always in need, always searching and always inventive.

Love is not a god but a great spirit (daemon) who intermediates between gods and humans. As such, Love is neither mortal nor immortal, neither wise nor ignorant but a lover of wisdom. The evil of ignorance is when those who are neither good nor wise are nevertheless satisfied with themselves. It is Love that moves us beyond the lethargy and accidie of our self-satisfaction – the love and desire to learn and discover more, to go in search of the beautiful.

When we are young, we need to be awakened from being in love with ourself to fall in love with the beautiful body of a loved one; thus, we realize we are not alone and learn love through another. Often after the heartbreak of the breakup of our first romantic attachment, we start to discover that Beauty is not confined to this one person, and we awaken to seeing beautiful bodies all around us. This can lead to a period of erotic feasting, sexual indulgence and addiction to sensuous pleasures of all kinds.

But soon, for many, this becomes unsatisfying, whereas those who get stuck at this stage become addicts who need more and more of what superficially and temporarily delights. Those who can mature in their love learn to appreciate that Beauty comes from the light of the individual's being – what some would call their essence, soul or spirit. This light shines through their eyes, their voice, visage and body and is superior to the superficial beauty of their physical appearance. Now we are able to love the inner being of others.

Only after loving the beauty of others' souls, Diotima suggests, can we start to love the inner beauty of the collective culture and its rituals, practices and customs. Only then can we experience the love and awe that can come from attending a music festival or sporting event, singing in a choir, partaking in a religious ritual or collective act of worship – the in-depth beauty of participation and collective effervescence.

Durkheim, the great sociologist, describes this process:

Collective effervescence stimulates various collective representations of social life, including various symbols, myths and ideas, through which individuals imagine the society of which they are members and the obscure yet intimate relations they have with it.

(Durkheim, 1995 [1912]: 227)

This can stimulate a desire to learn and to participate in the customs and rituals of other cultures and societies, to travel and explore in ways that liberate us from the constraints of our native culture. This, for Diotima, is the heart of philosophy, which in the Greek means the love of wisdom, which comes from fully embodied engagement.

The final stage for Diotima in the journey is to love and experience Beauty itself, rather than the various appearances of Beauty. This is why love is so important and why it deserves so much praise.

Hazrat Inayat Khan, the great Indian Sufi teacher who brought to the West a universal form of Sufism, in many ways follows the same stages as Plato, Socrates and Diotima. He writes (Khan, 1972: Vol. 11, Section 12) that our maturation in and through Beauty begins with finding beauty in objects, an earlier stage than any stage in Diotima's progression. Secondly, loving the beauty manifested by a living being. Then the beauty of their being – and how they connect and are in harmony with their place, their context and the needs of their time. Then, finally, finding love for the eternal and universal beauty that emanates from God.

Khan goes on to explore how we have to withdraw the projection of beauty from locating beauty in time and space and love the essence that emanates through the particular. Dante had to stop investing all his love in the hope of a lasting relationship with the beautiful young Beatrice and learn to love the opening to beauty that Beatrice had created in his heart. Only by following this, says Khan, will we eventually come to the divine beauty, beyond words and description, that Dante discovers in the 'Paradiso'.

We have to learn to love the act of loving, not just the object of our love. The object of our love will always eventually disappoint us; or we will become jealous of it, wanting to possess or imprison it, which in turn will destroy the love; or we become envious of the one we love, wanting to receive the love that we are giving to them.

   In exploring these levels in the progression of loving Beauty, I am reminded of the story of Hafiz, who grew up to be the greatest Sufi and poet of Iran. He was first a poor baker's delivery boy, who fell in love with the mayor's daughter in Shiraz, called Shakh-e-Nabat. He could think of nothing but her. But Hafiz could see no way that he, a poor 14-year-old boy, could be accepted by the daughter of the richest man in Shiraz. He was then told that if you stand supperless for 39 days and 39 nights at the grave of a great Sufi saint, any wish will be granted to you.

   His overwhelming love for the girl drives him to undertake this ordeal. On the final night of this fast, with lack of food and sleep, he is visited in a vision by the Angel Gabriel, who asks him: 'Hafiz, what is your wish?' He looks up and suddenly discovers that this angel is even more beautiful than the young girl. The angel asks again: 'Hafiz, what is your wish?' The young boy suddenly realizes that if Gabriel is so much more beautiful than the most beautiful girl in Shiraz, then God must be even more beautiful than Gabriel and everything else in creation. When Angel Gabriel asks for the third time: 'Hafiz, what is your wish?' Hafiz cries out from his heart and soul: 'Give me God. Give me God!' The Angel Gabriel responds by leading Hafiz by the hand through the back streets of Shiraz, where he knocks on the door of the Sufi teacher Hajji Zayn al-Attar.

   Much later in his life, when he was already a famous poet, and admired by the Mongol Emperor Timor (known in the west as Tamburlaine), Hafiz put his life in danger by telling the Emperor that he would exchange the great cities of Samarkand and Bukhara for the beauty of the mole of a particular woman (perhaps a heartfelt memory of Shakh-e-Nabat). Just in time, Timor realized that this was not an insult, implying that the great Empire he had fought for and built was worthless but rather that beauty and love were of more value than any material possessions.

   Let us now explore this story through Diotima's levels of Love.

First: Love for an individual person. Hafiz falls deeply in love with the beautiful Shakh-e-Nabat.

Second: Love for all bodies. Hafiz falls in love with the beauty of Gabriel.

Third: Love for souls. Hafiz realizes that Gabriel is an archetypal vision and that his beauty comes from the beauty of the divine light flowing through him.

Fourth: Love for communities, their practices, customs and culture. Hafiz, having already learnt the whole of the Koran off by heart by the time he was 14, goes on to learn by heart the poems of Rumi, Saadi, Farid ud-Din and Nizami and partake in other Sufi practices.

Fifth: Love for knowledge. Hafiz's teacher, Hajji Zayn al-Attar, was one of the greatest scientists of his age, a physician, chemist and author of one of the earliest pharmacopeias known. He guides Hafiz in his quest to expand his learning in all directions. Hafiz is a dedicated student, but all his life places higher value on learning from direct experience than from books. In his poems, he constantly praises Saki, the bringer of the wine, a metaphor for the wisdom that comes from direct experience.

Sixth: Love for love itself. Hafiz sees the beauty, both in its form and loves the beauty of love for itself, Hafiz put his life in danger by showing Emperor Timor that love transcends any material object that it is loved.

Patrick Curry (2019) warns us about the dangers of Plato's ladders that take us further and further away from the 'enchantment' in particular moments in the earthly world around us, and creates transcendent ideals, that leave behind and denigrate the material world. Curry (2019: 114) quotes Nietzsche: 'the worst, most durable, and most dangerous of all errors so far was a dogmatist's error-namely, Plato's invention of the pure spirit and the good'. In this, I am reminded of Bateson's plea that we never separate the transcendent from the imminent. Like Blake, we need to see and love the eternal in the moment and love the whole in the particulars. But the opposite danger is also present, that our love becomes fixated, on a person, an object, a tribe, a moment in time.

Here is the story of Charlemagne, as retold by Piero Ferrucci (2010: 25).

According to legend, Charlemagne, when he was already old, fell madly in love with a young woman – an embarrassing and difficult situation. The Holy Roman Emperor was losing his imperial dignity. Then suddenly the young woman died. Was the problem solved? No, on the contrary, it was still more embarrassing, because Charlamagne kept being in love with her. He had her embalmed and spent his days in adoration beside her body. The Archbishop of Reims, Turpino, suspected bewitchment and indeed found that the girl had a magic ring under her tongue. Clearly the ring had the power to make its owner irresistibly lovely and lovable. The Archbishop took possession of it, and sure enough Charlemagne fell in love with him. The Archbishop was not in the least interested, so he run away from the emperor and threw the ring into Lake Constance, you could guess what happened to Charlemagne: he fell in love with the lake and ended his days tenderly contemplating it.

From these varied stories of Hafiz and Charlemagne, we can move beyond seeing progression as a ladder that takes us away from the material world to seeing our individual capacity for love progressing systemically: from self-love to love of objects; to physical love of another individual; to love for the inner beauty of an individual; to love of a social group, its practices, rituals and culture; to love for learning; to the love of wider nature; to the love of love and loving.

Elias Amidon in his contemplation on 'Being the Beautiful' (Amidon, 2011) beautifully brings us back to earth and simplicity when he asks:

Why, after all, do we experience the beautiful as beautiful? Is beauty something we learn, or is there a capacity or sensitivity for beauty already in our beings?

My sense is that becoming the beautiful is not a matter of becoming something new, but 'becoming' that which we already are. It is a releasing of the constructed identities that have built up in our minds and in the ways we react to things. It is a simple 'opening out' into the innate spaciousness and light that is the essence of our being. This clear, identityless light we are, is itself the heart of beauty. It is a clear light or essence that resists all description. We can only say, with Sufi Inayat Khan, that it is 'the perfection of beauty – the transparent beauty we share with all being'.

(Amidon, 2011: 85–86)

Plotinus (204/205–270 CE), whom Amidon quotes, was one of the great teachers on love. In his teachings – which were collected by his disciple, Porphyry, into the great work known as 'The Enneads' – he shows how the role of beauty is to awaken desire and how desire draws us into the path of love. Unlike Aristotle, who took Plato's teachings and formulated logical categories and fixed ideals, Plotinus developed a more mystical, experiential and sensual approach of direct experience. In the Stanford Dictionary of Philosophy, Lloyd Gerson explains this concept of Plotinus as follows:

Everything with a soul, from human beings to the most insignificant plant, acts to satisfy desire. This desire requires it to seek things that are external to it, such as food. Even a desire for sleep, for example, is a desire for a state other than the state which the living thing currently is in. Cognitive desires, for example, the desire to know, are desires for that which is currently not present to the agent. A desire to procreate is, as Plato pointed out, a desire for immortality.

(Gerson, 2018)

The awareness of the 'poverty' of our current living and the 'resource' within us and around us in the wider world are the parents that give birth to the desire for beauty, which becomes our guide on the ever-expanding journey of love.

Love at the heart of creative evolution

One of the missing levels in this traditional developmental journey is the love of the wider ecology. In the urgent need to heal the split between the human and the 'more-than-human' world of wider nature, it is essential that we humans develop our capacity to appreciate the bountiful love of wider nature and to love every aspect of the world around us. As we mature, we can discover more and more ways of making love to and with nature. Andreas Weber (2017), as a subtitle for his book *Matter and Desire*, chose 'an erotic ecology', and as we saw earlier, Weber suggests that 'the Earth is currently suffering from a shortage of our love' (Weber, 2017: xiv).

Neo-Darwinian thinking has created the dominant and domineering story (see Chapter 6 on Beauty and Truth) that evolutionary life is rooted in 'survival of the fittest': competition at every systemic level – be it a cell, individual, tribe or species – motivated by a selfishness to ensure that their genes survive and dominate in the ecological niche. This, I believe, is not only a misrepresentation of Darwin's evolutionary thinking but also a dangerously atomistic and reductive way of seeing the basis of life.

Freya Mathews and many other eco-cosmologists provide a very different story of evolution. In developing a 'Living Cosmos Panpsychism' (2003 and 2023), Mathews is greatly influenced by indigenous Australian Aboriginal ways of understanding and learning from wider nature and also by early Daoist and Confucian writings, which see evolution as a constant interweaving to bring forth new patterns and forms of life. She builds on Spinoza's and Arne Naess's notion of 'conatus' or 'conativity', where not only are individual beings trying to self-realize but so are larger systemic levels such as groups, communities and ecological niches, which are all trying to ensure that their constantly emerging wholeness is more than the sum of its parts. Thus, each part is co-emerging, co-birthing itself in intimate relationship with every other being and element around it. Mathews writes:

> For this is a synergic pattern, one of mutually accommodating conativities. . . . A pattern characterized by the twin principles of (i) conativity, and (ii) accommodation and least resistance. In the biosphere, the behaviour of most species broadly follows these twin principles since this is a strategy that, being energy conserving, logically results from natural selection.
>
> (Mathews, 2023: 34)

Elsewhere in the same book, Mathews describes how we come to desire what our context needs us to desire, and through this, there is an accommodation. Through accommodation, a fitting-in with our ecological context, we are more likely to flourish and expend less energy and, therefore, in turn, are more likely to survive. Loving your neighbour is then not just a moral injunction, a new commandment, but also a biological necessity. As Weber (2017: 9) writes: 'love is an ecological phenomenon [which] is orientated towards relationships between life forms in the biosphere'.

New life is birthed out of a relationship, thus all nativity is a conativity, as it requires two parties to create a new third party. Love is the driving force of evolving life. Without our parents falling in love, or at least desire being present, we would not have been born; without the love for honey, bees would not pollinate flowers; and in all cases, it is beauty that opens the door to love. The whole history of our universe can be seen as being driven by love for the continuous process of creating what is new, beginning with the 'big bang', which constantly explodes outwards, creating new material, creating being out of non-being. Life continuously creates new, unique connections, patterns, forms and moments of living that never before existed. Creation is in love with becoming. Every moment is new and unique.

The story of the snow queen

In Hans Christian Anderson's fairytale *The Snow Queen*, the devil, in the form of a troll, makes a magic mirror that distorts the appearance of everything it reflects. The mirror blocks out all good and beautiful aspects of people and nature and makes the bad and ugly more prominent. The mirror is taken all over the human world to distort everything and even up to heaven to mock God and the angels. But as the troll approaches heaven, the mirror falls, shattering into billions of pieces. Some pieces become window glass, some spectacles and some get stuck in people's hearts and eyes so that they only see ugliness and fragmentation and become bitter and cold. It is the cold, frozen 'mirror of reason' that blights the world.

One such fragment falls into the eye of the young boy Kai, who until that time has been innocently playing and in love with Gerda. Once the piece of the mirror has tainted him, he no longer sees beauty or feels love. He becomes bewitched by the Snow Queen, who takes him off to her snow palace, where he is imprisoned. He sits alone on the frozen 'mirror of reason' and will only be freed if he can find the magic word that is fragmented into small pieces of ice.

It is only Gerda's love for him (and for the beauty of roses) that takes her on a long quest to find him. Her compassion and tears melt the ice in his eye, and Gerda and Kai's joyful dance of being reunited is joined by the fragments of ice that shape themselves into the word that is the key to Kai's escape. The magic word is 'eternity'. There are so many echoes of William Blake here – his 'Songs of Innocence and Experience' and the ability to 'see heaven in a wild flower' and 'Eternity' simultaneously, both in a particular moment and beyond time.

The path of love and beauty in leadership and coaching

As a leader – in an organization, sports team, community or country – we also have an expansive developmental journey to travel. When we first become a team leader, we may learn to empathize, love and care for the members of our team. This needs to grow into the collective love we have for our team's collective purpose (Hawkins, 2021) – what we can achieve together through collaboration. This, however, can become a collective egocentricity, our team against the world, with our internal love maintained by projecting all negativity out in the wider context.

To mature, we need to develop a love for the 'Team of Teams' (Hawkins and Carr, forthcoming; Hawkins, 2021a, 2022; McChrystal et al., 2015). We must learn to love and care about the relationship between our team and the teams above and beneath it; the teams upstream, who provide the support and services we need to do our work; and the teams downstream, who we support and for whom we provide goods or services. We need to develop 'wide-angled empathy' for all those in the wider organization.

However, this is not sufficient either, as we may just develop greater collective egocentricity, with our organization, and fail to realize that the organization is created to fulfil a purpose: that of 'co-creating value with, and for, all its stakeholders' (Hawkins, 2021a: 41). We need to develop an ethic of loving being in service of others – seeing all our stakeholders not as making demands on us but as partners whom we care about and find beauty through our co-creating together. These stakeholders include our customers or clients, our external suppliers and partner organizations, our investors or funders or the communities in which we operate and which provide the services that make our work possible.

We need to develop our capacity to work in partnership with all our stakeholders. For true partnership comes when we stop looking at and trying to get it right for each other but rather stand shoulder-to-shoulder, looking in the same direction. Our love comes from our joint love for what we can co-create and give birth to together but cannot do apart.

Our love also needs to expand its focus beyond the short-term, to learn how to be 'good ancestors' (Kryznaric, 2020) and have a love for the generations that have come before us and the generations that will come after us, to care about the health of the teams, organizations, communities and wider ecology we are bequeathing to future generations.

All the most impressive and successful leaders I have met through my long career have had an insatiable love for learning: curious about what was happening in other organizations and parts of the world, reading widely and constantly inquiring with others how to innovate what was needed next. Leaders everywhere need to love the process of learning and discovery – finding truth from beauty and beauty in truth, seeing every challenge as a generous lesson from life (Hawkins, 2023c) and loving being at the precarious learning edge, where true creativity happens.

Crucially, our love must also move beyond being anthropocentric to loving and caring for the living ecology in which we are nested and are just one small part. For as we explored in Chapters 1–3, anthropocentrism is at the root of our world crisis. As leaders, we need to go beyond strategies based purely on human sustainability and ESG policies; we need to learn from nature how to lead, shape and energize our organizations. Learning from new forms of 'net positive organizations' (Polman and Winston, 2021), biomimicry (Hutchins, 2012, 2016, 2022), cyclical and 'Doughnut Economics' (Raworth, 2017).

We then need to go further not just learning and applying these approaches as new methods and techniques for their utility but also coming from a deep respect and love for the 'more-than-human' world. To do this, we need experiential engagement with wider nature – for example, through nature retreats and immersions and vision quests. Through keenly listening to and contemplating the natural world, we can encounter its beauty both around us and within us, open up our inner channels of love and heal the split between humans and wider nature.

Love for love itself. Very few leaders arrive at the final stage of maturing through love. However, we can learn about it from those who know it intimately, such as Plotinus, Dante, Blake and Inayat Khan. With training from a good teacher, we can discover glimpses of the love of the emerging creative life force in us, through us and around us. As with Bergson's '*élan vital*' (Bergson, 1907), this life force is constantly flowing like a ceaseless river, each moment creating something new which has never happened before and will never happen again.

Coaches can help leaders on this journey but only if they, too, travel this road. To do this, coaches need to connect with the person they are coaching at the level of the heart and then help widen and deepen the exploration of any issues that emerge in the work. We will explore how to do this in detail in Chapters 12–14. For now, let me offer a short vignette of coaching a leader who is the senior vice president of a global company. The coachee starts and my interventions are in italics.

I struggle to really engage my people. I get criticized by them for being so demanding and yet uncommunicative. I am also worried my marriage may break down, as my wife tells me I am the same at home.

What do you need to communicate to them that you are not yet saying?

Well, I give clear instructions. I let people know what is happening in the wider company . . . so what are they not getting?

Have you asked them?

Yes, they just say you are not engaging us.

For them to feel engaged, what do you need to tell – either your wife, your team or both – from your heart?

[Long silence]

If your heart had a voice, what would it be saying to your team or your wife?

I really want to save our marriage and improve our relationship, but I don't know how to make it better.

[Long pause]

I really need your help.

I feel really vulnerable saying that.

I can really feel your vulnerability as you say that, and it makes me feel closer to you.

Thank you.

How might you also ask your team for help, from the same place of humility and vulnerability?

[Long pause]

I could let them know that I really want us to get to the next level as a team; share how I see the challenge, then tell them I cannot solve that alone and that I really need and want their help.

Can you try saying that now, as if I am the team you are addressing, so I and they can feel it coming from your heart and from love for what they and you can become as a team.

[The leader tries a rehearsal of this engagement several times, with feedback and encouragement from myself, until he lets out a deep breath and says:]

That felt really true and good.

Here, the coachee is discovering how to move from trying to manage the world around him to allowing his vulnerability and humility to be seen and ask for help. In this change, he is finding ways of showing his love for both his wife and for the team and how it could fulfil its potential.

Conclusion

The vignette earlier ends with the coachee beautifully opening himself up with Love and affirming that his expression feels true and good. The relationship between Beauty, Truth and the Good will be the subject of the next few chapters.

In this chapter, we have explored how Beauty opens us to the path of Love, which gradually deepens and widens, drawing us into greater maturity. We have explored how Love, like Beauty, is not located in the object of our love nor just in our subjective loving but rather, is a creative life force at the heart of evolution and human maturation and is essential to the future survival of our species.

Dante starts his journey of love when he first sees the young Beatrice and falls in love with her. It is many years later – after much suffering and descent into the terrible Inferno – that with Beatrice as his guide, Dante enters Paradiso. Finally, his love and the light of the Divine merge, there is complete union and all separation drops away.

As Plotinus teaches, we can only see the Divine with the eye of the divine and the oneness of being when we have surrendered all separateness. Our work is not to try and attain this or any other goal but to pursue the path of expanding love, with beauty as our guide.

The Sufi spiritual teacher, Fazal Inayat Khan, said to me: 'You can always love more'. Here, the 'more' is not just referring to the amount or degree of your love but also the reach and extension of your love. As bel hooks (2001: 162) shows in her book *All About Love*: 'when we practice love we want to give more'. In each moment, we can each deepen and widen our loving, our giving and the beneficial impact we create in the world. Another of my Sufi spiritual teachers, Elias Amidon (2021: 142), writes:

Spread your love out.
Include the room, the house, the whole neighbourhood.
Go farther, don't stop.
For this moment forgive everyone.

Chapter 6

Beauty and truth

Introduction

In this chapter, we will first explore the trinity of the 'eternal verities' of Beauty, Truth and Good, which have been explored by philosophers, mystics, artists and scientists throughout history. We will go on to explore the modernist split between objective and subjective truth and their roots in the different ways of knowing: of the left and right hemispheres of the neo-cortex, the limbic and amygdala, the heart and gut and the wider knowing of the body.

This will lead to seeing 'Truth' as always contextual, meaning it is embedded in an external context, with which it interrelates, and at the same time is always known through and mediated by the cultural lenses through which we experience the world.

This will take us to an exploration in the next two chapters of the Good and Ethics and how, like 'Truth', what is 'good' and 'ethical' is also relational, contextual, cultural and emergent, even though many philosophers, from Plato to Kant, and indeed professions and scientism, have tried to make it universal, fixed and absolute.

The trinity of beauty, truth and good

When Keats, in his sonnet 'Ode on a Grecian Urn' (1819), wrote 'Beauty is truth, truth beauty, That is all Ye know on earth, and all ye need to know', he was following a long tradition of Platonic and Neoplatonic thought. In this trinity, Beauty and Truth are two sides of the triangle, of which Good is the third. Sometimes they are seen as three sisters, daughters of the same mother, the family at the core of creation and living being. At other times, they are seen as co-arising, and each is the face of the other. Simone Weil (2005: 73) expressed this by changing the 'good' to 'justice': she wrote 'Justice, truth, and beauty are sisters and comrades. With three such beautiful words we have no need to look for any others'.

Beauty is the face of Truth, as Plato expressed when he said, 'Beauty is the splendour of the true'. In being the face of Truth, Beauty is also a possible

DOI: 10.4324/9781003349600-9

opening on the road to what is true. The Sufi mystic Ibn 'Arabi wrote in his treatise 'On Majesty and Beauty': 'Beauty is the welcoming openness of the Truth toward us'. This is echoed by Nadine Gordimer (2010) when she says, 'The truth isn't always beauty, but the hunger for it is', showing how the desire and longing for Beauty can lead us in search of what is true.

This is exemplified in the stories of Dante's love for Beatrice and Hafiz's love for the Mayor of Shiraz's daughter (see Chapter 5). In each case, falling instantly in love with a beautiful girl led them on a long, illuminating and sometimes perilous path in search of deeper truth. For Dante, Beatrice is his final guide to Paradise and divine realization. For Hafiz, his love leads him to find his great Sufi teacher and then to writing some of the greatest love poetry ever written.

Joy can emerge in the dance between beauty and truth and in finding Truth in Beauty and Beauty in Truth. One of Keats' contemporaries, William Hazlitt (1873), wrote:

> The contemplation of truth and beauty is the proper object for which we were created, which calls forth the most intense desires of the soul, and of which it never tires.

At the beginning of the 20th century, James Joyce (2013) wrote:

> Beauty, the splendour of truth, is a gracious presence when the imagination contemplates intensely the truth of its own being or the visible world, and the spirit which proceeds out of truth and beauty is the holy spirit of joy. These are realities and these alone give and sustain life.

Albert Einstein (1930) said, 'The ideals which have always shone before me and filled me with joy are goodness, beauty, and truth', showing that following these three sisters is not limited to poets and novelists.

As well as being the path to Truth and the bringer of joy, Beauty can also be the antidote to the fixity of rigid truth. Maurice Berman (1981: 53–54) indicates this when he writes 'without Beauty Truth becomes blind' – because it becomes blind to the wider context. We can also see that without Truth, Beauty may become seductive. Also, without the True and the Good, Beauty is adornment; but without Beauty, the True and Good may remain opaque and hidden.

The poet John O'Donohue (2003: 54) echoes Berman when he writes:

> without beauty, truth becomes blind and can be turned into a blunt and heartless imperative. When we hold truth and beauty together, truth will always have a sense of compassion and gentleness. Sometimes the so-called 'facts' of a situation actually tell us little or nothing about the heart of an experience. Only in the light of beauty can we come to see what is really present. Letting the light in so we can see the rich colour of the beauty that underlies truth.

Weber (2019) takes up this theme in showing how truth focusses on the external experience of things, but beauty on the interiority, subjectivity and inter-relationality of life.

What is true?

The English word 'true', or *treu* in Middle English, derives from the Saxon *triewe* and goes back to the proto-German roots of *treuwaz*. It has the meanings of being faithful, adhering to promises, being true to your friends. I recently asked a friend who teaches carpentry about the meaning of 'true' in construction. He explained how a mortise-and-tenon joint is true when the tenon fits perfectly into the mortise and how, without this truth, the structure it supports will not last.

The ancient Greek word for truth is *aletheia* and has a deep notion of correspondence: that which we see on the material plane corresponds to what is true at deeper levels of being. Heidegger (1962), in his writings on truth, goes back to the pre-Socratic philosophers, linking *aletheia* to the German word *unverbogenheit*, meaning 'disclosure' or 'un-concealedness'. Much of Heidegger's extensive writing explores the relationship of Being (with a capital B) and everyday being (with a small b). He explores how to uncover deeper Truth and deeper Being, which is covered by, but can shine through, everyday being in the material world.

The Latin word for truth is *veritas*. Mythologically, Veritas was daughter of either Chronos or Zeus, and the mother of Virtus or virtue. Interestingly, she is sometimes depicted as hidden at the bottom of a holy well, sometimes as a virgin dressed in white and sometimes naked – the naked truth, the truth disclothed and disclosed. Thus, in the European classical period, there is this deep sense that something is true if it is in accord and harmony with a deeper truth and that we discover truth through enchantment (Curry, 2019).

In all this etymology, we can see a pattern of truth being about harmony and 'fit'. Truth is found when what we say accords with the reality that we and others experience – when what we do fits with what we have promised implicitly or explicitly; when the two pieces of wood in a joint, or two marriage partners, are learning to fit together.

Then there is a deeper systemic level of true, where the actions of an individual are in alignment with the needs of the team, the actions of the team are in accord with the needs of the organization and the actions of the species are in harmony with the health of the ecological niche. Survival of the 'fittest', and the flourishing and health of what is most fitting, is played out between the systemic levels, rather than a neo-Darwinian competition within a level.

The notes of a Chopin nocturne are not competing with each other but rather, working in harmony to co-create the beauty of the music. This beauty also requires the co-creation between the composer, the pianist and the listener. Unless the composer is true to their inner inspiration and muse, unless the pianist is true to the score of the composition and unless the listener is fully present, listening without pre-judgment and not just with their ears, but with every aspect of their being, the true beauty of the music can never be realized.

Subjective and objective truth – mythos and logos

Much ink has been spent, and many ears wagged, by the dualistic arguments between the 'rational realists', who locate all 'truth' in an objectifiable material world, and the 'subjective relativists', who believe that the world only exists through our human perceptions of it. Underlying this dialectic is a more ancient duality and partnership between two very different forms of truth: the truth of *logos* and the truth of *mythos*. These can be seen as relating to the two hemispheres of the neo-cortex.

The truth of *logos* is about what is logically consistent, observable, measurable, repeatable and provable – the left-hemisphere ways of perceiving and making sense of the world. It is a form of perception that, since the Enlightenment and the growing dominance of empirical science and modernism, has come to dominate conceptions of what is true. Scientists and rational materialists tend to ask: 'Can you prove it? Where is the evidence? What are the facts?'

But there is a much older way of perceiving truth, more associated with the right hemisphere of the human neo-cortex – the truth of *mythos* and story that portrays the truth of pattern, connection and relationship. Bateson (1975) described stories as the 'royal road to understanding relationship'. He told a joke which went something like this:

A computer enthusiast searched out the latest and most powerful computer in the world, and programmed it to answer the question, will computers ever be able to think like a human being? After a very long wait the computer printer started to hum and the enthusiast rushed over to watch the computer printing the answer. There on the paper were the following words: 'Now that reminds me of a story'.

Stories constitute one of the fundamental languages that all human beings use to communicate what cannot be said through straight description. Bateson explores how, in the Western, post-scientific world, most of our language has become the language of things, which is the language of defining material objects. This is an important and useful language when used in the service of the empirical study of inanimate objects but a most inadequate language for conveying relationship or the underlying patterns that permeate living existence (Hawkins, 2005).

Einstein (1930: 195) also speaks of how this older and deeper way of knowing is the foundation for all true art and science:

The most beautiful thing we can experience is the mysterious. It is the source of all true art and science. He to whom the emotion is a stranger, who can no longer pause to wonder and stand wrapped in awe, is as good as dead – his eyes are closed.

Truth can never be captured or tied down, for it is always evolving and changing. Thich Nhat Hanh (1987), in the second of his 14 precepts for the Order of Interbeing, guides us:

> Do not think the knowledge you presently possess is changeless, absolute truth. Avoid being narrow-minded and bound to present views. Learn and practice non-attachment from views in order to be open to receive others' viewpoints. Truth is found in life and not merely in conceptual knowledge. Be ready to learn throughout your entire life and to observe reality in yourself and in the world at all times.

Even in *mythos*, truth cannot be contained or confined in stories, or even in great teachings, no matter how sacred or luminous they are. Truth flows through stories. Truth is a gift that wells up from the cracks between our stories. Our work as coaches or leaders is often to help open the cracks, just enough, so new truth can spring forth. To create the 'space for grace' (see Chapter 10), we need to be open and receptive to the emergent, to new life emerging through the opening, through *Ma*, the Japanese concept of the space between (see Chapter 13).

Ursula Le Guin, a contemporary weaver of myths and stories, wrote: 'Truth goes in and out of stories you know. What was once true is true no longer. The water has risen from another spring' (Le Guin, quoted in Eisenstein, 2013: 243).

None of this is true

Both times I attended talks by Krishnamurti, the Indian spiritual teacher (Brockwood Park, 1975 and 1979), he said, 'None of this that I am telling you is true, unless you find the truth of it in your own lives'. By this, I believe he meant both internally and externally.

More recently, I was coaching a senior leader and was tasked to share with him the 360-degree feedback that had been anonymously collected from his bosses, colleagues and subordinates. After listening to what others had said about him, he suddenly burst in, saying, 'But none of this is true'.

I asked him what he meant by that, and he replied, 'This is not what I am like'.

My response was 'You mean their stories about you do not match with your own stories about yourself'.

'But my stories are the true ones', he asserted.

'Be careful', I replied, 'the stories that most leaders tell about themselves often die with them, but the stories others tell about them live on and continue to evolve'.

We went on to explore the partial truth of his own self-story, and the partial truths of the stories and perceptions others had about him, and inquired into what would be the emerging truth that connected them.

When Irish people come together in great conversation, often accompanied by music and alcohol, they say, 'We had good *craic*'. The Irish Gaelic word *craic* travelled to Ireland from Scotland and Northern England, where it is spelled 'crack'. *Craic* means fun and jovial times when with good company, humour and conversational flow; we let go of self-concerns and self-importance. Truth does not reside in any song that is sung or in any individual's brilliant wit but in the love and creative connections that flow through the 'crack' we have collectively opened.

Literal or partial truth

By literal truth, I mean the truth that is found in our words, spoken or written, found in facts that are also formed in and by words or numbers. Numbers can be seen as a specialized form of abstracted words.

When we say something is 'factually or literally true', it is not sufficient; to be more truthful, we would need to add something like 'in this context', 'at this systemic level', 'at this time', 'if seen from this vantage point and compared to the following'.

I suggest that all literal and factual truth is contextual, limited to the systemic level we are exploring – comparative, temporal and limited by the location and lens of the perceiver. Let us explore each of facets.

Contextual: There is no text without context. Robert Louis Stevenson was a writer of stories and poems, particularly for children, and also a great travel-ler. In his book *The Silverado Squatters* (Stevenson, 1883), which describes his honeymoon travels around the Napa Valley in California, he wrote: 'There are no foreign lands. It is the traveller only who is foreign'. Likewise, when we describe something as odd or strange, we are saying that it is a stranger to us, feels out of place; I cannot see how it belongs or fits in this context.

Limited to a specific systemic level: What is true at one systemic level may be false at another. For example, 'every individual is a unique autonomous person, who has their own thoughts and is responsible for their own choices' can be a true statement at one level of systemic focus. If we shift our focus to a larger systemic level, 'the individual is the product of their family, relation-ships, society, culture and time, and their thoughts and actions derive from these contexts' can also be true. Here, the systemic lens has shifted to viewing a large whole, of which the individual is a part.

Comparative: When I say the leaves on this beech tree are green, I am compar-ing them to other objects we have agreed to class as and call 'green', which is a comparison of similarity. I may also be making a comparison of difference by contrasting the colour of these leaves with the leaves on another tree, such as a copper beech, where the leaves are a deep maroon. The original statement has no inherent meaning without its often unmentioned but implied comparators.

At this time: In the statement earlier, when I say the leaves on this beech tree are green, this is only true now, for when autumn comes, they may change to a different hue, yellow or brown, before falling. A statement is only true for a period of time. Not only is Truth contextual (it is also never absolute) but it is also always emergent. Truth is an unfolding journey, never a place of arrival. The Austrian philosopher, Karl Popper, in 1935 introduced the concept of 'falsifiability' – that a current truth of a proposition, statement, theory or hypothesis is only true until is proven wrong – and he proposed that it was through falsification that science progressed (Popper, 1959).

Perceived from this place: There is a lovely story about a father and a young boy who used to spend time together in their garden, watching planes take off from a nearby airport. When the son was 5, his father took him on his first flight in a plane. As they started to take off, the young boy turned to his father and asked, 'At what point do we begin to get small?' From the garden, the plane gradually diminishes in size, whereas from the perspective of the boy in the plane, he will discover it is his house and garden that diminishes. What you see depends on where you are looking from.

Perceived in this way: The quantum physicists discovered that a subatomic particle was only a particle if you fixed it in the dimension of space; if you looked at it as movement, it became a wave. Whether it was a wave or a particle depended on the way you were looking and the frame you were looking through.

From all these contingencies of literal and factual truth, I would contend that Truth is never true alone and only true when in true relationship with another. We need to recognize that we can only see a system of which we are part. As a part, we can never know the whole, only the truth of the whole, as perceived from the part we occupy.

Some post-modern advocates of deconstruction, such as Derrida, argue that everything is relative, and Lyotard (1979) wrote: 'I define postmodern as incredulity towards metanarratives'. Like them, I believe we should bring an inquiring mind and healthy scepticism to any claim of absolute truth. Similar to many social constructivists (Gergen, 2009), I would argue that truth is always contextual, contingent, temporal and rooted in a historical and a social context.

Post-modernists suggest there is no absolute or universal truth. Some suggest that all narratives are equally true – and that truth is always partial and 'at issue' rather than being complete and certain. I would suggest that this, too, is a very partial truth and, moreover, one that is very anthropocentric. Rather, I would say that we, as individual humans, can only speak and write partial truths and need the humility to recognize how what we say is contingent on our context, time, culture, the place we are looking from and the epistemological lenses through we are looking. However, I would contend that there are levels of Truth and that we can distinguish between less and greater validity.

Truth has greater validity when it is polyocular. By this, I mean a statement, a finding or a proposition has greater validity when what is studied has been looked at from many different perspectives, through different lenses and in different timeframes. However, as McGilchrist (2021: Chapter 13) argues, in our current world, increasing specialization and narrower and narrower academic silos yield less valuable new understanding. He quotes Arnold Toynbee (1961: 130):

> intellectual enquiry . . . debate is the source of advances in knowledge and understanding . . . the wider the field of advances in knowledge and understanding, and . . . the wider the field of discussion, the greater the chance of striking out fruitful new ideas.

We need to both zoom in and see the detail and pan out and see whatever we are seeing or saying in its wider context. We need to reflect on the external world, contemplate on the internal world and find the truth that unites them.

This echoes Hazrat Inayat Khan telling us that the spiritual seeker must look at everything from at least two different perspectives, as well as Blake's rallying call to move beyond 'Newton's one-eyed vision', both of which I have quoted elsewhere.

Deeper truth lies not at the surface of things, objects, individuals or parts but in what Bateson called the 'pattern that connects' and is arrived at by seeing the deeper pattern that emerges in the dialogue between different people studying through different disciplines, in different cultures and from different times. This has been the method I have attempted to use in this book.

The path of truth

In Shakespeare's 'Hamlet', Polonius mentors the young Hamlet: 'But this above all to thine own self be true'. And being honest with ourselves is perhaps the first fundamental step on the path of truth. When working with addiction treatment centres, I learnt the phrase: 'You can measure the sickness by the secrecy', vividly capturing a way of seeing all addictions as a disease of denial, which starts with lying to others, then family and then to oneself. Ferrucci (2010: 55) writes:

> To be honest with oneself is an invaluable form of inner training, and the aesthetic dimension is the ideal laboratory for practising this sincerity. It is a way to acquire bit by bit, a personal taste. When they feel too insecure, many individuals do not have their own tastes.

Learning not to go along with what we are taught to like by our family, friends or by hypnotic advertising but to find our own discernment can be learnt aesthetically from Beauty. Ferrucci (2010: 48) also shows how Beauty is discovered through spontaneity, what the Daoists call '*ziran*', 'to be what we are' and that spontaneity and naturalness, 'since it is not prepared or fabricated, it shows us the truest parts of who we are'.

bel hooks (2001: 157) shows how 'choosing to be honest is the first step in the process of love', and she shows how honesty and love are essential to each other, something as coaches and leaders we should never forget.

Instinct

Since Descartes and the growth of modernism, we tend to locate our living and our sense of who we are in our conscious and reflective thinking. More recent neuroscience, however, has suggested that 95% or more of what is happening in our bodies is outside this conscious awareness, and 40% or more of our actions are carried out through habit (Young, 2018). Increasingly, it recognized that, whereas the mind may be most self-conscious through the brain, consciousness cannot be reduced to our brains. The neuroscientist Dan Siegel (2010: 52) writes: 'The human mind is a relational and embodied process that regulates the flow of energy and information'. Our instinctual body is constantly regulating our heartbeat, blood pressure, hormone flow, digestion and many other aspects of our functioning, even when we are asleep.

When we drive a familiar journey, we might be talking or listening to the radio and be totally unable to remember anything than happened on the journey. It is as if we have been driving on automatic pilot. I find that I can find my way back to a place I have previously been to, even if it was many years ago, because my instinctual body-mind can feel which way to turn when it comes to a junction. However, if I took a wrong turning on the first visit, my body gets both anxious and confused when it comes to the junction where previously, I had gone wrong.

Intuitions

These emerge from the felt sense of our body, our heart and gut brain. In common parlance, we use phrases such as 'I sense in my heart' and 'my gut feeling is'. Our bodies can process a multitude of signals and information and provide a truth that the conscious left-hemisphere could not have arrived at by itself.

William James (1902: 73) wrote: 'If you have intuitions at all, they come from a deeper level of your nature than the loquacious level which rationalism inhabits'. McGilchrist (2021, Chapter 17) shows at length how our intuition is the natural processes of our wider brain and body constantly processing multi-levels of data and acting on the knowing that emerges from them, often without any so-called rational, left-brain intervention or awareness.

We can also know more about the world around us if we discover how it shows up inside ourselves. In Chapter 4, I described how the eco-systemic is holographic and fractal – that whatever systems we are nested within are also, in part, nested within us. Thus, another way of knowing the systems we are part of is to look not outwards but inwards, to how the larger systemic levels within which we are embedded are also embedded and enacted within us.

Inward contemplation

We can also follow Spinoza (1954) in moving from external reflection to internal contemplation. We can undertake an inward search, through a recursive inquiry back to where awareness has its source within us. Descartes said, 'I think, therefore, I am'; but let us examine this assertion through our own experience, by inward contemplation.

I invite you to try a short inward inquiry with me. In a moment, close your eyes and just watch the thoughts that emerge. Do not judge them or get attached to them; just watch them arrive and watch them leave. Be just lovingly present and impartial to any thought that comes and goes. Now ask yourself: Where did these thoughts came from? Where did they go? Which, if any, of these thoughts did you chose to think? Which arrived as if unbidden or uninvited, but guests, nonetheless?

Now we can go further. Close your eyes again, and watch the thoughts that emerge, stay for a while and then disappear. This time ask yourself: Who is the one watching these thoughts? Can you sense this hidden witness? It is hidden because it is the one that is aware, so cannot be an object of awareness. If it were an object of awareness, there would need to be another witness beyond this one.

Just sit for a while 'being in awareness' (where there is no 'me' because any 'me' we can describe would be an object in awareness and no 'I' being aware – well certainly not in the normal sense of my conception of who 'I' am). There is just presence being present to whatever emerges and departs, the constant mental chatter of the rise and flow of thoughts.

Now try the same exercise with your eyes open, looking out of a window. Watch whatever is happening, as you did your thoughts; just be aware of life, emerging and departing, always in flux, always becoming, always new.

Imagination

Blake describes in his poem 'Jerusalem' (Blake, 1968f):

> Trembling I sit day and night, my friends are astonish'd at me.
> Yet they forgive my wanderings, I rest not from my great task!
> To open the Eternal Worlds, to open the immortal Eyes
> Of Man inwards into the Worlds of Thought: into Eternity
> Ever expanding in the Bosom of God, the Human Imagination.

This is the search that comes from contemplation, not from reflection nor from measuring but from sensing; not from categorizing but from feeling the connections within me. This is what is alluded to when many Sufi poets talk about how the heart knows, what the eyes are searching for. This is echoed in the story of the wonderful, wise fool, Nasrudin. One evening, he is looking for his keys in the gutter, under the lamppost. His friends come and join him on the search, but one asks him, 'Where did you lose the keys, Nasrudin?' 'Inside my house', replies the wise fool. 'So why are we all looking out here?', the friend asks. 'Because there is more light out here', Nasrudin replies. Our tendency is to look outside for the truth, but contemplation takes us indoors, inside ourselves to find the lost key.

Beauty as a guide to the truth

Perhaps we recognize what is true and good, as we recognize the beauty within it. Through a recognition of inherent beauty in the person, being, thing or event, we sense an inner harmony and also that which is harmonious and fitting within its context and current ecological niche. When there is a 'fit' between the part and the whole, and the part is in service of the whole, then it is true and fitting. As explored earlier, in the English language, we still have the usage of the word 'true' to mean 'in alignment' or 'fitting', as when a corner of a wall or a joint in carpentry is said to be 'true'.

This notion of Truth being what is fitting and harmonious can also be found in the Chinese Taoist and Confucian concept of *Li*. This was developed by the great 12th-century Chinese sage Zhu Xi, who saw it as the organizing principles of the cosmos, the natural patterns of the universe that are continually forming and re-forming around us. For Zhu Xi, *Chi* was the energetic force that gave life to everything, but *Li* was the organizing and shaping force that worked through harmony. Both derived from *Taiji*, the supreme ultimate source.

In the work of this great philosopher and sage is the notion that not only is everything in the material plane constantly changing and evolving but so, too, is *Li*, the 'patterns that connect'; they, too, evolve on a different systemic level.

The sacred

As I have already expressed, there is a level of Truth we can sense but not fully know or comprehend. Some call it the divine, heaven, *nirvana*; others call it the realm of the archetypes, the Platonic forms and verities, while others call it the eco-spiritual.

Likewise, the beauty of Truth is that we can never fully know it, and the beauty of Goodness is that we can never own it. Truth and Goodness are destinations we can aim for and use to guide our journey but not places of arrival.

We can also approach this paradox systemically, for we can never know a system that we are not in some way part of and we can never fully know a system of which we are a part. We can only ever know the wider system from the perspective of our part within it and through how the wider system within which we are immersed shows up holographically within us, for we are just one of its many sub-systems or parts.

The Sacred is not just contained in places we humans designate as sacred sites, such as destinations for pilgrimages or sites that carry the energy of thousands of years of prayer and contemplation, although these can be of great value. Perhaps we should rename them as places where the sacred can be more fully sensed, or by using Joanna Macy's (Macy and Johnstone, 2012) term 'listening posts'. By making places sacred, we are in danger of making everywhere else secular or non-sacred, rather than embracing the realization that all places and all living beings are parts of the sacred Earth. As Wendell Berry (2012: 354) says in his poem 'How to Be a Poet': 'There are no unsacred places; there are only sacred places and desecrated places'.

The sacred is beyond our knowing and our grasping. We reside within it and are blessed by it. We encounter the sacred also when we get to the learning edge, the shore where our 'kennen', or left-hemisphere knowledge, runs out and we stand at the edge of the foggy sea of unknowing. This is the learning edge where all new knowing and new Truth emerge. For when we are in this liminal place, it is premature and rarely helpful to go searching for insight and answers or to rely on past experience. Here, neither the teacher nor the leader, coach or expert have the answer; something totally new needs to be discovered or birthed. It needs to come by Grace (see Chapter 10).

In one of my blogs (Hawkins, 2023a), I wrote about the 'eco-systemic prayer', in response to the many team coaches who have asked me how they can increase their confidence:

> When you encounter the panic at the learning edge, both in you and the team you are working with, do not react, or try harder, but instead pray. It does not matter who you pray to, as long as it is a greater system than you. Some people then ask: 'But what if no answer comes?'. My response: 'Be patient and pray harder?'

Conclusion

Truth is always relational, never alone and never fixed. It cannot be separated from its relational context, nor from the perceiver, nor from the systemic levels they are nested within and the level they are focussed on. We can only write and talk about contingent truth, but we can achieve greater validity through dialogue between different polyocular perspectives from multiple viewers, different cultures and periods of history and by discovering the pattern that connects them.

Truth lies in what 'fits' – what 'truly' conjoins across difference. Truth is found in the fitness of relationships – how elements, people, beings or musical notes fit together. Also, Beauty is found in the harmony of the patterns of *Li*, in the deeper patterns that connect. It is in the beauty of the 'fit', the beauty of the harmony across levels, that we experience the Truth, which is non-definable, living and emergent.

Truth lies in what connects the zoomed-in detail of the left-hemisphere perception with the wider panorama seen by the right hemisphere. It also lies in what connects that which is perceived through reflection on the outside, through the five windows of the senses, and what is sensed inside, through contemplation and by accessing the deeper layers of intuition, imagination and instinct.

Having met and learned from the second of the three verities, Truth, we will in the next chapter meet the third sister – the Good, or Goodness – and discover more about the connections between all three.

Chapter 7

Beauty and the good

Introduction

In the previous chapters, we have met two of the Verity sisters, Beauty and Truth, but now we will meet the third sister, the Good, or 'Goodness'. As with Truth, we will begin by looking at the etymology of Good, its origin and changing form. Then we will explore how Good never appears alone, for the Good is always in relationship with her sisters and involves doing good, as well as being good. Following this, we will look at 'doing the Beautiful – doing the Good' and explore the way in which these are interconnected. We will explore how Evil is the absence of Good so that by transcending the duality of Good and Evil, we find a deeper Good.

Etymology of 'good'

In ancient Greek, there were two words for good, *Καλόν*, or *Kalos*, and *ἀγαθός*, or *Agathos*. *Kalos* means someone who is beautiful and noble in their disposition, whereas *Agathos* describes the moral beauty and ethical virtue of a person.

The old English word for good was *gōd*, pronounced with a long 'o', probably originating from the proto-Germanic *gōda*, meaning 'fitting, suitable or belonging together'.

So just as we discovered in our exploration of Truth in the last chapter, Good has connotations of the fit between things, people and systemic levels; 'goodness' means it is 'fitting'.

The good person, good leader, good organization

In Daoism, the universal *Dao* also has its fractal echo within each individual, where it is known as the *De*, which is the 'power or potentiality of that person or being, or system, to manifest in accordance with the Dao whereas Dao denotes the intermeshed unfolding of things at the cosmological level in accordance with *Li*' (Mathews, 2023: 76). Here, *Li* means the deeper pattern out of which the

DOI: 10.4324/9781003349600-10

particular emerges. To be a 'good' person is not to focus on what we want to be but to discover and unfold our own potentiality, our *De*, the potentiality that is fitting to what is needed in the world around us and the needs of our times. However, Beauty helps us do this not out of a moral aught but because 'Goodness is the guarantee of the quality of beauty; as for beauty, it illuminates goodness and makes it desirable' (Cheng, 2013: 49).

When we meet an inspiring person, it is the beauty of their goodness that opens up our own aspiration for the Good. It is encountering the reflection of perfection in a person, an event or a work of art that inspires within us, the journey of unfolding of our own potential, of doing and being the 'Good'.

I propose that a good leader is someone who not only continually unfolds their own potential, and the potential of those around them, but also focusses on unfolding the potential of the organization they lead, the work to realize the collective De of a good organization.

At the heart of a good organization is an organization that co-creates beneficial value with, and for, all its stakeholders – that is, all the parties and elements that make up its wider eco-system. These at minimum include its customers/clients, suppliers and partner organizations, employees, funders/investors, the communities it operates within and the 'more-than-human' world of the wider ecology that it is both part of and dependent upon (Hawkins, 2021).

This leads us to inquire into the meaning of 'beneficial value'. The word 'beneficial' comes from the Latin and can have a sense of 'to make well or healthy', 'to confer benefit on others', 'to be helpful'. In this way, we can understand a good organization as one that co-creates goodness for, and flourishing in, the wider stakeholder eco-system of which it is a unique part. The organization is *auto-poietic* – that is, self-generating and continually self-creating and thus becoming more than the sum of its parts. At the same time, it is '*onto-poietic*' – that is, developing in response to the needs of the world around it.

I once heard an elderly rabbi say in one of his teachings: 'We are not born to have a good time but born to make the times good'. The relationship between a good organization and its wider eco-system is also '*inter-poietic*', creating not just a two-way benefit for the organization and its stakeholders but also how together in relationship, they co-create a new and better world. Polman and Winston (2021) provide many examples of 'organizations that thrive by giving more than they take'. And they and Hutchins and Storm (2019) show organizations that with their eco-system co-create a better world.

Doing the beautiful – doing the good

Through Beauty, we learn to desire that which our wider ecology desires us to desire. As Plotinus (1966–1988), in the *Enneads* (VI 7, 31, 17), puts it: 'The Soul loves the Good because, since the beginning, it [the Good] has incited her to love it'. In the same way, the beauty of the flower teaches the bee to desire its pollen; the bee teaches the plant to produce beautiful flowers in colour, scent and form: the bees feeding becomes the flowers cross pollinating. Through beauty, we discover that we receive what is good by doing that which is good for the world around us.

This can be seen as the wider eco-system flourishing and becoming good, through its self-organizing, its own auto-poiesis. Its goodness and flourishing are not just the sum of the organisms within it, each doing good. The parts are participating in good rather than just individually doing it. The ecological niche is also having to do that which is good for the wider systemic levels, of which it is just a part. In the case of an ecological niche, this would include the hydrosphere of the wider water systems that flow through it, the atmosphere of air and the lithosphere of the earth and rocks on which it exists. As Bateson (1972: 457) said, the 'organism which destroys its environment destroys itself. The unit of survival is a flexible organism-in-its-environment'.

We can go further and say that it is not just the unit of survival but also the unit of flourishing, which is never the individual organism by itself but the organism-in-and-with-its-environment. The unit of flourishing is never the individual human, team, organization, country or species but any one of these in dynamic relationship to the wider systems of which they are a part. Flourishing is always relational and involves multiple systemic levels. To do the Beautiful and to do the Good, and to co-create goodness in us and our world, we need to find the sweet spot where *De* and *Dao* are flowing and unfolding in harmony with each other.

To provide a breathing space from the density of the multi-levelled propositions we have just explored, let me retell a wonderful story of relational good. I first learnt this from listening to William Ury (he also recounts it in Ury, 2007: 77–80), founder of the Harvard Program of Negotiation, whose words I have summarized.

A young American, living in Japan to study aikido, was sitting in a half-empty train in the suburbs of Tokyo, with some mothers with children, and elderly people going shopping.

Then at one of the stations, the doors opened, and a man staggered into the carriage, shouting, drunk, dirty and aggressive. He started cursing the people and lunged at a woman holding a baby. The blow hit her, and she fell into the lap of an elderly couple. The woman ran to the other end of the carriage. This angered the drunk who went after them, trying to wrench a metal pole from its socket. The young student stood up ready for a fight.

Before he could do so, however, a small, elderly man in a kimono said hello to the drunk in a friendly manner. 'Come here and talk to me'. The drunk replied: 'Why should I talk to you?'. 'What have you been drinking?', asked the old man. 'Sake', he said 'and it's none of your business!'.

'Oh that's wonderful', said the old man. 'You see, I love sake too. Every night, my wife and I (she's 76, you know) warm up a little bottle of sake and take it out into the garden and we sit on an old wooden bench. We watch the sun go down, and we look to see how our persimmon tree is doing. My great-grandfather planted that tree'.

As he continued talking, gradually the drunk's face began to soften and his fists slowly unclenched. 'Yes', he said, 'I love persimmons too'. 'And I'm sure', said the old man, smiling, 'you have a wonderful wife'.

'No', replied the drunk. 'My wife died'. Gently, he began to sob. 'I got no wife. I got no home. I got no job. I'm so ashamed of myself'. Tears rolled down his cheeks.

As the student was leaving the train, he heard the old man sighing, 'My, my. This is a difficult predicament indeed. Sit down here and tell me about it'. He saw the drunk putting his head in the old man's lap, who then started softly stroking his hair.

What the young man was about to achieve by combat, the old man had achieved by doing the beautiful, with empathy and love.

Here, we experience Goodness, coming from an empathic, non-judgmental and loving response, to both a person and a situation. The old man didn't react to the behaviour of an individual, or take sides, but instead found a loving connection. The story moves beyond who is good and who is evil. This is what we will now turn to.

Good and evil

Plotinus (1966–1988), in part IV of *The Enneads*, describes Evil as the absence of the Good. We can all do Evil, just by not acting in the good way that the world around us requires. Organizations can become 'sub-optimal', when one part, one team or one function focusses only on its own success, its own flourishing or its own 'high-performance' (see Hawkins, 2021a: 39–41 and 2021b). Likewise, an ecological niche can become sub-optimal when one species tries to dominate and maximize its own numbers and power. Sound familiar? Focussing on maximally optimizing your part of the wider system to the detriment of other parts of that system or the system itself is, by Plotinus' definition, evil.

This focus on local advantage can have short-term benefits for those organisms that undertake it, but there is always a price to pay, as the diminishment in the flourishing of the wider eco-system will slowly but surely lead to the diminishment of all the organisms within it. Does this also sound familiar? As Bateson (1973: 473) warns: 'If the organism ends up destroying its environment, it has in fact destroyed itself'.

Hazrat Inayat Khan (1926: Vol VIII: [1972], 104) writes: 'nothing can be evil according to a fixed principle . . . [evil] is something that is devoid of harmony'. Evil is to be inharmonious, to sing out of tune with the people around you, to be out of relationship with nature and with life. Goodness comes from being in harmony with the natural order of things, from being in a state of flow and being true to what is. Goodness is harmonious and beautiful; evil is discordant and ugly.

As evil is to good, ugliness is to beauty and disgust is to desire. Our body reacts to ugliness with disgust, and the nausea we feel protects us from eating bad food that looks and smells ugly, turns us away from ugly and horrific images and makes us retreat from ugly snakes and insects that may be dangerous. Beauty is a built-in biological guide to the good. Ferrucci (2010: 161) tells us that word noise and nausea have the same Latinate root, which we can recognise when we see children grimace and put their hands over their ears when sounds are violent and ugly.

A flourishing ecological niche maintains a healthy and harmonious balance between all its constituents, by each species having a corrective predator that keeps its numbers and dominance in check. The ecology is sustainable because it is edible: each organism's life and death feed and support other organisms and, hence, the flourishing of the ecological niche, which in its turn supports the harmonious flourishing between and in each of its participating organisms (De and Dao dancing in flow together). Each is constantly evolving, unfolding their previously unrealized potential and co-creating new forms of life that have never previously existed.

It is in this mutual dance of unfolding that creation and innovation happen. They are two indivisible aspects of the evolving universe. Organizations and societies who wish to innovate in a good way need to do so at the boundary between internal creativity and the changing and unfolding of the world around them. To focus on just one or the other, or both out of relationship with each other, is to fail and fall.

Mathew Fox, formerly a Dominican and now an Episcopalian priest, writes about the sin of retreating to a private morality and the cultural underpinning in the sin of a dualistic perspective:

Violence and dualism, the refusal to do compassion and justice, contribute to the very shaking of the world's order and foundations. Behind this sin lies the basis of all sin, the dualism that human sexual, racial, economic exploitations are all about. No one can live in an isolated, privatized religion or world any longer. Interdependence is too much a reality of every nation today and of all global struggles for growth and peace making. Privatized salvations sin against the cosmos itself. They blind us to levels of ecological justice as well as human justice that we must be about.

(Fox, 1983: 296)

Beyond good and evil – revisioning righteousness

William Blake battled with the dualities of Good and Evil, Heaven and Hell and God and Satan in order to discover and create a high-order morality. In *The Marriage of Heaven and Hell*, Blake (1968b) wrote:

All bibles or sacred codes have been the causes of the following errors:

1. That man has two real existing principles, Viz., a body and a soul.
2. That Energy, call'd Evil, is alone from the Body; & that Reason, called Good, is alone from the Soul.
3. That God will torment Man in Eternity for following his Energies.

But the following contraries to these are true:

1. Man has no Body distinct from his Soul: for that called Body, is a portion of Soul discern'd by the five senses, the chief inlets of Soul in this age.
2. Energy is the only life, and is from the Body; and Reason is the bound or outward circumference of Energy.
3. Energy is Eternal Delight.

The poem ends with the line: 'For everything that lives is Holy'.

For Blake, like many mystics, sin derives from splitting and creating oppositional polarities and dualisms. Blake was not the first to call out the hypocrisy of many purveyors of religious morality. Jesus himself said: 'Except your righteousness exceed the righteousness of the scribes and Pharisees, ye shall no wise enter the kingdom of heaven' (Matthew 5:20). The word 'righteousness' in ancient Greek was *Dikaiosune*, a word much used in the Gospels and which, according to Frank Bullock (2000), appears 78 times in the Epistles of St. Paul – a word so common and yet very rarely explored. What does it mean? 'Righteousness' means to stand upright between the opposites (Nicholl, 1952), to be in balance, to not hold one truth against another but to see that all truths exist in relation to their opposite.

Maurice Nicholl, a psychiatrist and follower of both Jung and Gurdjieff, wrote:

The Greek word for righteousness (dikh) has the original meaning of being upright and so, between the opposites. The just man or righteous man, both of the New Testament and the Socratic teaching four centuries earlier, and of the teaching of Pythagoras as early as the 6th century B.C. is the upright man, the man who stands balanced between the opposites and is neither of them . . . the idea of the just man was directly derived from the ancient teaching about the opposites. **A one sided man could not be just. Nor could a man who**

lived in a small part of himself be just. To be righteous, to be just, is to be balanced. Do not misuse this word balanced, imagining that perhaps because you do not feel things so strongly as others, you are more balanced. To be balanced is not to be stupid but to be alive to every side of existence.

(Nichol, 1952: 326. Emphasis added.)

To be 'just' comes from 'doing the Good', which in turn is to be in both balance and harmony. However, balance is not static but dynamic. Modern science has shown that the only organisms that are in a stable state are those that are both dead and preserved or frozen and that evolution's creativity takes place in states far from equilibrium (Prigogine and Stengers, 1984). We must avoid making a new either-or dualism between balance and disequilibrium. Righteousness is about dynamic balance, about fully embracing both poles of the contraries, holding them in relationship and searching for a conjunction that marries the two together (see Chapter 13).

Bullock (2000) translates *Dikaiosune* as 'harmony' or 'living from the spirit'. But again, this should not be seen as a lovely, precious beautiful oasis with no conflict but rather, a dynamic harmony that flows between difference. For only by embracing the shadow can we be creative. Reconciliation arrives when that which is denied is fully owned, as when Prospero, in Shakespeare's play *The Tempest* turns to Caliban and says: 'this thing of darkness, I acknowledge mine'.

The Devil is known sometimes as *Diabolo* – doubleness, the prince of duality. Without his shadows, there is no light. God and Satan, said Bateson (Bateson and Bateson, 1987: 150), are 'so intimately joined that you will never disentangle them. . . . The first evil evidently was the separation of good and evil'. Here, perhaps, is a clue to Bateson's belief that any divinity governing ecological process must be both Shiva and Abraxas, both good and evil, life and death. In the words of Blake (1968b), 'Without contraries no progression'. Without separation, there can be no relationship; without relationship, nothing new can be created or new life evolved.

We all need creative enemies as much as friends or friends who are generous enough to act as our enemies. 'Opposition is true friendship', writes Blake (1968b). Friends can so easily become confluent and collusive, so we do not move on. What is more, they like us 'how we are' and may be a bit wary of what we might become. The creative enemy, the courageous coach and leader, all stand in the doorway, the entrance to the unrealized potential lying beyond, and challenges us to be fully alive and present, to become more than who we think we are.

To transcend, to transform, is to reach to the beyond, but the creative enemy might kill you if you waver in the process. The creative enemy may not just arrive in the form of an individual person; they may be collective or come in the form of a great challenge, which you cannot respond to without becoming more than you were previously. But as leaders, we need coaches who do not collude with our current way of being but are good for us because they help us see what is true and what is necessary.

Goodness and health

To be good is to be healthy, to do good is to create more health, wholeness and flourishing in the world you live in, to increase the fertility and fecundity of all that you encounter. The word 'health' has similar Germanic roots to the words 'wholeness' and 'holiness'. To be healthy is to be whole, and this requires both internal and external harmony and connectedness. There have been many experiments that have shown how Beauty can play an important role in healing, returning us to wholeness.

Ferrucci (2010: 85–95) quotes a wide range of scientific studies, including where patients who could see trees through a window from their hospital bed recovered quicker than those who could not, as did those who had images of beautiful scenery at the bottom of their beds; where beautiful music played in operations led to faster healing; and how the use of art, music and reading aided recovery. He ends his chapter by saying:

> Beauty is the perfect medicine. Rather than lowering our consciousness, as so many treatments do, it lifts us above our problems. Beauty has no side effects, its benefits last, the relief it brings does not diminish us in anyway, it creates no dependency, and it actually makes us feel clearer and stronger. . . . To enjoy its benefits we do not even need a prescription.
>
> (Ferrucci, 2010: 95)

Surgeons can stitch together the wounds in, or on the surface, of our bodies; but only Beauty can heal the soul and mend the disconnections within our psyche and between us and the wider eco-system. Beauty is good for us.

From disease to dynamic, harmonious balance

As individuals, we can become over-focussed on doing what our family, community and society teaches us in its moral edicts, or we can go to the other extreme and just follow our own instinct and needs. To overcome this duality, let me suggest five types of disharmonies – five varieties of dis-ease that arise from being out of alignment internally, interpersonally, collectively, globally and ecologically, failing to find the good or righteous balance between the contraries.

Individually

When we are out of alignment with ourself, we are in inner conflict, at war with ourself or dis-eased, unable to live at ease with what is within. The antidotes for this include such activities as providing time for inner reflection on our-self – time to go within, maybe through meditation or psychotherapy. Other creative processes include journalling, drawing or writing poetry.

Interpersonally

When we are out of relationship with those around us, we are unable to enter the flow of dialogue, where we let go of our own fixity and certainty so that something new can take form in the spaces between us. The antidotes for this include learning to listen empathically not just to the words of the other but also with compassion, with one's heart, to what the other is fully expressing. We not only stand in their shoes but also walk a mile in them with the laces untied. We can then practice entering conversations in the spirit of not knowing but rather, of seeking, not evangelizing or promoting our own current truth but discovering new truth together.

Collectively

Even in deep relationships, we are capable of creating a collective selfishness, an egocentricity made for two or more, or a collective egocentricity of our team or group, ignoring the wider community. Here, we need to strive not to ask the question: 'What does the community need?' For in doing this, we place our-selves outside of the community. Instead, we need to ask ourself: 'What can I uniquely contribute – in this group, to this team, this gathering, this organiza-tion, this community – so the wider system can flourish?'

Globally

Even in aligning ourselves vertically within, horizontally in relationship to oth-ers and by joining the flow of community, we are still in danger of being out of relationship with the wider human family. We can fall into the diseases of tribalism, sectarianism and nationalism: my family, my church, my team, my organization, my race. From this sin arises football hooliganism, religious big-otry, racial conflict and uncivil wars. The antidote for this sin is perhaps the hardest and the most urgent. For in our current world, the web of interdepend-ence that we have weaved means that we now truly live in a global village. What affects one group of people can very quickly affect the rest of the world so that the survival of the whole global eco-system is threatened. The antidote involves constantly focussing on the question: 'What does the whole world of tomorrow and today need that I, and we, can uniquely contribute?'

Ecologically

Thomas Berry (1999), in his book *The Great Work: Our Way into the Future,* explores how we need to link our individual and community purposes to the great work of our time. He shows the form of the great work has changed in each epoch of history and that now, the great work, the global challenge, is for humankind to move from exploitation of the earth and its resources to a new alignment with nature, from greed and over-consumption to creating a sustainable ecology and economy.

Putting them all together

If we put these five dimensions of health together into a unifying symbol, we have a vertical upright of inner balance and righteous goodness and a horizontal connection of dialogical co-creation with others: together, these make a cross. To this cross, we add the horizontal circle of the community dimension: the creation of a collective harmony that makes the whole community more than the sum of its parts. Then we add the vertical circle of the overarching and underarching purpose and alignment, where we are responding to the wider needs of the world and the ecology.

Together, these elements make a gyroscope that is only stable and upright or righteous when it is moving, embracing both opposing poles but has at its centre a righteous, still point that supports the moving dynamic balance. I have used this model of the gyroscope of dynamic balance in teaching leadership, moving beyond the traditional notions of authenticity to find dynamic congruence between the different levels of systemic engagement (Hawkins, 2018).

Here is a vignette of using the model to coach a senior leader.

I was coaching a senior partner in one of the world's largest 'professional services' firms, whom I shall call George. He was tasked with leading his part of the global business through a period of transformation. George talked of his challenge in getting partners to not only understand the challenges the firm was facing, but to 'buy into the new strategy'.

Step one: Self-congruence. I agreed to actively coach a rehearsal of his presentation and help him to increase his *Authority, Presence and Impact* (Hawkins and Smith, 2013). This involved my feedback focusing on how his message was matched and amplified, or mismatched, by the way he was standing, engaging and speaking. How the medium could be more congruent with the message.

Step two: Interpersonal congruence. This involved attending one of the many presentations George made to groups of senior partners. His talk was excellent, and he had now shared more of himself in the talk and there was a good match between the medium and the message. However, when it came to question time, he would respond to those questions that were in fact only faintly disguised challenges, by repeating what he had already said, only a little more slowly. I could see how the audience heard this as the leader being patronising and like a school teacher, who thought they were not able to understand what he was saying the first-time round. After this talk and before the next one, we worked on how he could tune-in to what the questioners were needing him to hear, and to be genuinely interested in the need behind the questions that are asked, and in the difficulties, others experienced when implementing the new direction.

At the next presentation, I watched carefully as he responded to questions, by asking the questioner to say more about their concern, or about what difficulty they fore saw in implementing the new strategy. Then he responded with genuine interest and exploration of how together they might address these issues. He also asked other partners, how they thought these concerns could best be addressed?

Step three: Collective congruence. Focussed on how this lead partner could be better at attuning to what was happening in different parts of the business and in different countries. George arrived at his talk to the Italian practice and instead of launching straight into his pre-prepared presentation, shared how he was aware that the practice had recently been through a very tough period and a whole group of partners had gone off to join a rival firm. He empathized on the difficult road they had been on and thanked them for the hard work they had put in to get the business back on track. He even spoke a few words of Italian.

Step four: Purposive and collaborative congruence. When George appointed his new leadership team, drawn from many parts of the business, he began his first meeting with the words: 'We together have a big challenge, and we have many thousands of stakeholders who we serve, that need us to succeed. That is our clients, our partners, our employees, the regions and communities where we operate. We have a large and exciting mountain to climb. For us to succeed with these challenges I need your help – that is help from every one of you individually, and from all of us as a team. We will only get to succeed together, if we discover how to become more than the sum of our parts'.

Step five: Ecological congruence. George, after we had belatedly talked about the wider ecology in our coaching and the firm's contribution to addressing it, engaged a whole cohort of leaders, who were being developed to be the future-partners of the firm. He shared his heart felt concern that the work the firm was doing was only making client firms more profitable and successful, while the ecology was burning and dying. He asked them to work in small groups, and then in three months share back with him, practical examples of where through partnering with client organizations in new ways, together they could assist the wider ecology back to better health. The groups were energized and dynamic and the ideas generated took the firm way beyond their previous ESG policies.

Now my coaching work is more dynamic and less linear, moving from the personal to the interpersonal, to the collective, to the ecological. Today, I would ensure that all dimensions were in play from the very beginning (see Chapter 14).

Beauty, justice and health

A healthy system is one in which every part has its place and is listened to. In an orchestra that plays beautifully, every instrument is heard and its contribution valued. In a beautiful picture, every colour has its part to play. Shakespeare's genius is that in his plays, we see the perspective of every character.

To create a better world that is good, it has to be good for everyone. There has to be equity, which does not mean everyone gets the same but that everyone's needs are listened and responded to. When one tribe or nation has exploited or persecuted another group, the persecuted so often becomes the next generation of persecutors. As Gandhi pointed out, the belief in justice, meaning an eye for an eye, ends up making the whole world blind. Only with compassion for all of humanity, combined with social and international equity and justice, will we be able to meet the challenge of the climate emergency and the multiple challenges of our times. Only by falling in love with the Beauty and Goodness of the wider world we are part of – and wanting to care for that world, responding to Goodness with Goodness and Beauty with Beauty – can both ecology and humanity not only survive but flourish (see Chapter 8).

Conclusion

Beauty inspires us and points us towards the Good. The Good, like Truth, is never alone but always in relationship – 'fitting' with the flourishing of all partners and the greater whole. Evil is the absence of the Good and can grow out of a pursuit of a local good, at the cost of the wider system and the world around us. Nothing can be evil according to a fixed principle, and evil is that which is devoid of harmony. We recognize harmony through its Beauty. The Good is also found in finding the third place that transcends our oppositional dualities, including Good and Evil.

But we have not yet finished with Good and Evil. In the next chapter, we will explore how the twins of Good and Evil get translated into Ethics. We will move from Veritas to her daughter, Virtus, or Virtue. We will explore how Ethics, like Truth and Good, can become separated from their relational context and become a false fixity and how aesthetics and Beauty can help Ethics transcend this danger.

Chapter 8

The ethics and aesthetics of Beauty

Introduction: without a new ethics, we will destroy the world

In the last two chapters, we explored the relationship between Beauty, Truth and Good, the three Verity sisters. In this chapter, we will explore how these three sisters can guide and deepen our ethical values and actions. The beauty of aesthetics can provide both depth and nuance to our ethics and values, for as the poet Gary Snyder (1995: vii) tells us, 'The key to ethics is aesthetics'.

Dostoyevsky struggled throughout his life and in his novels with questions of Good and Evil. He was concerned about the growing secularism in Russia and wrote, 'If God does not exist everything is permitted' (quoted in Cheng, 2013: 58). Cheng develops this concern of Dostoyevsky when he says, 'The truth is [that] when any notion of the sacred is banished it is impossible for humans to establish a true hierarchy of values' (Cheng, 2013: 58). Since Dostoyevsky's time, our human world has become even more secular, and with the growing global challenges outlined in Chapter 1, the need for shared values and a shared ecological Ethics has become ever more urgent and critical.

Different forms of ethics

There are many different forms of ethics, and here, I just introduce a few of the main ethical frames.

Behaviour

Looking at cause and effect and isolated behaviours is the simplest and most basic ethical frame. If we see a mother snatching a glass of liquid from a young child and see the child crying, we might think the mother is very cruel. But what if the child had taken their mother's glass of wine and the mother, having realized this, was protecting her child from a drink that would make them sick? In reverse, as in the well-known fairy tale, we might see an old lady offering Snow White a beautiful red apple and, like Snow White, say, 'How kind', not realizing it is poisonous.

DOI: 10.4324/9781003349600-11

Intent

This takes us from simply observing an individual's behaviour, in a short snap-shot of cause and effect, to looking at the intent behind the action – the mother trying to prevent her child drinking alcohol, the wicked queen trying to poison Snow White.

Moving from behaviour to intent creates its own complications. The leader accused of bullying and threatening their team might say, 'Yes, indeed, I shouted and demanded everyone stay late, but my intention was to protect them. If the order was not delivered, the factory would be shut down and they would have lost their jobs'.

When Jesus says that it is not enough to avoid sleeping with our neighbour's wife but that 'everyone who looks at a woman with lust for her has already committed adultery with her in his heart' (Matthew 5:28), he is not equating the two processes. Rather, he is saying that we are responsible for our intentions, as well as how we chose to enact them.

The fundamental tenet of all ethics is the Hippocratic baseline: 'Do no harm'. It is one that should be written into every profession's ethical code. Yet life's choices are rarely that simple or straightforward.

If we took 'Do no harm' literally, we would not move, eat or drink, as we would be too frightened of what small life-forms we might tread on, the harm caused to create every mouthful of food and drink we consume, clothes we wear or tools we use.

There is an old saying, 'All is fair in love and war'. In the heat of both love and war, our emotions can overrun our rationality, and we tend to act from instinct. This may be true of many other less 'hot' aspects of life. Many organizational leaders make hundreds of small and big decisions every day, without the luxury of examining all the evidence, weighing up the costs and benefits for all those involved and exploring the potential unintended consequences.

Disposition

Some writers on values in leadership say it is important that leaders have a 'moral compass' so that when they are in the midst of the storm, 'they know where their True North is' (George, 1997 and 2003). The implication here is that we need to develop an orientation to what is right and ethical before we go out into the storm.

Here, I believe we are moving to a third level of ethical discernment: one's guiding orientation or ethical *disposition*. There is a danger in the emphasis on finding your own individual 'True North', as if every person has to, or can, work it out for themselves. What if all our compasses read differently? Does the moral True North become totally relative and something we constantly have to negotiate?

In the modern Western world of the last 200 years, the dominant stance for collectively adjudicating what is ethical has been collective utility. This idea comes from the Utilitarian theories of Jeremy Bentham, for whom actions could be judged on how they led to the 'greatest happiness of the greatest number'. John Stuart Mill developed this further by stating that we needed to look at the quality as well as the quantity of happiness, but this still leaves many unresolved issues.

The first of these is that the most important values in life cannot be measured or quantified. We tend to measure what is easy to measure, and measuring is never neutral. By choosing to measure something, we make it important, we give it special status, and it can become a 'yardstick' for judging other people and events. Robert Kennedy (1968) pointed out how:

> the gross national product does not allow for the health of our children, the quality of their education or the joy of their play. It does not include the beauty of our poetry or the strength of our marriages, the intelligence of our public debate or the integrity of our public officials. It measures neither our wit nor our courage, neither our wisdom nor our learning, neither our compassion nor our devotion to our country, it measures everything in short, except that which makes life worthwhile.

We can lose sight of quality when our PowerPoint presentations are full of graphs and tables of quantities. Truth becomes only that which can be measured.

Measurement is always looking back at what has been. By the time you have measured something and made sense of your measurements, life has moved on. It is as if you are driving whilst looking in the rearview mirror, and yet decisions have to be made both in the present and about what is ahead of us along the road. Furthermore, the faster we travel, the further ahead our focus needs to be. I once travelled by car with a 'blue-light' driving instructor (someone who trains police and ambulance drivers to drive at speed with a flashing blue light). They said, 'Most of us only focus on the car immediately in front of us when we are driving – but to drive in an emergency at 100 miles an hour, you need to be aware of the driver 500 metres ahead of you, who might suddenly pull out; you have to sense this from their movements, even before they make a move'.

The world is not divided into ethical and unethical people. We are all capable of acting unethically, given the right circumstances. You cannot create an ethical profession just by having strict ethical codes and throwing out anyone who offends against them. Supervision, dialogue and teamwork are essential aspects of raising the standards of ethical functioning in all professions (Hawkins and McMahon, 2020; Hawkins and Carr, 2023). Indeed, when I have been part of a panel dealing with ethical complaints, or addressing ethical issues brought to supervision, my compassion for the so-called offender has been triggered by the thought, 'thus but by the grace of God go I'.

Eco-systemic ethics

From an eco-systemic awareness perspective, I would suggest that someone who is acting from an ethical disposition is always in service of the greater whole of which they are but a part. When acting from an unethical disposition, they might be trying to sub-optimize the short-term gain for themselves, or their particular part in the wider system, at the cost of the greater whole.

By this definition, a cancerous cell is unethical, but a healthy organ is ethical, by playing its part in serving the wider organism, recognizing that its thriving depends on the thriving of the whole body. Likewise, a team member is ethical when they are in service of the team as a whole succeeding and not just trying to use the team for their own next promotion or glorification. The organization is ethical when, in the words of Paul Polman (Polman and Winston, 2021), 'it succeeds by giving more than it takes', or in my own words (Hawkins, 2021a: 41), 'it co-creates beneficial value with, and for, all its stakeholders'.

I am aware that both these statements beg new questions such as 'Giving more than it takes of what?' and 'How do you define beneficial value?' As organizations trade in the exchange of a mixture of services, products and benefits of many different kinds – such as delight, utility, happiness, learning, employment, money and so on – how can these be compared, let alone measured, in the judgment of giving more than taking?

One way out of the Utilitarian reduction of trying to measure and quantify everything on the same measurement scale is to link value back to prime values. It can help if we stop and ask how we arrive at a human consensus of what core human values are, ones that are foundational to wellbeing. But here lies the danger of returning to the Utilitarian trap of attempting to measure the greatest happiness of the greatness number. In doing this, we are replacing GDP (gross domestic product) with GDH – gross domestic happiness. This is, at least, a step forward, as it moves away from merely measuring the scale of economic activity, whether good or bad, to something we all experience. However, the problem is that they are both gross and both domestic! My country's happiness versus yours. Wellbeing and happiness have become popular concepts in both modern psychology and modern business writings. But arising out of the modern Western tradition, they are located in individuals. Collective wellbeing then becomes the sum of every person's individual wellbeing, rather than the wellbeing of society as a whole.

Global ethics

The United Nations has made brave attempts to arrive at some 'universal givens' that unite us all, particularly in two landmark documents. The first is the *Universal Declaration of Human Rights* (United Nations Declaration on Human Rights, 1948) which was drafted by representatives with different legal and cultural backgrounds from many regions of the world.

The second is the *UN Sustainable Development Goals* (United Nations Sustainable Development Goals, 2015), also known as the global goals, which is a universal call to action to end poverty, protect the planet and ensure that by 2030, all people enjoy peace and prosperity.

The UDHR, written in the wake of the Second World War, is about the 'rights' of individuals, which should not be taken away from them by governments. It is couched more in terms of 'freedom from', than 'freedoms to'. As such, it is very much in the paradigm of the Western modernist tradition of individualism and human-centrism. The global goals go some way to balancing this by showing not just our individual rights but also some of our collective responsibilities. However, it is not until we get to Goals 13–15 that it really starts to become less human-centric and to look at our human responsibility for what we are inflicting on our wider ecology – our atmosphere (13), our hydrosphere (14) and our earth (15) (United Nations Sustainable Development Goals, 2015).

We may all agree that 'peace and prosperity' are good things, in abstract. But peace at what price? And when does one group's prosperity have disastrous consequences for other human groups and/or the wider ecology we all share?

Value

McGilchrist (2021) argues extensively that the post-Enlightenment scientific and materialist paradigm brings with it enormous scientific, economic and social benefits, particularly for the early adopters, who used it to achieve power and advantage over others, but that it has been out of step with the vast majority of cultural paradigms, both throughout the world and over the course of human history.

If we want to find more widely shared values, we need to look beyond this limited perspective, as it has been dominated by left-brain perception and reduces everything to human utility. In our modern world, value has simply come to be equated with monetary value. The value of a person has become the electronic numbers registered in their various savings accounts, and the value of a company has become what it can be sold for on the open market. The value of a person's life then presumably becomes how much monetary wealth they have accumulated in their life and can pass on to others.

Jesus said (Matthew 6: 19–21):

Do not lay up for yourselves treasures on earth, where moth and rust destroy and where thieves break in and steal, but lay up for yourselves treasures in heaven, where neither moth nor rust destroys and where thieves do not break in and steal. For where your treasure is, there your heart will be also.

In today's world, material wealth has moved beyond metal that can rust to electronic numbers that have even less substance.

Some people invest value in a belief in a future life in which they will be rewarded for good behaviour. Others invest value in how much they are admired and liked (celebrity-ism), measured by the numbers of 'likes' on their Facebook, X (formerly Twitter), Instagram or LinkedIn posts.

What if we invest instead in making our best contribution to co-creating a better world right now on this planet? To realize that we are not here to have a good time but to make the times good. To realize that one of the urgent tasks in the world right now is to develop a shared ethical code, which, in turn, needs to be built on shared core values.

Many companies and organizations in recent times have worked at developing core values that can underpin their culture, strategy and leadership. Indeed, I have facilitated many such processes. Many arrive at similar terms. Some of the most common include words like honesty, transparency, trust, teamwork, customer-focussed. Many of these describe behaviours that the company wants to encourage, and some have usefully created examples of the behaviours that exemplify each value and the behaviours that are contrary to it. This exercise is very useful in moving a culture towards developing a shared moral code and defining acceptable behaviour, but it does not elucidate the value we are here to co-create.

Tim Cook, the CEO of Apple, in his love for simplicity said in a call to investors in 2019, 'We believe that we're on the face of the Earth to make great products'. But this begs the question of what determines whether or not a product is great.

With the help of others who have been on this journey before us, we will now explore a deeper sense of beneficial value – value that increases the wellbeing of the whole and by so doing benefits the parts, rather than the other way round.

Reverence for life

In early summer 1915, Albert Schweitzer took a boat trip up the Ogooué (or Ogowe) River in what was then French Equatorial Africa, now Gabon. He was depressed about the terrible war going on all across Europe and troubled by how his writing and teaching criticized current civilization, while not providing a positive way forward. He spent two days sitting on the deck of the boat, filling his notebook with unsatisfactory ways to create positive ethics for his times. In his autobiography, he describes the following:

> Late on the third day, at the very moment when, at sunset, we were making our way through a herd of hippopotamuses, there flashed upon my mind, unforeseen and unsought, the phrase: 'Reverence for Life'. The iron door had yielded. The path in the thicket had become visible. Now I had found my way to the principle in which affirmation of the world and ethics are joined together!

(Schweitzer, 2009: 154–155)

He goes on to say:

> In spite of the great importance we attach to the achievements of science and human prowess, it is obvious that only a humanity that is striving for ethical ends can benefit in full measure from material progress and can overcome the dangers that accompany it.
>
> The only possible way out of chaos is for us to adopt a concept of the world based on the ideal of true civilization.
>
> (Schweitzer, 2009: 155)

What he meant by true civilization, he further elucidated in his book *The Philosophy of Civilization*, in which he writes: 'Ethics are responsibility without limit toward all that lives. . . . Love means more, since it includes fellowship in suffering, in joy, and in effort' (Schweitzer, 1987: 317).

It is interesting that Schweitzer uses the word 'reverence', or in the original German, *ehrfurcht*, which combines the notion of deep respect and awe. His teaching goes well beyond respecting and protecting life, as it encourages us to be in service of all life. As a young child, he was concerned that the prayers he was asked to say each night were only for human beings; and so, after lights were out, he would add prayers for all creatures. As he matured his ethics, he went further and embraced all that lived, not just animals. For Schweitzer, progress went beyond human science and invention to the constant evolution and emergence of all life on our shared planet.

At the other end of the 20th century, and at the other end of the world, another philosopher and naturalist addressed the same urgent need for expanding our ethical maturity. The Norwegian ecological philosopher Arne Naess would retreat to his remote mountain cabin, where he would go on long walks, immersing himself in the 'more-than-human' world that surrounded him. It was here that he developed the foundational principles of 'Deep Ecology'. He differentiated this from 'shallow ecology', which is the study of our eco-systems as if they were separate from ourselves. He showed how much of the writing of shallow ecology is human-centric, looking at ecological sustainability in terms of how it best benefits human survival and flourishing (Naess, 1987).

The core principles of Deep Ecology (Naess & Sessions, 1986: 2) are as follows:

1. The wellbeing and flourishing of human and non-human life on earth have value in themselves. These values are independent of the usefulness of the non-human world for human purposes.
2. Richness and diversity of life-forms contribute to the relation of these values and are also values in themselves.
3. Human beings have no right to reduce this richness and diversity except to satisfy vital needs.

4. The flourishing of human life and cultures is compatible with the substantial decrease of the human population. The flourishing of non-human life requires such a decrease.
5. Current human interference with the non-human world is excessive, and the situation is rapidly worsening.
6. Policies must, therefore, be changed. These policies affect basic economic, technological and ideological structures. The resulting state of affairs will be deeply different from those of the present state of affairs.
7. The ideological change is mainly that of appreciating life quality (dwelling in situations of inherent value) rather than adhering to an increasingly higher standard of living. There will be profound awareness of the difference between big and great.
8. Those who subscribe to the foregoing points have an obligation directly or indirectly to try to implement the necessary changes. It is this principle that highlights the importance of deep questioning as the process by which to follow/develop/enact the other principles.

Naess argued that humanity urgently needed to develop a higher form of maturity. Traditionally, models of adult development – such as those espoused by Maslow (1962), Kegan (1982) and Torbert (2004) – have shown how, as human beings, we move from being egocentric, through developing a social self, to developing a richer authentic self that can make a difference within the world. Naess argued that we have to extend this continuum of development to include a higher and more expansive mode of development, which he called the 'ecological self'.

Naess (1986: 24) was one of the early leaders who showed the following:

> One of the great challenges today is to save the planet from further ecological devastation, which violates both the enlightened self-interest of humans and the self-interest of non- humans and decreases the potential of joyful existence for all.

Naess believed that creating the necessary changes in human consciousness cannot be achieved by rational argument and a simple appeal to 'universal moral duty'. Rather, he argued, we need to fundamentally shift our human consciousness in a way that expands our sense of self to include the wider world of nature, of which we are part and upon which we are totally dependent. Only by stopping making nature 'other' and instead see nature as part of us, and ourselves as part of nature, will we start to naturally care for the wider ecology in the same way that we naturally care for our immediate family.

> The requisite care flows naturally if the Self is widened and deepened so that protection of free nature is felt and conceived as protection of ourselves. . . .

If reality is experienced by the ecological self, our behaviour naturally and **beautifully** follows norms of **strict environment ethics.**

(Naess, 1986: 45. Emphasis added.)

Naess (1986: 44) suggests that 'in environmental affairs, perhaps we should try primarily to influence people toward beautiful acts'. Naess drew on the earlier writing of Aldo Leopold (1887–1948), a pioneer in ecological ethics who wrote that 'A thing is right when it tends to preserve the integrity, stability and **beauty** of the biotic community. It is wrong when it tends otherwise' (Leopold, 1949: 224–225). Leopold developed what he called a 'Land Ethic', which 'simply enlarges the boundaries of the community to include soils, waters, plants and animals, or collectively the land' – an ethic that 'changes the roles of *Homo sapiens* from conqueror of the land-community to plain member and citizen of it' (Leopold, 1949: 204).

Bateson (1972, 1979, 1991; Bateson and Bateson, 1987) also wrote extensively about paths back to ecological wisdom from our current destructive thinking: learning from the wider ecological systems of which we are a part and through aesthetic engagement, which we will explore in Chapter 14.

To develop a global ecological ethic, we need to create a new marriage between science and aesthetic and embodied engagement. Ursula Goodenough (1998), like Bateson, is a scientist in search of 'the sacred depths of nature', searching for a way of understanding the world that transcends both mechanism and superstition. She argues that science must develop a religio-poiesis, a way of speaking 'that can call forth appealing and abiding religious responses' (Goodenough, 1998: xvii). She calls her approach 'religious naturalism', in which she suggests:

the story of Nature has the potential to serve as the cosmos for the global ethos . . . only if we all experience a solemn gratitude that we exist at all, share a reverence for how life works, and acknowledge a deep and complex imperative that life continues.

(Goodenough, 1998: xvii)

Note the echo of the word 'reverence', taking us back to Schweitzer and Naess.

Goodenough (1998) charts a path that starts with empathy, progresses through awe and wonder to compassion and produces fairness, justice and the Good. For if we are to transform humans – from extractors, exploiters and abusers of the Earth and destroyers of a great deal of biodiversity – to healers, we need to go beyond the statistics and lessons of science. We need a transformation based in our emotional feelings and spiritual wisdom, in a 'religio-poiesis' – a language that transcends concepts, edicts and rules; a language that springs from a longing to partake with compassion and love in the places where Beauty, Truth and Good conjoin.

Building on the inspirational writings of Albert Schweitzer, Aldo Leopold, Arne Naess and all those who have developed Deep Ecology even further (Sylvan and Bennett's 'Deep Green Theory', 1994; Mosquin and Rowe, 2004; Plumwood, 2006; Mathews, 2021, 2023), I would argue that we urgently need an evolutionary leap in human consciousness. We need a collective ethical maturation in which we expand our capacity to be in service – beyond our own immediate and apparent self-interest, beyond the service of humanity and future human generations – to being in the service of life. And in service not just of what is already living but also of what is emerging and, at times, struggling to come into being.

My own contribution to this development has been to argue that we need to develop an eco-systemic understanding and epistemology and an eco-systemic ontology or way of being.

As I laid out in Chapter 4, there is an essential difference between system thinking, systemic thinking and eco-systemic awareness. System and systemic thinking have been useful in helping us move beyond reductive, atomistic ways of viewing the world, which have been at the heart of scientific modernity. It has been the great system and systemic thinkers of the 20th century – such as Gregory Bateson, Maturana and Varela, Prigogine, Capra and Senge – who have created the intellectual groundwork in which systemic awareness can grow. We need a new perceiving, new feeling, new sentiment of the heart, new responses from the gut instinct and a comprehensive new eco-spirituality.

Curry, in his second edition of *Ecological Ethics* (2010), expanded the whole section on the essential spiritual contribution to set out a living ecological virtue ethics. More recently, Curry (2019) has written about how 'enchantment' and 'wonder in modern life' are essential aspects for the human turn to virtuous living in an ecological world. His work is paralleled and supported by the work of Keltner (2023) on awe (see Chapter 5).

The importance of ecological aesthetics in developing ecological ethics

Cheng (2013: 48) writes: 'There can be no aesthetics without Ethics'. I would add to this that there can be no Ethics without aesthetics: no understanding of what is 'good to do' without its sisters, Beauty and Truth.

The Age of Reason brought with it a philosophy of trying to create universal truths. Kant argued that to lie was always wrong, so even if someone was hiding in your house, and soldiers came searching for them to murder them, you should not lie to save their life. Rationality, empirical science and the left-hemisphere neo-cortex love certainty, fixed rules, commandments and absolutes. This can also be said about the Pharisees and Sadducees at the time of Jesus. They wanted to know whether or not Jesus believed in the laws of the prophets and the commandments of God, as delivered by Moses. Jesus said that we need to live under the laws of our context and give unto Caesar what is Caesar's and to God what is God's (Mark 12:17) – that is, live in accord with your context. Jesus's commandments were not rules but rather, guiding principles. He urged us to love God with all our hearts and minds and to love our neighbour as ourself.

Insight may come from the investigation of the left-hemisphere way of thinking, but personal, relational and cultural change are always embodied, involving many parts of the brain, the body and feelings. Without love, ethics becomes a dry concept that fails to take root and grow within the person. Beauty is the vehicle through which Love flows. If we are to find a new ethic that enables the healing of the spirit between the human and the-more-than-human world, we need one that comes from the heart and from where Beauty, Truth and Good meet.

You cannot have a fully-lived ecological ethic without an ecological aesthetic. In this book, I have shown that rationalism and the Cartesian split are a foundation stone of the modernity that has led humans down the catastrophic and ecologically destructive path to ecocide. White Western ethics, since the time of Plato and Aristotle, have been dominated by rational and linear logic of the (mostly male) commentators on life.

To make the necessary change, we need an embodied, relational and engaged ethics that flows through not only how we think but also how we feel, respond and interact moment to moment in relation to the world around us – both the human and the 'more-than-human' world. We need not a conceptual aesthetic of the observer and analyser of objectified beauty nor a relativist subjective aesthetic that privileges the individual but a relational aesthetic ethic.

The great educationalist John Dewey (1934), who argued for the importance of 'hands-on' engaged learning, wrote about how aesthetics enhances the intensity of everyday life.

An experience is a product, one might almost say biproduct, of continuous and cumulative interaction of an organic self with the world. There is no other foundation upon which aesthetic theory and criticism can build.

(Dewey, 1934: 220)

Aesthetics give depth and feeling to relationships, whether between humans, living creatures or living beings and their ecology. One of the key roles of Beauty is to draw the individual's attention to what lies beyond them. Beauty engages not the left-hemisphere, objectifying gaze in search of utility, but rather, the right-hemisphere, embodied engagement of being-to-being and presence-to-presence – to cause the person to lift their perspective from self-interest and to feel, see and hear the world beyond their grasp.

Through Beauty, we find Love; and only then, when we begin to love those who were previously other, do they become part of our extended circle of intimacy, and we begin truly to care for the wider world. When we experience Beauty in the connection with what was previously other, we not only experience receiving love by Grace (see Chapter 10) but also are moved to reciprocate and to express our love from whence it came. Aldo Leopold (1949: 263) wrote how 'The landscape of any farm is the owner's portrait of himself', echoed by Wendell Berry, farmer, eco-philosopher and poet, who commented on Twitter (now X) on June 24, 2018: 'A good farm is recognized as good partly by its beauty'.

What we see in life is also a reflection of who we are. William Blake (1799), in a letter to the Reverend Dr. John Trusler, wrote:

The tree which moves some to tears of joy is in the eyes of others only a green thing which stands in the way. Some see nature all ridicule and deformity . . . and some scarce see nature at all. But to the eyes of the man of imagination, nature is imagination itself. As a man is, so he sees.

Looking at a wood, the urban child may see a dark place of terror, the entrepreneur may see a valuable tranche of saleable wood, and the tourist may see a cool place to wander in the shade. But an indigenous woodlander sees an ever-changing home, from which they are constantly learning and in relation to which they are constantly developing and evolving.

In my writing on learning from the woods, where I live, I describe the difference between someone who studies woods or is a visitor who uses the wood for their own enjoyment and a true woodlander.

Woodlanders, those who live and work in the woods, know the woods from living in their interstices. Their knowledge is embodied and diurnal as they breathe differently each day in syncopation with the woods. As visitors we can never know the wood fully, but we can open all our senses and let it teach us how it lives. Woodlanders learn from their environment that everything resides in relationship with everything else, and that every organism is gifting itself to the great whole.

(Hawkins, 2022: 3)

True woodlanders can identify a tree by the noise it makes in the wind and fungi by their smell (Deakin, 2007). Most of us in so-called 'developed economies' have lost our connection with earth and with the Earth that supports us. But we can rediscover this essential connection and attune our desires to what the ecology needs us to desire in order that we play our full part in the larger whole (Mathews, 2017).

The Native American Luther Standing Bear (1868–1939), Chief of the Oglala Lakota peoples, said in 1905:

> The old Lakota was wise. He knew that a man's heart away from Nature becomes hard; he knew that lack of respect for growing living things soon lead to a lack of respect for humans too. . . . The old people came literally to love the soil and they sat or reclined on the ground with a feeling of being close to a mothering power.

Conclusion

To follow Schweitzer in developing a reverence for life, we have much to learn from the indigenous peoples of the world. Our respect must mature into reverence, and this reverence must bring with it a humility and an openness as a species to learn from the wider and wiser parts of nature. Robin Wall Kimmerer, a professor of botany who has spent much of her adult life rediscovering the teachings of her Native American ancestors, writes (Kimmerer, 2020: 9):

> Within Native ways of knowing, human people are often referred to as 'the younger brothers of Creation'. We say that humans have the least experience with how to live and thus the most to learn – we must look to our teachers among the other species for guidance. Their wisdom is apparent in the way that they live. They teach us by example. They've been on the earth far longer than we have been and have had time to figure things out.

Later, Kimmerer (2020: 222) says: 'The land is the real teacher. All we need as students is mindfulness'. This mindfulness involves us deepening our reverence into feeling the beauty of the earth in the core of our being. Only then does this participation in and through Beauty naturally flow into love – beyond the human realm, beyond philosophical knowledge and science – to a love for Gaia, our Mother Earth, and all our wider ecological family and home.

I argued earlier in this chapter that we need to expand our ethical focus from behaviours to intentions and ethical dispositions: from trying to establish universal moral codes, which involves measuring everything through its utility, to looking at what provides the most expansive, beneficial value. I went on to define, from an eco-systemic awareness, an ethical perspective – whether of an individual, a team or an organization or, indeed, a country or species – as one that is always in service of the greater whole of which it is but a part. I then showed how an unethical disposition is one that is trying to sub-optimize the short-term gain for their particular part of the wider system, at the cost of the greater whole.

To develop this ethical disposition, we first need to develop eco-systemic awareness in order to ascertain how we can best serve the wider system, rather than constantly react to the latest demand from our environment. We need to ask ourselves not just once but regularly: 'What can we uniquely do that the world of tomorrow needs?' Then we need to ask how we can best make this contribution in a way that increases the radiance of Love, Beauty, Truth, Goodness and Grace.

In the next chapter, we will explore in greater depth how a reverence for life needs to be deepened by a reverence for the transience of life and for death and how suffering, dying and death are not just located at the end of life but are at the heart of living.

Chapter 9

The Beauty of death and transience

Introduction

We have looked at some of the companions of Beauty and the role they play in our return journey to fuller consciousness. In this chapter, we explore what, for some, is a surprising companion to Beauty and encounter the role that death plays, both as a core aspect of Beauty and in deepening our appreciation of life.

To make the return journey to participative consciousness, we need to realize that death is part of life, not its opposite. We need to learn to 'die before you die' as the Koran, Marcus Aurelius and many great spiritual teachers and philosophers have taught throughout the ages. Montaigne (1893) wrote, 'To philosophise is to learn how to die'; but as Ernest Becker (1973) and Roger Scranton (2015) show, modern humans are on the run from death, and many tech billionaires and others seek to defeat death and achieve personal immortality (Harari, 2016: 21–29), while the Earth, the rest of humanity and all living beings pay the cost.

Death in life

In unexpectedly taking on responsibility for 37 acres of land, I had to learn what the terrain needed in order to be healthy, with the requisite ecological diversity. I learnt how the fields needed small numbers of different domestic animals rotating through them. How, after the wildflowers had spread their seed in early autumn, sheep were needed to clean up the grass so the flowers could come through fresh in the spring. How a small number of cattle would tread the seeds into the earth and would eat the long grass down to the length where the sheep could take over. Then there were the goats, who are bush eaters. They would chomp through the rampant blackberry bushes and ivy that love to take over as much of the field as they can and strangle small trees.

I became very fond of these different animals, feeding them apples by hand and giving them our own stored hay when the ground was frozen or snow-covered in winter. We, and then our grandchildren, also gave them names. But the hardest

DOI: 10.4324/9781003349600-12

and deepest lesson we took from these animals was to see them put into the trailer to go off to the abattoir and then to receive one of them back as butchered meat for eating. Before we eat them, I pause and give thanks to them, often by name, for their life and the gift of their death. From this experience, I composed the following grace to say before a meal:

> We give thanks for all that dies that we might live.
> We give thanks for all that lives that we might die.
> And in partaking in this food,
> We remember that life and death are one.

Death is an integral part of life, for it is the dying of organisms that feeds the next cycle of living. Andreas Weber (2017: 59) writes: 'Death is unavoidable, but only death makes life legible'. He writes beautifully and poetically of watching a wood in winter and how the dead trees provide shelter and nourishment for woodpeckers, other birds and insects. In doing so, the trees continue, in death, to be part of 'the circle of giving', because humans had not yet come along to remove them as 'dead waste' (Weber, 2017: 197).

Both my parents, as the end of their lives came closer, decided they were ready to transition from life into death, my mother aged 89 and my father aged 91. They had both faced a series of illnesses, which made living very difficult, and they were exhausted. Both consciously stopped eating and then drinking. They died peacefully and with equanimity. My father had asked that I do a personal farewell to his coffin at the cremation, on behalf of the whole family, as I had done for my mother.

The cremation was just for the family and was followed, later the same day, with a memorial service. As it came to the last hymn, I had my 4-year-old granddaughter on one knee and my brother's 4-year-old granddaughter on the other. I told them I needed them to get off, as I was going to say farewell to their great-grandpa. My granddaughter immediately said, 'I am coming with you', which was followed by her second cousin saying, 'I am coming too'. I walked to the front of the crematorium supported by two young girls, each holding one of my hands. I asked them both to hold my left hand so my right hand could rest on the coffin. The next moment I will never forget. Suddenly, I could sense the electricity of the generations before me and after me, flowing through my outstretched arms – the continuous flow of the river of the generations, of which I was just one small part.

Beauty in transience

The Japanese have a beautiful concept of *mono no aware* (物の哀れ), which I am told is very hard to translate into English. It has the sense of pathos and sensitivity to the transience of things. There is a recognition that everything is in the process of dying and an awareness of the transience of all living things, which heightens appreciation of their beauty. Thus, the Japanese meditate on the falling of cherry blossom in late spring and of the leaves in autumn. The gentle, nuanced feelings that this brings can increase our empathy with all things. The nearest we have to this sentiment in the European tradition is probably the Latin phrase *lacrimae rerum*, from Virgil's *Aeneid* (Book I, line 462), meaning 'tears of things'.

François Cheng (2009: 15) shows the following:

> All beauty collaborates precisely with the uniqueness of the moment. True beauty could not be a perpetually fixed state. . . . It is the reason why beauty seems nearly always tragic, haunted as we are by the awareness that all beauty is ephemeral.

The great Sufi Ibn Arabi teaches how 'self-disclosure never repeats itself' and 'The renewal of creation is at each instant' (IW28).

All living is transient, yet as the sons and daughters of modernity, we want to collect, categorize, own and control life – life reduced to our museums, souvenirs and photo collections. The great poet and mystic William Blake wrote the following lines which we have quoted before in this book:

> He who binds to himself a joy
> Does the winged life destroy
> But he who kisses the joy as it flies
> Lives in Eternity's sunrise.

This was at a time when collecting butterflies in a net, pinning them on a board in a glass cabinet and classifying every aspect of nature was becoming popular. A time when rationalistic, scientific enlightenment thinking was on the rise in Europe and giving birth to modernity, with humans becoming eager to control the world around them and view it with atomistic eyes – a world of separate, disconnected things.

We, too, can learn from seeing how fragile and fleeting is the beauty of nature. A flower opens in the morning, and its petals may have fallen by the end of the day. The painted lady butterfly that adorns our flower meadow has died within the month. We are reminded that every separate being dies and feeds the next phase of life. We can learn to see the beauty of this constant cycle of birth, life and death and see beauty in all its phases. In so doing, we can become less attached to the passing of our own seasons. We can start to notice the birth, the life and the dying of each day, of each project, of each moment and of each life. And discover the beauty and equanimity of non-attachment.

Some of the great Roman philosophers spoke of how birth and death are at the heart of all life. Ovid (1922, *Metamorphoses*, 5.177) wrote:

> There is nothing constant in the universe, all ebb and flow, and every shape that is born bears in its womb the seeds of change.

Lucretius wrote in his classic text *De Rerum Natura* ('The Way Things Are'):

> Nothing can dwindle to nothing, as Nature restores one thing from the stuff of another, nor does she allow a birth, without a corresponding death.
>
> (Lucretius, 2020)

More recently, Wallace Stevens (1967) in his poem 'Sunday Morning' writes: 'Death is the mother of beauty'.

Idolizing growth and denying death

In modernity, we have created a polarization of life and death. Beauty is associated with spring, new life coming into being, the bright sunshine of midday light. We have become deniers of death. The rich elite are investing in cryogenics and planetary escapism to inhabit Mars or other planets, escaping from the massive death and destruction that they, and other humans, have created on our shared planet.

One of my spiritual teachers told me: 'The degree to which you can fully embrace life is equal to the degree to which you can fully embrace death'. Life and death are one. Death is not something that comes at the end of life, or ends life, for it is an inextricable part of life. But we have banished it to the periphery; we have tried to conquer death, but at the price of diminishing life.

In coaching, we have been addicted to growth and to everything and everyone 'developing' (Hawkins, 2017b). We want the beauty of a perpetual spring and early summer. As James Hillman (1975), the founder of archetypal psychology said, growth is good and appropriate in spring, childhood and the beginnings of a cycle but that growth in middle age is over-consumption, obesity or cancer. Francis Weller (2015: 23) echoes this sentiment:

> It is challenging to honor the descent in a culture that primary values the ascent. We like things rising – stock markets, the GDP, profit margins. We get anxious when things go down. Even in psychology, there is a premise that is biased toward improvement, always getting better, rising above our troubles.

This is also reiterated by the American poet and friend of James Hillman, Robert Bly:

> How can we look at the cinders side of things when the society is determined to create a world of shopping malls and entertainment complexes in which we are made to believe that there is no death, disfigurement, illness, insanity, lethargy, or misery. Disneyland means 'no ashes'.
>
> (Bly Quoted in Weller, 2015)

In the privileged white Western world, we want to focus only on one arc of the circle of life – that of spring and new growing life. Both capitalism and personal development are built on the notion of continuous exponential growth. Gregory Bateson (1972) and the Club of Rome (1973) point out that limitless growth on a finite planet is impossible. David Attenborough (2013) quotes Kenneth Boulding, President Kennedy's environmental advisor, as saying: 'Anyone who believes in indefinite growth in anything physical, on a physically finite planet, is either mad – or an economist'.

In my years of reading books on organizational, team and individual development and coaching, I have read many books on 'team building' and creating 'higher performing teams', but it is nearly impossible to find books on contracting teams and teams ending well. Likewise, there are many books and programmes on 'on-boarding' managers and leaders and how to get the most out of the first 100 days. Very little, however, can be found on 'off-boarding' and the last 100 days and how to leave well.

Endings as transitions and rites of passage

Over 25 years ago, I was coaching someone whom I shall call Richard, the CEO of an international financial company. One particular session, as far as I can recall, went something like this:

Richard: I think the time has come for me to retire from this role. I think I have done what I could uniquely do for this company, and it needs someone else to take the reins.

Peter: What are the signs and signals, inside you and outside, that are giving you this message?

Richard: I no longer feel the same passion at the beginning of the week, and externally I can feel new challenges coming over the horizon. As I listen to the voices of the Board and the different stakeholders, they are requiring a new direction, a new phase in the life of this company.

Peter: It sounds like you sense a new transition for the company, different from the one you and your team have been leading and enabling over the last four years.

Richard: Yes, that is right, but I have not yet told any of my colleagues. To be honest I don't know how to. Some will be keen to see me go, while others will try and convince me to stay.

Peter: Before we explore how to tell them, perhaps it would be helpful to explore how this leadership transition needs to happen. What do you need to finish? What do you need to hand over and hand on? How do you need to pass on different roles, responsibilities and tasks and to whom?

Richard: Part of me just wants to walk out and let the Board and Executive team get on with it; but I know that is what happened when I took over, and it was very costly to me and the company.

Peter: It sounds like, as with Odysseus, after the long battle there is a journey home to be navigated. Let us explore how I can support you in designing this journey.

Together, we designed a draft framework for the transition of his role, seeing it as a process rather than an event. It was a draft framework, as the transition was not just his and needed to be co-created with the Board and his team and, indeed, the person and people who would carry on his work.

Since then, I have further developed an off-boarding process, helping a number of senior leaders to leave well and end well, both of which are subcategories of learning how to die well. For death is not just something that happens at the end of life but is a process that is at the heart of living.

Coaches are in the business of helping leaders manage transitions and rites of passage, and many anthropologists, following the classic work of Van Gennep (1909), have found that most transition rituals start by honouring death. The wedding in Western cultures is preceded by the wake of the 'hen night' or 'stag night' (or weekend!). In some Jewish weddings, the bride and groom crush wine glasses under their feet to demonstrate the death of their previous state of being. In many traditions, the bride wears white and is veiled at the start of the wedding, an echo of the shroud and the death of being single. In many indigenous coming-of-age rituals, the children are taken away from their villages, thus leaving behind their mother, in order to die to the familiarity of childhood and come back from their initiation in the wild, into a new phase of being.

In modern leadership and coaching, however, we often want to pretend we can transition to the new without a death of the previous phase.

In my garden, I have a stone Celtic cross next to my compost heaps. They are deliberately juxtaposed: the cross is the symbol of new life, coming from the sacrificial death of Jesus; and the compost heap is the symbol of dying into living, home to literally billions of worms, insects and microbial beings, which turn rotten and dying vegetation into new living earth.

Inspired by a favourite Easter hymn from my childhood, I wrote this poem in 2022 to connect the two entities.

The Celtic cross and compost

There is a green hill
Not far away
Within a garden wall,
Next to the place

Where I survey
The wondrous cross
And all that died
To feed us all

Die before you die

In our modern Western world, we have regulated death to the end of life and hidden it away. Death is what happens to other people, not us. Jem Bendell, a British professor of sustainability leadership, explored the emotions that underpin the dangerous beliefs that are creating the 'climate chaos' and ecological catastrophe:

> It is useful to recognize how phobias around impermanence and death are at the root of the habits of e-s-c-a-p-e (entitlement, surety, control, autonomy, progress and exceptionalism) and how those phobias mutually consolidate separative ways of experiencing and understanding ourselves and the world, thereby diminishing our affinity for all life.
>
> (Bendell, 2021: 149)

To heal the split between the human and more-than-human world, to re-experience our 'affinity with all life', we need to learn to embrace death as part of life. In earlier times, and still in many parts of the world, death and dying are constant companions. For most of human history, before we became adults, we would have witnessed the death of siblings, parents and neighbours. Each would have been a deepening experience, often one that helped us more fully embrace life.

In the Koran, there is a short, beautiful injunction: 'Die before you die', which is developed in Islamic Sufism with the practice of *fana*, which is best translated as 'unselfing' – letting go of the attachment to our self, our identity, our fame or success and who we think we are. Similar approaches can be found in the Eastern Orthodox Christian church, with its practice of human 'kenosis' (emptying of oneself), or in the Hindu practice of leaving one's role in work and the family and becoming a *sanyasi*, a wandering mendicant, relying on the help of others.

The focus, not only of coaching but also of a great deal of psychotherapy and counselling (Hawkins and Ryde, 2020), is about developing our identity, strengthening our ego, building our self. But little is taught about how, as leaders and coaches, we help people to let their ego die, become unattached to their success and their role and see the beauty of letting go.

In my coaching, I have met many leaders, including myself, who find it very hard to ask for help. They have been promoted for being strong, decisive, independent-minded and being able to work things out for themselves. They believe that leaders should not show weakness in front of their followers. One of the hardest lessons for me and for many of the people I coach is to stop being attached to being the one who knows, the one with the answers, the one who can hold it all together.

Many of the leadership teams with whom I have worked have found that the most important breakthrough has come when the leader has learnt to say the following to the team from their heart:

> This is how I see our major future challenges, but I cannot work out by myself how we can respond to all of these. I need help from every one of you, as well as from us as a collective team.

This is a small act of *fana*, of dying from the role of the strong leader with all the answers and, for a brief moment, becoming a *sanyasi* asking for help.

The role of suffering

Gautama Buddha taught the four practices (*jhanas*) of 'The Four Immeasurables' (*appamana*).

1. A feeling of love and compassion for everybody and everything.
2. Learning to suffer with other people, beings, systems and things through empathy.
3. A sympathetic joy in the happiness, success, life and joyful being of other people, beings and things.
4. Equanimity – similar to what we explored in Chapter 6 on *diakosone*, the person who can stand calm, upright and unreactive between the opposites, embracing all that is.

The second of these, learning to empathically suffer with others, is not just about caring and being kind to others. It is also about how we deepen our own souls. It is not just those close to us or just other humans that we need to accompany in suffering. Rather, we need to feel the suffering of everything that lives, of the many species that we humans have driven to extinction: the fish struggling because they are trapped in discarded nets or from ingesting plastic; the ancient tropical forests, razed to the ground for financial gain and to create cattle 'burger farms' to satisfy human greed.

I have written several times in this book and elsewhere (Hawkins, 2019; Hawkins and Turner, 2020) about the practice of wide-angled empathy: to enter into the suffering and joy not just of the person who is with you in the meeting or coaching room but also every person, being and system that emerges in their stories, to enter into the joy and suffering of others and of life and to let that joy and suffering enter into you.

However, it is important not to take on and carry these joys and pains, yourself becoming elated or suffering and feeling burdened but rather, to feel and resonate with the different waves of feeling, to watch them arrive, flow through you and leave.

Every funeral we go to is a practice in embracing death, if we can allow ourselves to fully engage with all stages of this important rite of passage: the celebration of the life that was lived, the grief and mourning for the loss of the bodily presence of the one who has departed, the realization that this is the death only of the form that connected the living parts of their material body and their individuated consciousness, their personality as we knew it – to recognize that their spirit lives on in and through the lives of others, as the material aspects of their body return to be part of the wider cosmos.

The Old Testament of the Bible contains the extraordinary story of Job, who undergoes many trials and tribulations. First, Job loses all his animals – oxen, sheep and camels. Then his house is struck by a thunderbolt, and all his children are killed. Then he suffers an awful affliction, with his whole body covered in ulcers. He curses his fate and will not be comforted by his companions or look at his own part in what has happened. Job argues with God, demanding to know why such a good man as he should be so afflicted.

Karen Armstrong (2022: 70) sees God as helping Job to stop the following:

whining self-indulgently as he, like all of us human beings, need to realise we are not the centre of the world and learn from the animals who have far nobler values than the humans that exploit them.

God praises the behemoth of the Nile (hippopotamus) whom Armstrong says:

symbolises the harmony of conflicting opposites in nature that epitomises the sacred. Thus, nature shocks us out of our human complacency and forces us to confront the limitations of our vision. In nature we have a harmony in which violence and beauty, terror and serenity, mysteriously coexist, defying our own restricted categories.

(Armstrong, 2022: 71)

Faced with this vision, Job 'humbly . . . puts his hand to his mouth, a ritual expression of awe in the presence of the sublime'. His words, complaints and self-centredness have been blown to pieces. He becomes a wise prophet to whom has been 'revealed the beauty, strength and mystery of sacred nature that pushes against the limited horizons of human beings' (Armstrong, 2022: 72).

It is through suffering in life, and feeling the suffering of others, that our human hearts become open and tenderized so we can learn to become less self-centred and arrogant. Through suffering, we can learn to see we are not in control of life and what happens, become more accepting of what life brings, be less arrogant and full of hubris and be prepared to learn from wider nature.

I remember working with the Bristol Cancer Help Centre in its early days of pioneering alternative approaches to help cancer patients. One beautiful elderly lady told me the story of her many spiritual quests in India and other Eastern countries. She said to me, 'Despite all my travels and the amazing people I met, I did not find my true spiritual teacher until I returned home'. 'Who was this teacher?' I asked, hoping in my naivety I could learn from them too. 'My cancer', she replied.

Many people have written about how near-death experiences, or the sudden loss of a loved one, has transformed their lives and helped them be less goal-driven and more able to enjoy each moment of life. Others have shown how meeting the overwhelming force of nature, in its fierce beauty of wildfires and storms at sea, the silence of a long desert journey, the crashing of mountain avalanches or the eruption of a volcano has helped them realize how small and fragile our own lives are in comparison and be in awe of the Beauty of nature even in its destructive wildness.

In Coleridge's poem 'The Rime of the Ancient Mariner' (1798), the old seafarer of the title, like Job, undergoes many afflictions. His ship becomes becalmed in the fog, and the crew runs out of water and food, suffering great thirst and hunger. He and his shipmates believe their misfortune has been caused through his shooting of an albatross. He has to bear the guilt of watching all of his 200 companions die terrible deaths, with an accusing look in their eyes, before finding himself alone on the ship, his only companions the slimy sea snakes that surrounded the ship.

> The many men, so beautiful!
> And they all dead did lie:
> And a thousand thousand slimy things
> Lived on; and so did I.

What saves him from this terrible ordeal is that, when he is at his lowest, he suddenly sees the thousand slimy things as beautiful, and the beauty of nature brings a blessing of grace spontaneously from his heart.

> Beyond the shadow of the ship,
> I watched the water-snakes:
> They moved in tracks of shining white,
> And when they reared, the elfish light
> Fell off in hoary flakes.
>
> Within the shadow of the ship
> I watched their rich attire:
> Blue, glossy green, and velvet black,

They coiled and swam; and every track
Was a flash of golden fire.

O happy living things! no tongue
Their beauty might declare:
A spring of love gushed from my heart,
And I blessed them unaware:
Sure, my kind saint took pity on me,
And I blessed them unaware.

The self-same moment I could pray;
And from my neck so free
The Albatross fell off, and sank
Like lead into the sea.

Like Job and the Ancient Mariner, it is easy for us to see suffering as a curse and to ask: 'Why me? What have I done to deserve this?' Even when listening to, and empathically feeling, the suffering of another, we can experience them as the victim of what has unfairly happened and been done to them. But Coleridge and the *Book of Job* teach us to switch our perception, to see suffering as a visitor – not invited but nevertheless a guest who needs to be welcomed and listened to so we can discover what this visitor has come to help us learn.

Faced with suffering in someone we lead or coach, we might remember that the Ancient Mariner, after this life-changing experience, still needed to stop a stranger and have them listen to his extraordinary tale. The story, with all its trauma, has to be heard and received by another. It is, therefore, essential that, as coaches and leaders, we listen deeply to people and can move through the stages of hearing and resonating with their suffering through empathy, finding ways to express our compassion in ways that are appropriate to the situation and are also heartfelt. We can then help the other, over time, see how this suffering is also a generous lesson that life is providing.

The Japanese have a lovely concept of *kintsugi*. This involves taking a beautiful pot that has become cracked and making it even more beautiful by highlighting the crack in gold or another colour. They teach and show how it is only through the crack that the light can come in.

Suffering can, with our help, become a welcomed visitor, even if it has arrived uninvited. This is beautifully expressed in the poem of Mevlana Jalaludin Rumi (2004) called 'The Guest House', where he likens our personal being to a guesthouse, every day being visited by many different emotions and events, and how we should welcome whatever comes as a gift and a learning from the larger life.

Nature, whether through its overwhelming and frightening force, or when it is the bringer of affliction, or in moments of tranquil beauty, can be our best teacher.

The beauty of non-attachment

Often, in leadership and coaching, we focus on the development of the new and fail to focus on what needs to die and be given up for the new to flourish. We add new projects to an already full agenda, without first deciding what we must stop doing to free up the time, space and energy for the new to thrive. I regularly teach leaders how to be 'radical weeders'. I ask them to enter in their calendars every three months: 'Radical weeding day'. On this day, they review their calendar and action lists and work out how they can remove 10% of their commitments and activities, to free up space for the new. Without first weeding, fresh plants will not have the space or nutrients to grow.

Like many who I ask to do this, I struggle with giving things up, as they are the habits and ways of doing what is familiar and what we are good at. The new is harder and requires change and learning. In my research on leadership (Hawkins, 2017a), I interviewed a very impressive CEO and asked him about his leadership development journey. He shocked me by saying, 'At each stage of being promoted, I had to learn to eat my children'. I had no idea what he meant and found the image shocking. He explained, '*I had to consume, digest and destroy what made me successful at the previous level in order to discover how I needed to be at this next level of leadership*'. What is necessary in one role and one stage of our lives must often be unlearnt in order that we can learn what is required from the next fresh encounter, phase or role. This is echoed by Roger Scranton:

> Practise of learning to die is the practise of learning to let go: learning to die means learning to let go of the ego, the idea of the self, the future, certainty, attachment, the pursuit of pleasure, permanence and stability. Learning to let go of salvation. Learning to let go of hope.
>
> (Scranton, 2015: 92)

There is an old Welsh saying, 'Pure love arrives with the first grandchild' – a phrase I have shared with many first-time grandparents to prepare them for this special gift and blessing. When I eulogize about the pleasures of being a grandparent, many say to me that grandchildren are such a joy because you can give them back to their parents once you have had enough. I do not deny that this has some practical benefit as you get older and tire more quickly but that is not the essential blessing that comes with grandchildren. The pure love comes from loving them for who they are, without expectation or judgment, of either them or your own parenting. This is not about trying to give them what you wanted or missed out on as a child, or aiming to be a perfect parent, or trying to do it by the book or from some pet theory. Rather, it is about watching, listening, being present to what emerges.

As I have grown older, my gardening has also changed. Gone are the days when I would plan schedules, follow formulae or read up on what I should be doing. Now I wander through the garden, look and listen and ask the garden what it needs from me. It shows me plants that are desperate for water or need feeding; weeds that, if not removed, will spread seeds and dominate; compost that needs balancing or turning; roses that need deadheading; and fruit, ripe for the picking.

The garden and grandchildren are my teachers in 'partnering with life' and how this requires a softening of my ego-will, a quietening of my overeager mind and a patience that I often lack – a curiosity for what appears when you are not looking too hard. Delight in moments of beauty that spontaneously emerges from apparent disorder.

Coaching requires these same qualities – non-attachment to outcome or to being seen as helpful or liked by the coachee. A gentle, curious interest in what emerges, not as issues to be sorted but previously unrecognized patterns and connections, surprising images and metaphors and fresh, spontaneous learnings that come as gifts coach and coachee alike.

Leadership, too, requires our willingness to let favourite projects be killed off, to become unattached both to fame and to seeing the organization's success as our own, letting go of what we were previously good at or being the one with all the answers. Each stage of leadership development requires a death of the previous stage. But dying well is rarely taught in business schools.

Conclusion

We have explored how finding beauty in transience, wildness, suffering and death can deepen our engagement with life, which is perpetually in flux. It can help us learn to let go of idolizing growth, clinging to a sense of certainty and a false sense of being in control; it can help us welcome whatever comes as the next lesson we need to face.

Beauty helps us learn the arts of non-attachment, wide-angled empathy, humility and a love for the ever-changing. This, in turn, creates the space for grace, which is the subject of the next chapter: an appreciation of all we have been given freely and a loving gratitude for the ever-changing beauty of life.

There is an old story about a seeker who travels to visit a great teacher on the other side of the world, who is renowned for his equanimity and perpetual happiness. When he arrives, he bows deeply to the revered master and asks him, 'What is the secret of your serenity?'

The master smiles and removes the ring from his finger. 'All my wisdom is written on this ring'.

The seeker takes the ring and reads, 'This, too, will pass'. He looks up at the master, who says to him, 'It is important to say this to yourself not only when you are suffering but also when things are going well and you feel your life is blessed'.

'This, too, will pass'.

In the next chapter, we will conclude this section of the book with a chapter on Grace, having now explored how embracing death can open our gratitude for the Grace of life.

Recently, as I stood contemplating the beautiful Celtic cross and beautiful compost heap in my garden, I heard emerge from my heart a spontaneous prayer:

May my death be a gift to life, as death has been such a gift to my life.

Chapter 10

Beauty and grace

Introduction: opening to grace

In Chapter 9, we took a deep dive into the depths of loss, suffering, death and grief. We discovered how suffering, loss and death of what we love, and those we love, can open up our hearts and hollow out the space where the drum of love can beat more resonantly through us and our lives. When our life and work are going well, we can quickly become complacent and take the rich bounty for granted, not noticing how blessed we have been. Often it is only when we experience setbacks and losses that we can appreciate what we have. When a friend dies, in the poignant grieving, we can feel the richness of what we received from them.

In his 'Ode on Melancholy', Keats (1819) wrote: 'She dwells with Beauty – Beauty that must die'. We could reverse this and say: 'Because Beauty is transient, we savour beauty in each passing moment'. Elias Amidon (2021: 23) wrote:

Because everything perishes, we have sorrow.
Because this Presence doesn't, we have love.
Because both are true, we have beauty.
Because of beauty, we have thankfulness.

What is grace?

Before I explore the different meanings and origins of Grace, I invite you to engage in your own contemplation of Grace.

Reflective practice on grace

Please write down your responses.

- Think of an animal, a bird, a tree and an insect that you find graceful.
- Think of piece of music that, for you, has the quality of Grace.

DOI: 10.4324/9781003349600-13

- Recall a person who you know who is graceful in their movement and demeanour.
- Think back to a conversational dialogue you have had with another person that you felt was graceful.
- Now review your responses and notice the pattern that connects the different aspects of Grace you have recalled.
- Write down three words or phrases that, for you, capture the qualities of Grace.

When I have tried this practice with small groups of coaches and leaders, some responses have come up several times:

- **Graceful animal** – Gazelle, deer, cat, leopard, grass snake
- **Graceful bird** – Heron, bird of prey rising on a thermal, woodpecker
- **Graceful tree** – Willow dancing in the wind, reflections of a tree in a still lake, silver birch
- **Graceful insect** – Dragonfly, butterfly, long-legged spider
- **Graceful music** – Chopin nocturnes, Irish ballads, Tchaikovsky's 'Swan Lake', Palestrina, Débussy's *'Le Prélude à l'Après-midi d'un faune'*.
- **Graceful art** – Chinese calligraphy drawing, the paintings of Leonardo da Vinci, the landscapes of Paul Cézanne.
- **Graceful people** – People who glide into a room and whose gestures are balletic; people who gently lean their head towards you receptively as they listen to you; a contented baby, wide-eyed and open to the world; a pianist, harpist, cellist or other musician, their hands flowing into the keys or strings and the music flowing back through them. Some recalled memorable moments such as men in Georgia, who I saw riding horses together; performers in Japanese *Noh* theatre; Balinese dancers; Chinese women doing Tai Chi in a park; a Maasai woman carrying water in a pot on her head while holding her child's hand. I find myself touched by Levin in Tolstoy's *Anna Karenina*, when he is moved by watching over 40 men with long scythes harvesting the hay.
- **Graceful dialogue** – One that flowed from one person to another, weaving a joint colourful tapestry of words that emerged from the conversation.
- **The qualities of Grace** – Flow, glide, being in tune, gentleness, humility, effortlessness, curvaceousness, stillness combined with movement.

When I think of a graceful coach, my mind goes to my good friend and long-time colleague John Leary Joyce, who founded the Academy of Executive Coaching. He intersperses being a coach and teaching coaching with wood-turning and tango dancing. In his wood-turning workshop, which is next to where he practices tango, he showed me how he was learning to follow the grain of the wood and to work with minimum effort and tension in his arms, allowing his body to move smoothly with the turn of the lathe. In tango, he has led workshops on tango and coaching, learning to both lead and follow, learning to be led by the music, your partner and the space between you and to move from deep inside yourself.

The Three Graces

'Grace' is a graceful word, which carries within it many meanings and evocations. Here, we will explore three different but interconnected aspects.

1   Grace we freely receive, every moment of our lives

The first meaning of Grace is that which comes to us, not earned, but as 'manna from heaven', from the bounteousness of wider nature and ecology. If we reflect on all that makes life possible, nearly all of it is gifted to us by the wider systemic levels within which we are nested. The sun provides our light and warmth; the wind and clouds freely give us rain, which becomes the rivers and the water we drink. Together, sun, rain and water, in partnership with the earth, provide fungi and plants, the basis for all the food we and other animals feast upon. The atmosphere provides the air we breathe, each breath a gift of life and a blessing. And the atmosphere takes back the air we need to exhale and uses it for other parts of nature. John O'Donohue (2003: 228) expresses it with a poetic religious sensibility as 'grace is the permanent climate of divine kindness'.

2   The grace of gratitude

The second meaning of Grace is the 'grace' we may say to express gratitude for what has arrived by grace – the thankful response that flows from the heart when food arrives or when we view a beautiful sunset.

Emerson (1841) wrote in his 'Essay on Friendship':

> Cultivate the habit of being grateful for every good thing that comes to you, and to give thanks continuously. And because all things have contributed to your advancement, you should include all things in your gratitude.

Sometimes graces have words, and indeed, my father did a collection of his favourite graces to say before a meal. But sometimes grace is a silent, graceful response of thanks from the sigh of the breath or the slight bowing of the head and body.

3   The grace displayed by the graceful

The third meaning is to move with grace, to be graceful, as we explored in the exercise at the beginning of this chapter. The grace of a gazelle moving across the savanna, or a deer moving through the trees. The dancing of *corps de ballet*, or a gymnast, or the music of Mozart's 'Solemn Vespers'.

I suggest we can see these three meanings not as separate but as a 'trinity of Grace'. In this trinity, we can simultaneously recognize and partake in the Grace we constantly receive in every moment of our lives and our own responsive Grace of thankfulness. In this cycle of receiving Grace and responding with Grace from the heart, we begin to move, flow and relate gracefully. We become part of the three Graces flowing and dancing together.

It is Beauty that opens this dance and provides the music, as Mevlana Jalalu-din Rumi writes in the Mathnawi that it is Beauty that beats on the drum of our heart, which then responds with thankfulness.

This helps us to further understand gracefulness and the other words and phrases it evoked earlier – flow, in tune, glide, effortlessness, gentleness, humility and harmony. Gracefulness is not a property of certain animals, trees or people but a way of being – responding to Grace with Grace. It is a response to Beauty, by both being grateful and moving gracefully. Certainly, some people seem to live in a more graceful way, whilst others have to cultivate it in their lives.

Aesthetic intelligence and aesthetic grace

Aesthetic grace is what I believe Gregory Bateson spent his life exploring and also those who have followed him such as Noel Charlton (2008) and Peter Reason (2017). All three are concerned with how we develop 'aesthetic intelligence' as an antidote to our restrictive atomistic left-brain thinking and a crucial step in healing the split between the human and more-than-human world.

Bateson taught that we do not live in a world of things but a world of relationships. On many occasions, he would invite his students to look at their hands and report what they were aware of. 'Four fingers and a thumb, lines, rings, dirty nails'. Having used this exercise many times, I get similar responses in nearly all parts of the world. I joke that I am waiting for someone to answer: 'I am aware of the hand offering itself for the eyes to see – or the eyes and hand coming into relationship!' Even today, the latter answer would probably seem mad to most people. It is more difficult for us to understand that, at some level, everything we see is in relationship to everything else. Bateson (1991: 310) said in his 'Last Lecture', which I attended:

> I recommend you to take your hand home and take a look at it. . . . Very quietly, almost as part of a meditation. And try and catch the difference between seeing it as a base for five parts and seeing it as constructed of a . . . pattern of the interlocking of relationships, which were the determinants of its growth. . . . If you can really manage to see the hand in terms of the epistemology I am offering you, I think you will find that your hand is suddenly more recognizably **beautiful** as a product of relationship that as a composition of countable parts.

We live in a meshwork world of entangled relationship, not a world of separate things. Our knowledge about the world comes through our senses. We do not actually see things but differences; we see outlines where there is a difference – in shape, size, colour and so on – and our thinking mind fills in the outlines and gives them names.

Bateson spent his life teaching people to see the 'pattern that connects', whether in anthropological studies in New Guinea or Bali, or in disturbed families, or in cybernetics, or in the behaviour of dolphins or wolves or in our own hand. He urged us to stop focussing on the notes and hear the harmony and flow of the music, to focus not on separate dancers but on the dance.

The pathways for this, he suggested, were aesthetic – music, poetry, communal singing, dancing, rituals – all of which work through metaphor and relational pattern. McGilchrist (2009, 2021) would say that these are the languages that are better understood through the right-hemisphere neo-cortex and are nonsensical to the left hemisphere.

The pattern that connects can be seen as similar to the Daoist concept of *Li*, the deeper pattern that organizes and gives shape to what is – a pattern, which, like our ecological niche, is also co-evolving. Beyond 'patterns that connect', Bateson suggests, must be an even deeper level. Bateson (1991: 265) tells us:

> Pathology is a relatively easy thing to discuss, health is very difficult. This . . . is one of the reasons . . . there is the sacred, and why the sacred is difficult to talk about.

Bateson never fully defines or pins down his concept of grace and leaves us to see the pattern that connects his different passages on Grace. He says that 'This sacredness', the one we reach through aesthetics such as 'art, poetry and rhythmic prayer', 'has something to do with this covering and uncovering deeper components' (Bateson, 1991: 304).

I suggest that with aesthetic grace, we need to move from being a grateful recipient and observer of Beauty to a full, embodied participant. Rather than following Heidegger's notion of 'uncovering' deeper meaning and understanding, Chinese philosophy points to the process of seeing, listening and sensing *through* what shows up in the everyday world. To do this, we need to stop seeing things; instead, we need to allow life to be translucent so that the relational patterns, the *Li*, the organizing patterns and the sacredness can shine through. The beauty of translucence is that light does not just shine on life from outside but also through and from all that lives. This is reflected by Charlton (2008) when he writes:

> The qualities of experience that are dominant when such aesthetic appreciation is taking place are sensory acuteness, the perception of unity, the awareness of inextricable involvement and simultaneous understanding of awe, and humility.

We need to go further than sensing through, to be drawn into Beauty – what Curry (2019) calls the world of enchantment – by entering Beauty beautifully, through music, singing, dancing, painting, sculpting, writing poetry, cooking and sacred ritual.

Many of you may have taken part in communal dances, or sung in choirs, and experienced how dancing and singing both start from listening with, and through, your body to the wider system – listening not just to the other group members but also to the music, the movement and to the harmony that plays through them. To enter beauty, we need to attune ourselves not just internally and externally but also 'in-ex-ternally' – where the internal and external conjoin and transcend their separateness. This attunement is an essential aesthetic ethic not just for being a dancer or a singer in collective, harmonious beauty but also for doing the beautiful as a leader, coach or an ecologically attuned human (see the practice of inter-poiesis in Chapter 14).

It is through embodied sensuous participation that we experience and know Beauty, beyond what our rational mind can appreciate. This is why Bateson (1972: 146) writes:

> purposive rationality unaided by such phenomena as art, religion, dream, and the like, is necessarily pathogenic and destructive of life. . . . Unaided consciousness must always tend toward hate.

This is echoed by Goodenough (1998: 565), who encourages us to study life both poetically and scientifically, in a way that invokes 'awe and wonder', so we increase 'our capacity to walk humbly and with gratitude in their presence'.

Bateson later (2000: 452–453) writes about ways of overcoming the dangers of conscious left-brain purpose and short-term goals:

> it is appropriate to mention some of the factors which may act as a correctives – areas of human action which are not limited by the narrow distortions of coupling through conscious purpose and where wisdom can obtain. Of these the most important is love . . . there is religion.

To move from hate to Love, we need to cultivate Grace, gratitude and gracefulness and develop our 'aesthetic intelligence'.

Piero Ferrucci (2010: 18) describes three aspects of 'aesthetic intelligence':

1. aesthetic range – the range of place and forms in which we can appreciate beauty;
2. the depth at which we can experience and be moved by beauty; and
3. our capacity to integrate beauty into other aspects of our lives.

From my explorations earlier, I would add:

4. our capacity to listen and see through the surface of what presents to the underlying '*Li*' and the 'patterns that connect';
5. 'aesthetic grace', a full participative and embodied engagement with, and in, the Beauty of each moment; and
6. to move from love, through eros and joy, to awe, which we will now explore.

The journey of our senses through grace to awe

There is another way we can consider the path to Grace and how Beauty progressively opens our emotions. For many years, I have been teaching leaders and coaches how to connect with the seven base emotional rhythms, as identified by Manfred Clynes (1977 and 1989), called 'sentic states'. I mentioned this in Chapter 5 and have written about this more in Hawkins and Smith (2006: 221–223).

In his research, Clynes identified seven basic emotions, all of which he saw as having a biological and evolutionary importance. Each sentic state has a distinctive rhythm and bodily movement, which transcends cultural differences, so that even if you watch a foreign film without subtitles, you can still identify the emotion that is being expressed. The seven basic emotions are as follows:

- **Anger:** The emotion that sets boundaries and limits – saying 'no', 'stop', 'enough'.
- **Hatred:** Probably better defined as 'gut determination' – important for mobilizing energy, pushing through obstacles, ending projects and relationships. Without this sentic state, you become constipated and cluttered and never throw things away.
- **Grief:** The rhythm of surrender, letting go, mourning – but also empathizing with the sorrow of others.
- **Love:** The rhythm of welcoming, including, appreciating, embracing and showing care.
- **Eros:** The rhythm of sensuality, exciting interest and desire in the other. Without eros, a vision is just words and a trainer fails to elicit bodily or emotional engagement in those they teach.
- **Joy:** The rhythm of delight – congratulating and celebrating, a 'Mexican wave' at a sporting event, singing at a birthday or wedding.
- **Awe:** Attending an event, watching a spectacle such as a beautiful sunset, being in the presence of a person or in a place that inspires us, moves us, incites a sense of wonder or takes our breath away.

Awe can come from a spontaneous response within our bodies to Beauty that we are either witnessing or partaking in. A realization that the Beauty is so much greater than we are and yet we are connected with it; we are a part of what we experience.

On the journey to Grace, it is *Love* that opens our hearts and our desires for Beauty and for a fuller, more engaged life. Love more fully opens all six of our embodied senses – touch, taste, smell, sound, sight and movement – into deeper sensuous engagement, the *eros* of life. Through sensuous eros, we find *joy* and delight in listening to music, seeing a beautiful vista, tasting a sumptuous meal, making and sharing love with others and the world in so many ways. As the *joy* grows, we open in *awe* at the wondrous depth, breadth and richness of life and a thankfulness and gratitude for being so alive.

In his book on awe, Keltner (2023: 7) writes: 'Awe is the feeling of being in the presence of something vast that transcends your current understanding of the world'. As this realization takes root within us, awe gives way to humility, gratitude and a sense of connection. Keltner (2023: 40) goes on to say:

> In moments of awe . . . we shift from the sense that we are solely in charge of our own fate and striving against others to feeling we are part of a community, sharing essential qualities, interdependent and collaborating.

Whereas joy brings us delight, excitement and pleasure, awe takes us closer to Grace. Keltner (2023: 56) quotes global research by Daniel Cordaro, which shows that across different cultures, people respond to awe with a raising of eyebrows, a spontaneous smile, jaw dropping and head tilting up. For some, there would be tingling on the back of the neck, a shudder through the body, a sharp intake of breath.

We respond to joy with high fives, clapping, cheering, slapping people on the back; but with awe, we respond with a quiet bow of the head. In some cultures, this might be accompanied with hands held together as if in prayer or a greeting of *namaste* in India (meaning 'I honour the God within you') or with the right hand held over the heart, which is more common in Arab or Islamic cultures. People in white Western cultures are more likely to say 'Whoa!' responding with the rhythm of joy and rushing to get out our phones to take a picture of the sunset, the overwhelming thunderstorm or a beautiful vista. In our embodied response of awe, we experience humility and our relative smallness amidst the wider and wilder beauty of life; we experience gratitude for the Grace of what we have just experienced and received.

But all these different forms of levels should not be construed as linear, where we leave one stage behind and move on to a higher stage, but rather as a spiral, where each turn includes and incorporates the levels beneath it. When something delights me and initiates a physical response within me, it has already been pleasing to my senses. When I fall in love, I have been attracted and moved by someone or something beyond myself, and this has awakened something in me prior to any thought or consideration. This spiral is an inclusive hierarchy, not a hierarchy of power or importance. The higher turns of the spiral are not intrinsically better, for they include and rely on the lower circuits; they just go further and include more.

Love and flow

A fulfilled craftsperson loves their work; they would be drawn to do it whether or not they were paid or recognized. They love gifting, making things for others. They love the wood, the stone or the clay they work with, the rhythm of working, finding joy in the creative process itself. This is similar to what Mihaly Csikszentmihalyi (2000) describes in his work on flow states, where the being of the person is in tune and in harmony with their doing and with the material world with which they are engaged.

When you are in flow, it is not you that is doing the flowing nor are you being flowed; you are neither the subject nor the object of the flowing, neither the doer nor the one done to. You become in harmony with the flow of the river of life. In turn, the river does not flow where it wants to but flows where the terrain requires. The terrain is shaped not by what is aspires to be but by how the river, wind and rain have moulded it. All evolution is co-evolution. All creation is co-creation.

Leading and coaching with grace

Humans are, by nature, creatures who focus on the proximal. We respond to what we can see in front of us, what we can touch and hear. In the UK, we failed to respond to the Covid-19 pandemic until it was already overwhelming hospitals relatively near to us in northern Italy. Our news is more concerned with one death in our locality than with thousands of people dying from a natural disaster on the other side the world. We empathize most easily with people who are like us and with the suffering of our own species. We can then make 'other' those who are not like us; and this process is at the root of localism, sexism, racism and anthropocentrism.

Only when we can increase our kindness and extend our circle of kinship can we reduce this divisive process of othering, which destroys global collaboration. Othering is a deeply ingrained process at the root of our splitting of the human and the 'more-than-human' world, a process that stands in the way of a deep adaptation to the emerging world challenges (Carr and Bendell, 2021: 179).

To have 'active hope' (Macy and Johnstone, 2012) that we can respond successfully to these challenges, we need to discover that not only our friends and family but also all humans, all sentient beings, are part of our family; that the ecology is not out there, it is in us; and that we are a small, inextricable part of the wider eco-system.

The role of leaders and coaches is to help others to extend the family of connection: from their own family and team to the whole organization and community; from there to the wider interconnected human family, to other sentient beings and the whole Earth ecology and then to the whole living/dying cosmos (see the practice in Chapter 9, Chapter 10 and Chapter 15).

One of the great works on the graceful leader is the *Shujing*, which was written down in the 4th century BCE, though the roots of its teaching go back to the 23rd century BCE (Armstrong, 2022: 169). The *Shujing* is one of the Five Classics of ancient Chinese literature. It is a collection of rhetorical prose, attributed to figures of ancient China, and became a foundational text of Chinese guidance on leadership for over 2,000 years. De Bary, Bloom and Lufrano (1994: 29) translate the *Shujing*'s description of the virtuous or graceful leader as one who is the following:

> brings affection to the nine branches of the family. When the nine branches of the family had become harmonious, he distinguished and honoured the hundred clans. When the hundred clans had become illustrious, he harmonized the myriad states. The numerous people were amply nourished and prosperous and became harmonious.

The role of the coach is to help their coachee move beyond short-term goals and problem-solving to discover the beauty in their work and their love for it, as well as love for all the people and eco-systems for whom the work creates value. This helps the coachee see the short-term and local in the context of opening the wider arc, the larger perspective, liberating their inquiry from self-centricity, problem-solving and short-term concerns – the journey out from the proximal, in terms of both space and time, the small dark prison of our concerns, to the free air where we can experience the grace of all that is given to us and experience gratitude for all our blessings. Only then can we live and move gracefully.

Cultivating grace: practices of grace for leaders and coaches

There are many practices all human beings can do to help us cultivate Grace and gracefulness in our lives. Here, I share just a few, and I will suggest ways in which these can be applied to our work.

1 Start and end each day with a practice of gratitude

Say out loud or silently 'Thank you' for everything and every blessing you have received from friends and family, from nature and from the wider cosmos. It often helps to start with five statements of gratitude, then extend it to ten, then 20 and then 30. As you go to higher numbers, you may find that you include people, events, beings and aspects you had previously taken for granted and not focussed on or appreciated.

2   Say a short grace, or expression of gratitude, before every meal

There is an example in Chapter 9. Another grace is 'back to source', where you look at the plate of food in front of you and first give thanks for the person who cooked and served the food, then for the people who shopped for the ingredients and the shopkeepers who sold them. Then you give thanks to those who transported and harvested the food; the farmers who tended and grew the food; the earth that provided the nutrients for the food to grow; the billions of small organisms that made the soil nutritious; the rain that watered the plants; the clouds and wind that brought the rain; and the sun that provided the warmth, heat and light for plant and animal growth.

3   Practice graceful, physical movement

Learn and regularly practice graceful exercise routines such as Tai Chi, yoga, graceful dance or walking meditation.

4   Play or listen to graceful music

Singing or dance to the music.

5   Practice graceful art

Examples include Chinese calligraphy, free painting with your non-dominant hand, making collages from nature, sculpting.

6   Practice doing daily activities gracefully

Chopping vegetables, cooking, sweeping floors, cleaning, washing dishes, turning wood – and then saying 'Thank you' to the vegetables, wood or stone as you sense their beauty.

7   Breathing meditations

These help us experience the graceful coming and going of each breath. 'How gently it enters me, this breath: and how silently it leaves again' (Amidon, 2021).

8   Meditate in flow with the wider world

Meditate – with your eyes open, if possible – looking at the outside world, either looking out of the window or meditating outside. As you breathe in, sense that you are drinking in the Beauty of the world around you. Then hold your breath as this Beauty flows through your whole body. As you breathe out, imagine your breath is carrying love and gratitude to the wider world. Do this ten times.

9   Working with nature

One of my granddaughters takes great delight in helping avocado stones develop roots over a glass of water. When they are strong enough, she plants them in composted soil. She loves to dig potatoes, unearthing the buried treasure that nature has provided. She also loves to plait strings of harvested onions and garlic so they hang like nature's necklaces, drying in the autumn sun.

Research has shown that older people in residential care who were given a plant to look after and water lived longer than those who were given a plant which a nurse or care staff looked after for them.

10   Looking after animals

As I watch my grandchildren caring for their pets, I become aware of the capacity for Love and Grace growing within and through them. I feel the same when I go out and feed the animals on our small hobby farm. Caring for animals, including domestic companions, as well as caring for nature, has been shown to increase our vagal tone, oxytocin and other beneficial chemicals in our bodies.

Applying these to your work

1. **Graceful setting.** Attend to your office or meeting room so that it has a graceful feel (Chapter 12).
2. **Graceful being.** Pause before entering a room, let go of any thoughts or worries and take a deep breath out, exhaling any stress and then a long inhale, drawing up energy from the earth and drawing energy from the sun and sky. Draw up your spine; open up your chest. Discover how to walk into the room with calm, poise and grace. Adopt a graceful way of standing and sitting, gently and receptively leaning in towards the person speaking. Adopt 'postures of gratitude, that acknowledge the giftedness of life' (Wirzba, 2021: 139).
3. **Graceful leaving.** Discover how to leave the room with a 'Thank you' with deep gratitude and appreciation. Tell the people you have been with what you have appreciated specifically and what has touched your heart. When we can enter a room gracefully, with thankfulness in our heart for what has happened, what is about to happen and the beauty of this moment, the meeting will flow with Grace. The emergent engagement will feed and nourish us, and the work will be effortless effort – what the Daoists named *Wu-Wei*.
4. **Graceful receiving.** Hear everything that is shared as a generous lesson, coming by grace from life. In our work, we often get colleagues and clients who we do not necessarily like or want, but we can treat each one as a teacher who can teach us valuable lessons about life.

   It is also important to learn how to receive feedback, compliments and gifts gracefully. For many people, receiving gifts gracefully is harder than giving, but to allow yourself to be given to is a way of honouring the generosity and thoughtfulness of the giver. I remember the first time I was standing on an underground train (subway) and a young woman stood up and offered me her seat. My first reaction was 'Do I really look that old and infirm?' But then I caught myself, accepted the gift and said, 'How thoughtful of you. Thank you so much'.

5. **Graceful inquiry.** Ask yourself, 'What do you think this event, person or happening have come to teach you?' or 'What can I or we learn from this?'

6. **Gratitude.** Regularly saying 'Thank you' to your team members or coachees for the stories and reports they bring, the feelings they share, the contribution they are making. You can do this either with words, or silently in your heart, or with a look or a gesture.

In closing

If we look with a graceful eye and listen with a graceful ear to the world within us and around us, we will discover so much more beauty, as John O'Donohue (2003: 19) expresses when he writes:

The graced eye can glimpse beauty anywhere. . . . When we beautify our gaze. The grace of hidden beauty becomes our grace and sanctuary.

Later, O'Donohue (2003: 145) says:

When our eyes are graced with wonder, the world reveals its wonders to us. . . . The quality of our looking determines what we come to see.

We see and hear through what manifests before us, to see the Beauty of the web of connection, the pattern that connects, the *Li*. With practice, we can experience the flow of the *Dao* and be embodiedly, sensuously and aesthetically engaged to the constant, emergent fecundity and fertility of life – not just the 'being' of life but its continual 'becoming', always giving birth to the new. When we can realize the world is constantly giving freely to us, we can learn to respond with thankfulness in our hearts and we, too, can learn to give freely.

In this section of the book, we have explored the interplay between Beauty, Love, Truth, Good, Ethics, Death and Transience; and in this chapter, we have looked at Grace, which in some ways flows through all of them. As Andreas Weber (2017: 193) writes: 'The "flesh of the world" is a network of reciprocal grace, an unfathomably interwoven practice of giving'.

Part 3

Doing the Beautiful

Introduction to Part 3

Leaders and coaches both have an important role in shifting human conscious-ness not just imparting new knowledge but also transforming themselves and others to new ways of thinking, being and doing.

The traditional style of executive coaching is to ask questions. A typical style of consultants and directive leaders is to provide solutions and answers. The for-mer helps us to think through our own way forward but within our current ways of thinking, doing and being. The latter may help us align to what is collectively needed but also increases our dependency and passivity and fails to grow collec-tive ownership and responsibility. The necessary transformation does not come from either being told by a leader or a consultant or by being asked questions by a coach.

In this final section, we explore how to apply all that we have learnt – from the many aspects of Beauty we have been exploring to the demanding and important roles of leadership (Chapter 11) and coaching (Chapter 12). We shall then go deeper into two central capacities that both leaders and coaches need in order to be both effective and transformational, in enabling all those they lead and coach to move beyond the prison of left-brain dualistic and problem-centred thinking (Chapter 13) and develop a co-creative language and dialogue of 'inter-poiesis' (Chapter 14).

'Inter-poiesis' is a term I have created for a key process that we have lacked the language to express. 'Poiesis' is a beautiful word, meaning the emergent coming into being, or becoming, of something or some knowing that previously did not exist. I have added the prefix 'inter' to show how new knowing and inno-vation happen relationally and inter-subjectively.

The creation of this concept has arisen out of relational engagement with the two important and related concepts – that of 'auto-poiesis' (Maturana and Varela, 1980) and 'onto-poiesis' (Mathews, 2009) – the former describing the processes of organisms and systems self-creating and the latter the creative evolution between an organism and its ecological context, in which both are changed and renewed.

DOI: 10.4324/9781003349600-14

All these chapters provide practical examples and vignettes of leadership and coaching using these new Beauty-guided processes. In each chapter, I also suggest simple practices you can undertake to grow your aesthetic capacity, for experiencing, doing and being the love and beauty the world so desperately needs.

Having offered practices for leaders in Chapter 11, for coaches in Chapter 12 and for both in Chapters 13 and Chapters 14, in the final Chapter (15), I offer personal practices that can expand our humanity so we can become that which the ecology and the future require us to be.

Chapter 11

Beauty in the art of leadership

Introduction

The 'art of leadership' is not just for CEOs and those appointed to senior roles but for everyone. Indeed, leadership is not a role but an attitude, which begins when we stop blaming others and making excuses, step up to do what is necessary and ask others to join us (Hawkins, 2005). Leaders are not appointed; they are always volunteers. Rabbi Jonathan Sacks (2018) said:

> Not all of us have power, but we all have influence. That is why we can each be leaders. The most important forms of leadership come not with position, title or robes of office, not with prestige and power, but with the willingness to work with others to achieve what we cannot do alone. . . . Always choose influence rather than power. It helps change people into people who can change the world.

In this chapter, I will integrate all the different aspects of Beauty we have explored in Chapter 3 and Chapters 5–10 and suggest how these can be developed into practical guidance for the 'art of leadership'.

In Chapter 4, I outlined the new paradigm of leadership, having first shown how for many years leadership development in the West was classroom-based, cognitive and analytic, often studying case histories of past individual leaders and so-called 'excellent' and 'successful' organizations. Leadership was seen as something that was done by individual leaders – and mostly men. 'The great man' theory of leadership was handed down to us by Thomas Carlyle, Henry Gibbon and other 19th-century historians and biographers. This paralleled and grew out of the atomistic, Newtonian view of the world.

Only gradually have we learnt that leadership does not reside in leaders but is always relational and co-created, involving a leader, followers and a shared purpose. We have also learnt that leadership in a complex world needs to be collective, where a leadership team takes collective responsibility for the whole and the team functions as more than the sum of its parts. In addition, leadership needs to be in service of all the wider stakeholder and eco-system in which it is

DOI: 10.4324/9781003349600-15

enmeshed, as well as the future generations that will inherit the consequences of the decisions made and actions taken.

The qualities of the great leader have often been portrayed as decisive, determined, self-reliant, confident, analytic, strategic and charismatic. The role models were drawn from military commanders and politicians. Only in the last 30–40 years has there been a greater emphasis on the emotional and relational skills of the leader – the need for the leader to develop their self-awareness, their emotional intelligence (EQ) (Goleman, 1995), their social intelligence (Goleman, 2006), their collaborative intelligence, We Q (Hawkins, 2021). These enable their teams to be more than the sum of their parts and to partner effectively with all stakeholders.

We have also realized the importance for leaders to be global in their outlook (Hawkins, 2017a; Ghemawat, 2012) and be able to focus on longer and multiple timeframes (Sharp, 2013; Kryznaric, 2020). In the previous chapter, I have shown how developing 'aesthetic intelligence' (AQ – not to be confused with AI, which has little or no AQ!) is also an essential capacity for human consciousness to evolve. In his research on Beauty, Ferrucci (2010: 10, 16) found the following:

> Those who felt most at home with beauty were also more in touch with their feelings, had a richer inner life, and were more capable of using their own resources, were stronger when in difficulty, and more adaptable in changing strategy when they faced a variety of predicaments. They were not invulnerable, but when they met crisis they could cope more competently. . . . Those with a limited aesthetic range have not only a more restricted world, but also a personality which is less rich and flexible.

Ferrucci (2010: 17–18) later argues:

> To gain cognitive flexibility open to other ways of living and being, has never been as urgent as it is now. Beauty can be an easy way to promote a universal outlook beyond provincialism and parochialism. Several studies have shown that even a brief contact with literature and art increases our capacity for empathy.

He shows how 'Those with a vaster aesthetic range will have a greater capacity to understand others and adapt to their way of thinking' (Ferrucci, 2010: 18). The further good news is that a number of studies have shown that increasing your aesthetic intelligence increases your health and your longevity.

Some simple practices we can do to increase our AQ are, at least once a month, to do one or more of the following:

1. Read a novel or book of poetry, preferably by someone from a different cultural background from your own.

2. Go to a play, opera or concert and allow yourself to be immersed within it.
3. Take a long walk in nature, allowing your attention to be led by surprising moments of beauty around you.
4. Go to an art exhibition, and with at least one work of art, spend time entering the feeling of the piece and the artist who created it, and discover multiple levels of Beauty.
5. Keep a diary of the Beauty you have experienced.

In this chapter, I will offer teachings of leading with and through Beauty, which I have gleaned from the rich traditions we explored in the earlier chapters. But a word of caution: I have discovered, over many years of failure, that you cannot learn these lessons just by reading. As I have said elsewhere in this book, all change – and, therefore, all learning – is always embodied; it happens not through information or insight but through experimentation, spiritual and craft practice, ritual and developing new habits. Therefore, I have offered a simple practice to go with each of the ten lessons.

Self-cultivation

Many years ago, I was fortunate to meet the wise ex-CEO of Hanover Insurance, Bill O'Brien, who said: 'The success of an intervention depends on the interior condition of the intervenor'. The main instrument of leadership is the being of the leader, an instrument that needs constant maintenance, tuning and upgrading. Executive and leadership coaching, as well as systemic team coaching, have played a major role over the last 45 years in helping leaders develop their self-awareness (EQ), their relational and collaborative intelligence (WeQ) and their wider 'whole intelligence'.

Malcolm Parlett is one of the leading pioneers in the fields of Gestalt coaching, psychotherapy, organizational development and education. In his book *Future Sense: Five Explorations of Whole Intelligence for a World That's Waking Up* (Parlett, 2015), he describes five key capacities that are essential for individuals, teams and organizations.

- **Self-recognizing** – This includes self-awareness of one's strengths and weaknesses, one's habits and patterns, but also goes beyond this to recognizing what is required and being able to constantly reflect and learn.
- **Responding to the situation** – The ability to see what is needed in the challenges we are presented with and take responsibility rather than reacting or being a bystander.
- **Inter-relating** – The capacity to engage others, to listen deeply, to empathize and show compassion; to effectively lead teams and partnerships, engage in generative dialogue, use a wide range of emotional engagement; to motivate, celebrate, energize and focus.

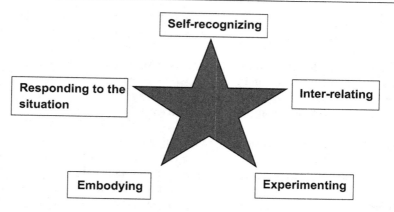

Figure 11.1 Five key capacities: Malcolm Parlett (2015)

- **Embodying** – Attending to our emotions, feelings and gut sense, rather than just operating from our analytic mind.
- **Experimenting** – Co-creating new thinking and doing; trying out new actions and ways of being; constantly learning

This provides a more rounded and wholistic curriculum for leadership. In talking with Malcolm Parlett (Parlett and Hawkins, 2023), I was reminded of a much earlier model of five capacities of leadership – one that was developed in the 4th century BCE by *Wuxing* in China, in a treatise on 'Inward Training' (see Puett and Gross-Loh, 2016). *Wuxing* had five virtues that needed to be cultivated:

- **Goodness** – Doing what is needed or required.
- **Propriety** – Including respect, appropriateness to the setting you are in, decorum.
- **Knowledge** – Going beyond conceptual and practical knowledge to include learning poetry by heart and calligraphy, both of which develop an aesthetic appreciation and a way of being aesthetic in one's being and ways of relating.
- **Ritual** – Confucius taught that leadership is developed through how we behave, which is often rooted in our habits. Habits, he argued, are best changed through new ritual practices.
- **Sagacity** – Spiritual wisdom.

Like Parlett's (2015) five areas, each one of the earlier virtues helps and is interconnected with the other four, and they cannot be developed separately. They are the five points of a bright star, and the light of the star is more important than mapping the points (see Figures 11.1 and 11.2). Parlett sometimes describes them as different gateways to a walled city (Parlett and Hawkins, 2023). Each requires constant practice and action learning, reflecting on what was helpful

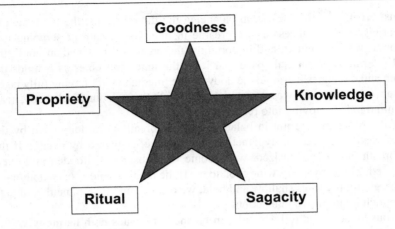

Figure 11.2 Wuxing: Five virtues

and what was not and what required further refinement in the next daily cycle of practice. In the ancient Chinese tradition, the 'Ruler' and the 'Mystical Sage' were not opposites but two aspects of the same person.

The Western approach to personal development, largely based in humanistic psychology, has been very influential in helping liberate people from outdated, restrictive ways of being, so they can connect with more of their, and others', emotions and express themselves more fully. However, this approach has many shadow aspects, which I explored in depth in my 2015 talk, 'The Necessary Revolution in Humanistic Psychology' (Hawkins, 2017b).

The motivation for self-development for many coming to coaching or personal development workshops, unlike that of the ancient Daoist teachers, was about developing 'my' self, enhancing 'my' being for 'my' personal success. Humanistic psychology can become trapped in individualism, human-centrism and dualistic thinking. Leaders often come to coaching for self-improvement so they can be 'higher performing', 'polish their personal brand', get their next promotion or grow their company's 'bottom-line' profits.

In contrast, the Daoist notion of self-cultivation is not simply either inner or outer but the flow between the two, learning to respond in harmony with what is arising in the outer and inner world, developing the capacity to be in touch with the *Dao* – the source of both the outer and inner worlds – and the *chi*, or vital energy that continually flows between them. This can be seen in the Daoist central concept of breath, which is seen as the vital connecting energy of 'interbeing'. Cheng (2009: 104) writes:

> The Breath constitutes the fundamental unity, and at the same time it continually animates all the beings in the living universe, connecting them into a giant network of life-in-process called the Tao, the Way.

Daoist breath practices focus on balancing the three breaths: the *yin* breath of receptivity and gentleness as we breathe in; the *yang* breath of stepping into action as we breathe out; and importantly, the breath of the 'median void', the vital intermediary, liminal space that joins the inner and outer as it holds the breath and circulates it around the body. In the 'median void', having fully taken in the world around us, we sense and experience it through our whole body, heart and mind before moving into response.

If these breaths are not in balance, and our breathing is dominated by the *yang* breath, we become hyperactive and reactive, triggered by events. If the *yin* breath is overemphasized, we become over-absorbent, flooded and over-whelmed, blown by every wind around us. If the median void is over-dominant, our breathing becomes shallow and held; we can become frozen, neither able to take much in nor move into action.

If our breathing is full and fully in balance, it creates both harmony within and without and harmony between the inner and outer. We breathe in the Beauty of the world, we let the Beauty flow through our whole being, until we become the Beautiful, and we breathe out, doing the Beautiful in our movement, our speech, our presence, in how we engage others and how we respond and move into action.

Practice

Sit with your feet flat on the ground, in touch with the earth; your spine straight, reaching up to the heavens; your hands, palms upright, resting relaxed and open at each side of you; and your eyes open.

Breathe in the *yin* breath, taking in everything that is around you, through all your senses – seeing, listening, smelling, tasting, feeling.

Hold the breath in the 'median void' and feel the breath flow through your body.

Breathe out the *yang* breath, sensing your body moving out to engage with all that surrounds you.

Repeat the exercise and notice to what degree these three breaths are in balance. Does one dominate more than the others? How much is there a harmonious flow between them?

Managing our shadow: from reaction to response

The much-publicized failures and scandals of once successful leaders are rarely based on their lack of intellectual capability or decisive determination; on the contrary, they are most often rooted in their over-determination and confidence in their own beliefs. This failing has been made worse by their so-called 'charisma', seducing others to blindly follow them. It is the lack of self-awareness of their shadow side, and their failure to encourage others to give them challenge and feedback, that becomes their undoing.

Carl Jung is reputed to have said: 'The greater the light, the darker the shadow'. But many years later, many still want to place their faith in bright-shining leaders and to deny that those leaders have a shadow. In Hawkins (2021: 11), I open the book with a true story of a senior team I was working with in the 1990s:

I was working with the senior executive team of a leading financial company. After an exploratory round of individual meetings, I was struck by how much of the views of the team were focused on what was wrong with their chief executive. I was aware that they had had a number of chairmen and chief executives who had quite short tenures and there had been competition before the latest (internal) appointment. After my first few months of working alongside them in their meetings and facilitating a team off-site, I was still being lobbied in the corridor about the CEO's weaknesses. At the next meeting I said to the team: 'I am fed up with you all telling me what is wrong with your chief executive'. The chief executive who was sitting next to me, turned and looked at me with shock and anger, and the team members all looked down at their papers! I continued, somewhat in trepidation: I think you are all delegating leadership upwards and playing the game of 'waiting for the perfect chief executive', or 'waiting to be the perfect CEO'. Well, I have some bad news for you. In all my years working with a great variety of organizations, I have never met a perfect chief executive. So the question for you as senior team members is: 'How are you as a team going to take responsibility for his weaknesses?'. The team coaching had begun.

Power tends to corrupt in a number of ways. The pressure to be a decisive person of action, always on the go, can take the individual away from their connection to their heart-mind and leave little time for wider reflection. Leaders are taught to develop their 'leadership brand', their own narrative and manifesto. But many leaders start to believe their own rhetoric, propaganda and constructed story and lose their sense of self within this constructed story. They have to enact the part they and others have created, no longer being their fuller self. They can fall in love with their own power and status, losing their humility and forgetting that their power is only a means to an end, to lead others in making a positive difference in the world. They become their own caricature. I am sure you can think of recent political and corporate leaders for whom this is true.

Being trapped in power is exacerbated by how leaders can attract sycophantic followers and adoration, as well as envy and competition. No longer is the world around them reflecting just them back to themselves; they are in receipt of many people's projections. Many leaders I have coached have talked of the pain and pressure of being surrounded by so many people who see them in so many ways that do not fit with how they see themselves.

'Citizen Kane' is an iconic film about business power and leadership – the leader who, as he became more and more powerful, became more isolated and lonely, longing for the innocence of his poor childhood and the one thing he loved: 'Rosebud', the sledge that carried him down the snowy slopes near his house. But this love was locked away in the attic with the ageing Rosebud. Innocent love that seeks no return, no profit, no dividend. Love that is complete unto itself.

In Chapter 4, I outlined the relational and triangulated models of leadership – how, for leadership to happen, it requires a leader, followers and a shared endeavour or purpose. Leadership is a verb, not a noun or an acquisition or something you can own. Leadership cannot be learnt theoretically in the classroom but rather, through action learning or coaching at the learning edge, experientially engaging with real or simulated challenges, trying out new ways of thinking, engaging, relating, organizing activity, receiving feedback, reflecting and learning.

A brilliant and competent leader can be undone by just one moment of instinctual reactivity, leading to an action they will regret the rest of their lives. All good leadership development helps individuals and collective leadership attend to their shadow and their 'triggers' and 'derailers'.

Practice

Think of a time when you got angry and frustrated, ending in you shouting at somebody. (You might even have gone on to blame them for making you angry.)

Reflect on the series of events, trying to see and hear them as clearly as you can.

What was the very first point you can recall when you can recognize the irritation beginning to spark?

What happened immediately prior to that?

What were you telling yourself at this time?

What other situations in your previous life, stored in your emotional memory of your amygdala and hippocampus, might have been activated by this event?

In your calm state of today, can you ask the you who became emotionally reactivated back then what it was they most needed – both in the situation where they shouted and in the situation that had been reactivated?

Now ask what would have been another way of expressing that need other than the one you instinctively used?

Leading with love

When I was invited to give a speech in Istanbul on 'What Europe could learn from Turkey about leadership', I searched through the whole of the *Mathnawi* by Mevlana Rumi to find what he had to say about leadership. I was rewarded by the one-line jewel: 'Leadership is a poison, unless you have the antidote in your heart'.

Earlier in this chapter, we explored this poison, which comes with the shadow side of leadership, as leadership often brings with it power, privilege and being surrounded by people who tell you what they think you want to hear rather than what you need to hear. Leaders can easily lose their sense of who they are, lost in their own rhetoric and stories, which followers play back to them. What is the antidote that Rumi speaks of that will cure the poison of leadership, if we have it in our hearts? The antidote is love. It is easy for leaders to become in love with their own power and status, losing their humility and forgetting that it is only a means to an end, to lead others in making a positive difference in the world.

In Chapter 5, we explored the path of love that Socrates learnt from Diotima, the arduous path of Dante and the Sufi path of love, of Hafiz and Inayat Khan. This is a path that is necessary for every leader and aspiring leader. It is love that helps us develop what the Daoists call the *xin* or 'heart-mind', which integrates our thoughts, emotions, consciousness and spirit from *suxin* (unaligned with the *Dao*) to *Wuxing* ('awakened nature'). The awakened leader is characterized by stillness and clarity, or *qingjing*, and emanates peace, presence and love (Komjathy, 2014).

Practice: loving more

1. Write down ten moments when you have experienced deep loving in your life. Try to include love of nature, individuals, groups, moments, music, art and writing.
2. For each one of these, write how you could bring this quality more alive in your daily work.

Truth

In Chapter 6 on Truth, we explored how the journey of truth in leadership starts with being honest to oneself. It then proceeds by creating a 'holding space' in your team, with enough psychological safety for all team members to speak the truth from their perspective, in such a way that all perspectives are acknowledged and a greater collective truth can be discovered. Both in teams and between teams, and between organizations and partners, honesty is critical for building both trust and collaboration. Structured feedback between all parties that is 'clear, owned, regular, balanced and specific' (Hawkins and Smith, 2013) is an essential practice in this.

As leaders, we also need to train ourselves in depth listening – hearing not just the words that are spoken but also listening empathetically to the feelings that are often conveyed indirectly, noticing and hearing the non-verbal emotions and listening to how the patterns of the wider systems are manifesting through this person or group: to be able to listen to the 'diversity' of different perspectives and hold that although they may be contradictory, they all hold a separate part of a greater truth; to listen to the 'conversity' of the potential pattern that connects and flows between them; and to facilitate a collaborative inquiry, to discover the 'eversity', the 'emergent truth' that is coming into being.

Practice

1. Write down three truths about yourself and then read them out loud to someone close to you.
2. With your team, try the 'secrets exercise' (Hawkins, 2021a: 122). Team members are asked to write or type on a piece of paper something they believe needs addressing but that people avoid mentioning. These are then mixed up and reallocated; each person shares the one they have been given, speaks to it as if it was their own and the issue is discussed. This ensures issues are collectivized and people are not punished for being the messenger.
3. Sit in a meeting and focus on listening to the spaces between the separate contributions, hearing the unrecognized connections between separate points of view.

Good and justice – service

Last night, a colleague from South America was telling me about her father, now in his nineties, who loves life and all it brings, every day. Her father had been a well-known neurosurgeon, who loved his work and his colleagues and, above all, everyone he treated. He was unconcerned with rank or how much he earned, and he was dedicated to every patient's needs whether they could pay or not. His poor patients, whom he treated without any charge, would often later bring him fish, vegetables or flowers as tokens of their love and appreciation, and he would say this was greater reward than any money. He would see the good in everyone, curious about what he could learn from the homeless begging in the street or the waitress in the café. Life was good, living was beautiful. A life of service that constantly gave back a fuller and more beautiful life to him, which he could then share with his family and community. A circular economy of Beauty and Good.

A life of service, of seeing what is needed and doing what is necessary. We are all given that opportunity, and the rewards are many.

Practice

Create three columns.

- In column 1, write down all the people, groups, communities and aspects of the eco-system for whom your work and life create beneficial value.
- In column 2, write what is the beneficial value you co-create with and for each of them.

- In column 3, write how you could co-create greater beneficial value with and for each of them.
- Then plan your first steps in bringing this Beauty and Goodness alive.

Grace and gratitude

As we explored in Chapter 10, it is through gratitude that we become graceful. Our posture changes from being tightly held with face thrust forward – looking for the next challenge, the next opportunity for profit – to being grounded, relaxed and flowing, in tune with other humans and all life that is around them.

As a leader, I had to learn not to respond to work done for me by others by immediately telling them how it could be improved; but first to thank them and tell them what I appreciated in their work. I was unaware how demoralizing my responses were in my drive for constant improvement.

My saying 'Thank you' went from five, to ten, to 20 times a day – not just at work but also to the ticket clerk at the station, the person who made the coffee, the cashier in the cafeteria, the people who came to the team meeting, those who showed up for one of my training sessions, my wife and children. I also adopted the practice of starting the day by opening the curtains, seeing the world around me and saying, 'Another day in paradise', and ending the day by counting at least ten blessings, each day different.

My sense of joy in the world and bodily relaxation greatly increased, and my easily provoked irritation lessened.

Practicing gratitude

Choose one or more of the following:

- Double the number of times you say 'Thank you' each day.
- Experiment with walking into work or entering a meeting with grace and poise.
- End each day naming what blessings you have received that day – from people, from the wider nature and from life.

An ecological ethic and aesthetic

Gratitude just for the human world is not enough. We can develop gratitude for all the daily gifts we receive from nature that we have taken for granted. We can say 'Thank you' to the wind, clouds, rain, rivers and lakes for every glass of water we drink. To the trees, earth and mycelium for every piece of paper we use or packaging we receive. 'Thank you' daily to the sun for all the warmth, energy and life it gives.

We need to develop an ecological ethic and aesthetic, as we explored in Chapter 8, and realize that the more-than-human world is the largest investor in every business – our most important stakeholder, whose welfare cannot be delegated to a small environmental, social and governance (ESG) team, but the wider ecology, who needs a seat and voice in every team meeting.

The National Assembly of Wales in 2015 passed the 'Well-being of Future Generations (Wales) Act', appointing a Minister for the future, who comments on all new proposals from the perspective of future generations. I have worked with other governments, encouraging them to have a Minister not just for future generations but also a Minster for the more-than-human world. I have worked with some enlightened teams who have adopted a practice, at each team meeting, of having a different team member wearing the hat of the ecology and giving voice to the ecology's needs. The ecology is not just out there or in the future; it is part of us and affected by everything – yes, everything – we do.

Practice

1. Take a walk each day, and see what beauty catches your attention – breathe that beauty in.
2. Bring ecological beauty into the workplace: fresh flowers, shells, stones, pictures.
3. Have a chair for the ecology in every meeting, and have someone speak from that chair on behalf of the 'more-than-human' world.
4. Do the 'Deep Time Walk' (https://www.deeptimewalk.org/).

Embracing death and transience as a beautiful part of life

Gratitude does not end with life, but we need gratitude for all that dies that we might live. Life is sustainable because nearly all living matter including us are edible and recyclable (Weber, 2019: 39). Our life is dependent on the past dying of other planets. The earth is dependent on the constant death of vegetation and microbial insects. It is death that gives birth to life. Yet as modern humans, we live in fear of death.

Baldwin (1963) says:

one day, for each of us, the sun will go down for the last, last time. Perhaps the whole root of our trouble, the human trouble, is that we will sacrifice all the beauty of our lives, will imprison ourselves . . . in order to deny the fact of death, which is the only fact we have. It seems to me that one ought to rejoice in the fact of death – ought to decide, indeed, to earn one's death by confronting with passion the conundrum of life. One is responsible to life. . . . One must negotiate this as nobly as possible, for the sake of those who are coming after us.

There is an old, wise saying: 'live as though your will die tomorrow, but garden as if you will live for 300 years'. This can equally be applied to leadership. Many great leaders and teachers have realized their wisdom through a near-death experience, as when we realize our time on life is short and unpredictable, then we embrace life to the full and can focus on serving life and our legacy.

Practice

Write a farewell letter to be read after you die, either to your family, your work colleagues or your current self. Include what you have most valued, appreciated and loved and what would be your wishes and hopes for them.

Eldership

The art of leadership does not end at retirement or at the peak of one's career. I vividly remember being on a flight in South Africa, sitting next to one of Mandela's first cabinet members, who told me he was going to stand down at the forthcoming election. He proudly showed me pictures of his family, and I casually remarked, 'I guess you are looking forward to retiring'. He looked sternly at me and said, 'In my culture, leaders do not retire. They become elders. Elders have an important role. They stand back and watch, and they hold the new leaders to account, helping them see the bigger picture'.

In our white Western world, we have lost the practice of eldership. For many years, I have been supporting my good friend Trevor Waldock, who has been taking leadership training from the UK to communities in Africa and then bringing back learnings about eldership from Africa to the white Western world (Waldock, 2017, 2021). Trevor quotes Nelson Mandela from his speech in Johannesburg, South Africa, July 18, 2008:

> an elder . . . people who use their collective experience, their moral courage and their ability to rise above the parochial concerns of nation, race and creed, they can help make our planet a more peaceful, healthy and equitable place to live.

The work of eldership begins long before we retire, for one of the most important tasks of leadership is to develop the leaders of tomorrow, through role-modelling, coaching, mentoring and a caring interest. As elders, we know tomorrow's leaders will face far bigger challenges than those our privileged generation has had to face. But the work of eldership does not end with retirement. Some say our last great responsibility is to show others how to die well.

Anita Sanchez (2017: 16–18) teaches us how the indigenous peoples, who still have participative consciousness, understood eldership:

> Elders are people who are steeped in the traditions or the passed-down knowledge of a community or tribe. People who have taken on the role of healers, cultural leaders, and spiritual teachers.
>
> An Elder can be truly funny . . . a twinkle in their eye. . . . The innocence of a child and the deep wisdom of the ancient. They know magic exists and are playful with it. They know how to balance things, creating harmony and connection. They hold the understanding that every thought and action has an impact that either lends support to or destroys our interconnected life and community.
>
> They share the message that the honor of one is the honor of all; and the hurt of one is the hurt of all. They understand we are all connected.

Reuel Khoza (2006) in writing about African leadership said, 'Elders are the cradle of leadership'.

Practice

1. Ask whose potential leadership you could help develop.
2. Choose one of these people or groups. Meet with them, and explore their hopes and dreams and how you could support them.

Conclusion

Having included eldership as the last lesson in the art of leadership, we should not wait to the end of our leadership journey to learn the art of eldership but combine its qualities with a beginner's mind, the humility of being a lifelong learner and the playfulness and awe of being a child.

We all need to be carriers of the four sacred gifts (Sanchez, 2017: 3):

> the power to forgive the unforgiveable . . .
> the power to heal . . .
> the power of unity. The power to come together . . .
> the power of hope. The ability to dream, to see wellness and the powers to attain it.

Sanchez (2017: 16–17) continues to show how critical and urgent it is for all humanity to find their way back home, to an Earth-connected way of being:

> The re-emergence of the felt experience of belonging in the larger consciousness (our collective interdependence and evolution), not only on our own lives but in our connections to all things, requires action from all of us, you and me. . . . This wisdom is necessary for humanity to move forward and evolve.

Chapter 12

Beauty in the art of coaching

Introduction

As I hinted in Chapter 11, the art of Beautiful leadership cannot be achieved alone, for it requires the involvement and support of others, colleagues, trainers and, particularly, coaches and mentors who can practice the art of beautiful coaching. Future-fit leadership requires coaches, who are not just technically proficient, with all the right attested competencies, but also ones who are dedicated and passionate about coaching as a relational art and craft that gives birth to Beauty. These coaches may be full-time dedicated professional coaches or leaders coaching their teams or its individual members.

Minna Salami (2020: 188–189) in her book on *Sensuous Knowledge* writes:

> Do beauty, dear reader. Do beauty like your life depends on it, because in many ways it does. All our lives do. Beauty in action is art, and the more we strive to make of life an art, the more beautiful our world and ourselves will become. I have never seen a person, no matter what age, look, ability, height, this or that, be passionate about life and not be beautiful.

To watch a woodturner create a beautiful handle, a potter a fine jug and plate and a flower arranger a display of mixed fresh flowers in an elegant vase is to witness people who love their work, where they have achieved mastery in doing the beautiful. For leadership and coaching to be crafts where we do the beautiful, we, too, must love and delight in our work. Our craft is in relationship, in sensing with all our senses, listening through the words of the other to the pattern and narrative that connects what is shared. Feeling through limbic resonance, the flow of feelings of the other. Seeing through the embers of loss and lack, to the spark that can be blown on and ignite new possibility. It is the path of creative conversation and co-discovery – the art of creative inter-poiesis as we will explore in the next chapter, which leads to finding new expression, weaving a new story which creates new ways of thinking and being and liberates people from the small dark prison of the atomistic mind.

DOI: 10.4324/9781003349600-16

Beautiful Coaching

Satish Kumar (2021) writes about how he learnt about doing the beautiful from his upbringing as a Jain in India, long before he became a great eco-spiritual teacher.

> My mother used to teach me that whatever we produce and consume should have three characteristics.
>
> **Number one, whatever we make or use should be beautiful.** Beauty is food for the soul. Our senses and spirits are nourished by beauty. Beauty ignites creativity and inspires the imagination.
>
> **Number two, the beautiful should also be useful.** Beauty is and should be an integral part of making and producing. Neither is there nor should there be any contradiction between beauty and utility. Form and function must be harmoniously combined.
>
> **And number three, what is beautiful and useful should also be durable.** What we produce and make should have long life. Built-in obsolescence is violence and sin against nature.

So how might we apply this BUD formula (Beautiful, Useful and Durable) to the craft of coaching?

- **Beautiful.** We should create beautiful settings for our coaching. Our attitude as coaches should reflect and be in the service of the beautiful. We should make our engagement, and our conversation, beautiful.
- **Useful.** Our coaching should create change, both live in the room and in what comes next, and should create beneficial value not just for the coachees but also for all their stakeholders, including the more-than-human world.
- **Durable.** We should coach with an awareness of 'deep-time', the seven generations who come before us and the seven generations who hopefully will come after us. A focus on how we become good ancestors (Kryznaric, 2020) and not just focus on short-term goals but how we create sustainable contribution to a more sustainable world.

Where do we learn these BUD aspects of our craft? My colleague Giles Hutchins (2012 and Hutchins and Storm, 2019) shows how we can learn from 'biomimicry' – from how nature operates. Satish Kumar (2021) also shows how nature is our best teacher:

> We can learn about the BUD formula in the university of nature. For example, trees are beautiful; they are lovely to look at, they have natural balance and appropriate proportions, but they also have great usefulness; they absorb carbon and provide oxygen, birds nest on their branches and humans as well as animals enjoy their fruits. And trees have long life. An oak or a yew tree can last for a thousand years.

In Chapter 4, I outlined the new paradigm of coaching, and you might want to revisit that before reading the rest of this chapter. Leadership and coaching have traditionally been focussed on people and problems, and the language has been prosaic. Now, with the challenges of our times, both leadership and coaching need to move to a focus on purpose, planet and be poetic. Purpose: What is the work that life is requiring us to do that will create value for all stakeholders? Planet: How will our work serve not just human needs but also create beneficial value for the more-than-human world with which we share this planet and which daily sustain us?

In the next chapter, we will explore how this requires us to move from a prosaic conversation between two left-hemisphere neo-cortexes, with a language of questions and answers, and objects to be sorted and problems to be solved; to a poetic dialogue of collaborative inquiry, where together, we are finding new language for what is emerging that needs addressing: a new language of the heart, the whole brain and the whole body, a new inter-poiesis.

Preparing the outer and inner space

When we coach or meet with people, do we invite them into a beautiful space or a cluttered, uncared-for room? Does the space feel open, receptive and welcoming? Does it have aspects of the wider nature within it, such as plants or living flowers, or at least pictures of the more-than-human world?

Even when we are meeting people in a public meeting room, we can find moments of Beauty. I remember coaching leaders in Canary Wharf, the banking hub in the east of London, and having battled through security, reception and the crowded lifts, walking to a faceless office on a very high floor. Before starting the sessions, I would walk with the coachee to the window, pause alongside them and ask them what attracted their attention in the world beyond our room.

When the Coronavirus pandemic led to lockdown, suddenly, all my trainings and coaching went online and felt flat – the group became a chequerboard of tiny faces. Often, I could only see the face and ceiling of my coachee. We were both pinned in our seats. Suddenly, I realized this does not have to be. I asked my coachees to adjust their screens so we could each see each other's hands and hearts. I committed to always having, immediately behind my left shoulder, an arrangement of fresh flowers from my garden. On one occasion, as I was teaching a global webinar, the evening light came in a side window and lit up the flowers, leaving me in twilight. How appropriate the flowers were in the spotlight, not the speaker.

Preparing the external space is important but not sufficient. As coaches, we need also to prepare the internal space before the coachee arrives – to be prepared, open, present, centred and connected. We do not put on the costume or mask of Beauty but connect to the source where Beauty flows up from the earth and from the air around us, where Beauty flows in from the light we allow to flow through us.

Becoming fully human and developing our 'presence' is a lifelong journey of learning and unlearning for each of us. This involves developing what the Sufi's call our '*adab*', an Arabic word meaning a behavioural etiquette. There is the *adab* of the host and the *adab* of the guest, the *adab* of the teacher and the *adab* of the student, the *adab* of the parent, grandparent and neighbour. Kabir Helminski (2000), a current Mevlevi sheik, writes:

> *Adab* is the ability to sense what is appropriate to each moment and to give to each its due – a continuous process of refining one's speech and actions. To have *adab* is to be cultured.

In developing our *adab*, we offer an elegance and gracefulness towards self and other; we are continuously creating and recreating conscious relationship within and without.

Opening the seven levels

For a number of years, I have had the privilege of being an inter-faith spiritual celebrant, facilitating weddings, child blessings, funerals and other rites of passage. In more recent years, I have trained other spiritual celebrants in this important work. One of the core practices happens before the ceremony and is for the celebrant to prepare themselves, through the practice of opening to seven levels of awareness.

1. The first level is to open to the individual or individuals, who are central to the forthcoming event, and to picture them with love and compassion.
2. Then to refocus on the relational connections. In the case of a wedding, the relationship between those marrying; for a child blessing, the relationship between the parents, siblings and new arrival; and for a funeral between the relatives and the deceased.
3. Third, to open to the wider community of family, friends and neighbours who will shortly gather.
4. We then move our focus to those who will not be present because they are ill or have died or have not been invited – the previous wife or husband, the estranged sibling, the parent with dementia.
5. The attention then moves to the whole, interconnected human family, all 8 billion of us who share this planet.
6. Then to the more-than-human world of all the sentient beings that surround us and the elements that support and flow through us.
7. Finally, we open the door to the mystery of oneness – that which connects everything, beyond time and space, beyond words and certainly beyond our own limited comprehension.

Every coaching session is, in some way, *a rite of passage*, so this is a practice we can do as coaches before each coaching meeting. Picture the individual, their important relationships, the community they talk about in their sessions and the community they leave out and ignore. Then the one human family, the more-than-human ecology and, finally, the mystery of oneness.

What we know from the experience of many practitioners is that when you open to some new awareness within you, even though you never mention it, the client starts talking to that same level, as though they had only been awaiting your readiness.

How we start sets the tone for what follows

In the Beautiful art of leading and coaching, how we start new relationships and how we open meetings and coaching sessions Beautifully, as a loving craftsperson, is essential for what will follow. We love our craft, what it creates and with non-judgmental compassion and care for our partner(s) in the conversation. Like all good craft workers, we realize that we need to get our ego and personal needs out of the way and be in service of the work.

A traditional first meeting in coaching

Chris:	Tell me about you?
Terry:	Well, I am Head of the UK sales team for a business that sells domestic plumbing materials. I have been there about four years; before that I was a salesperson for a furniture company.
Chris:	What brought you to coaching?
Terry:	My boss recommended it to me – thought it would improve my leadership skills.
Chris:	What do you want to work on in coaching?
Terry:	I guess how I show up in the UK executive team, and also in the international sales meetings; and also how I manage my team members?
Chris:	What are your goals for the coaching?
Terry:	Well, I want my boss to see me as a competent leader. He might then recommend me to be international head of sales when that job comes available.
Chris:	What do you most need from me to help you achieve those goals?
Terry:	Help to be a better leader.

Notice the coach is asking stereotypical questions, as if interviewing this new coachee or they are coaching out of the habit of using well-tried, and possibly tired, questions.

A different approach

Now let us play this conversation again but differently. As you read this, notice what different feelings you have.

Chris: Tell me the story of your life from when you were born, to being here with me right now, in under two minutes?

Terry: Wow! Well, I was the oldest child with three younger siblings, for whom I did a lot of looking after, especially when my Mum went back to work as a nurse. My Dad was also working – he used to sell brushes door-to-door, and then got promoted and moved into selling for a big pharma company. I did ok at school, worked very hard, but there was no discussion about going to university, which my youngest two siblings did. Somehow, I was expected to go out to work. Support the family coffers. Worked in a shop, then in a bank, then got a job in sales for a printing company, then a furniture company and now an international plumbing business. Have I had my two minutes?

Chris: No, still time for more of the story – what about beyond work?

Terry: Well, I am married, no children. We both are into restoring vintage cars and take them on rallies. We also spend a lot of time looking after my partner's mother who is very frail and lives on her own; she is very reliant on us.

Chris: Take me to a moment when your heart was singing?

Terry: When we were driving our lovingly restored, beautiful Alfa Romeo, with the top down, and the wind was blowing through our hair; and we suddenly came over the hill and could see right along the coast, and the cliffs were all lit up. I felt so happy and alive.

Chris: And at work?

Terry: Rarely. I guess when I get a really appreciative letter from a customer, or my boss tells me I have done well.

Chris: So, I'm curious about who and what do your work and life serve?

Terry: I love pleasing customers and I like to see the company do well, although we have been struggling recently with the pandemic slowing down building work and supply chains.

Chris: Who else beyond your customers, investors and employees?

Terry: Well, the money I earn means we can support my mother-in-law, and also my sister and her kids who are really struggling.

Chris: And beyond your family, where you have always been a great support?

Terry: I lead our company's campaign to support cancer relief, which is close to my heart, as both my parents died from cancer, quiet young.

Chris:	It feels like that loss is still very present for you.
Terry:	I still miss them. Going for walks in the countryside with my Dad, working with him in the garage.
Chris:	If your Dad was here now, what would he be encouraging you to use this coaching to explore?
Terry:	(Thoughtful – closes his eyes) I think he would say: believe in yourself more, stop doubting yourself; also get out more.
Chris:	He would say: 'believe that you are'.
Terry:	As good as others, stop waiting for approval.

This time, the coach comes from loving interest and curiosity about this new person. Rather than asking questions for the coachee to give them information that the coachee already knows, they are inviting the coachee to say things they have not said or thought before. They are inviting heart contact and moving towards the learning edge where neither has an answer but where they can explore together.

Where we focus changes the tone

Now let us look at coaching in an ongoing relationship between a senior leader (Sam) and one of their team members (Anne).

Sam:	So, what do you need to talk about today?
Anne:	I have got a real problem customer, Diablo; they are always complaining, and I have offered them a reduced price to make up for our late delivery of the new product; I even put Josh, my best salesperson, on it.
Sam:	Well, Diablo have been an important and big customer for years, so what else do you need to do?
Anne:	I don't know, but they are eating up far too much of my time and I have so many other things to get on with.
Sam:	What would success look like in the relationship with Diablo?
Anne:	They got off my back.
Sam:	How will you achieve that?
Anne:	I don't know.

Like many leader meetings with one of their direct reports, Anne is working from the assumption she should share a problem that the leader can help her solve: in this instance, what to do about the customer, Diablo. The leader has been encouraged to adopt a coaching style, which they think means that they should just ask questions and get their direct report to come up with her own answers.

Another version of the same conversation

Sam: What is the work that your world and your stakeholders need us to explore today?

Anne: Well, we have a number of unhappy customers, like Diablo, and my team are looking to me to come up with ways of getting them back on side.

Sam: This sounds important. How could we develop, together, new ways of you engaging your team in creatively exploring the pattern beyond the individual complaints, and co-creating together new ideas for addressing these?

Anne: I feel they leave it to me as the team leader, the General that must come up with each day's battle plan.

Sam: So it's a perpetual battle, at war with. . . . .

Anne: The difficult complaining customers.

Sam: So, tell me about you best customer, your most beautiful customer relationship, and what makes it so enjoyable and creates real beneficial value for them and us.

Anne: Well, with Circum, it feels like a partnership. Like we are facing in the same direction. They always tell me about their challenges with their customers, and I see what we can do to help them with those. I have also got them involved with our R&D team to develop with them new products that will work with their pre-assembled houses.

Sam: That feels like both valuable and enjoyable partnering.

Anne: Absolutely. I'm sure there are others that my team have.

Sam: I wonder if it would help to spend time with your team to discover together the key ingredients of these successful partnerships.

Anne: Yes, I can see this could be a useful inquiry. We could also explore how these could be baked into some of the more challenging relationships.

Sam: Let me know if I can help you at all with the co-design of this session. I would certainly be interested in hearing what the team and you come up with together.

Here, the leader is starting the conversation – outside-in, coming shoulder-to-shoulder so they can focus on the needs of both Anne's world and its stakeholders. Sam picks up on Anne's feeling that it is all down to her, and she is a 'general in a battle'. From this, Sam invites in exploration of the positive, enjoyable and beautiful aspects of partnering in the work, rather than battling alone. Sam also positively models partnering in the relationship between them and encourages partnering, not just with the customers, but also Anne with her team.

In Beautiful leading and coaching, there is a Beautiful synergy and harmony between 'what' is being explored and 'how' it is being explored. The conversation moves beyond talking about the change out there to finding ways of co-creating the needed change in the relationship, here and now in the room.

There is an old expression: 'You don't get a second chance to make a first impression'. We could also say: 'You don't get a second chance to set the tone of a meeting'. This is why a conductor, before the music starts, gently raises their baton, looks at all the musicians and pauses, with a gesture and look that sets the tone. And it is certainly how a relationship starts that sets the tone for how it will unfold. Once the relationship has found its groove, it is hard to change course, so it is important how you start a new relationship and how you open every meeting.

Starting team meetings

This is also true of team meetings. Here are a number of opening lines that I have heard team leaders use. Please imagine what tone each will set and how you think the meeting will progress. Which do you think will lead to a Beautiful meeting, where team members will leave more energized, connected and focussed?

1. Is everyone here?
2. Should we wait for the latecomers or get going?
3. So what's first on the agenda?
4. Let's see if we can get this done quickly and finish early today.
5. Item one.
6. It is really lovely to see everyone and have the chance to be creative together.
7. Let's do a check-in and hear one moment of success you have had in the last week.
8. I would love to hear, from every one of you, something that you are grateful you have received from another member of the team, for which you would like to thank them.
9. Let's go round the table and hear the most important thing you each want us to leave having collectively achieved.
10. Please can we agree what we need to have worked out together, and decided, by the time we finish today's meeting?
11. Can we all share which of our team's many stakeholders we think we need to hold in mind in this meeting.

Imagine what tone and feeling you think each of these openings will engender in the meeting and how it might play out. Which of these have you experienced or used in teams? Which would you prefer?

You could choose to take one of these and experiment with using it to start your team meetings.

Coaching from beauty

Here are some further coaching practices once the coaching or team meeting has got underway.

Seeing the unrecognized beauty in the coachee

A good manager catches someone doing something right – a Beautiful coach catches the moments of Beauty that so easily get buried in life's busy-ness. Noticing and showing you have noticed small moments of Beauty is important. Echoing phrases like 'how beautiful', 'what a gift', 'nicely put', 'how lovely', 'say that again so we can savour it together' or 'let me play that back so we can feel the depth of what you said' and 'as you say that, your light shines through'.

Coaching questions that open the door to beauty

There are many coaching questions that invite Beauty into the coaching conversation. Here are just a few.

1. Pause, look around you. Where is Beauty speaking to you right now?
2. Tell me when Beauty has deeply moved you in your life.
3. Share with me your favourite work of art, music, poem, novel or place and what it means for you.
4. What do you need to give birth to in your life?
5. Where does the wild still live and dance in you?
6. How could you invite Beauty more into every aspect of your life?
7. How could you make your work more Beautiful?
8. I wonder how our coaching can best serve Beauty and be a delight for both of us and produce joy for others.

We also need to remember that questions are only one of the many ways coaches can respond to their coachees. Coaches are not investigative journalists but collaborative explorers with their coachee partner. Questions possibly should not be more than 50% of the ways we respond; otherwise, it is an interview, not a coaching session. Great conversations are not built on one person asking the other question after question and the other searching for answers.

Remember back to when you were at school and the teacher turned and looked you in the eye and asked you a question. By looking in the eye, we trigger the left-hemisphere neo-cortex. We hypnotically put the other into feeling back at school, panicking because they don't know the answer or trying to come up with the right answer – the one they think you want to hear.

But the coach is also not there to provide the answers or make judgments or interpretations.

Hobson (1985), Bohm (1987, 1996) and Zeldin (1998) have all shown how conversations, generative dialogue and collaborative inquiry co-create new awareness and new thinking: not through questions and answers or through exchanging pre-cooked thoughts but thinking together, cooking new understanding and meaning, co-creating new possible stories of the future. Here are a range of interventions that are not questions.

Joining words

In engaging in dialogical inquiry with another, some of our best helpers are the little words, short phrases or echoes. In contrast to the big words that present themselves as objects and things that want to stand out and be noticed, little words open new spaces and invite connections. They are the joining threads that weave together the not-yet-connected.

Too often in exploring an issue, situation or feeling, we fall back on asking complicated questions, which require the other to leave the flow of their own emerging sensing and thinking to make sense of our question, to work out what we are asking about and what sort of answer we might require.

In contrast, small words or phrases can join the flow of their own inquiry and, chosen well, can be the keys that unlock the door we have already tried to open.

Simple words, like 'with', 'to', 'about', invite the speaker to go further in their inquiry and become more specific. Here is a simple example:

Anne: I need to communicate more.
Coach: With . . . .?
Anne: My colleagues in the team.
Coach: About . . . .?
Anne: What they find useful and what I could do to make it more helpful.

Inviting intention

Another group of simple words, such as 'because', 'in order that', invite the speaker to discover the purpose in what they are exploring. The word 'be-cause', if we break it down, is a rather beautiful word – how we need to be in order to cause something to happen, or the cause of how we need to be.

John: I need to be less directive
Coach: In order that . . . .?
John: I leave space for my team to do more of the thinking.
Coach: About . . . .?

One-word reframes

There is a third set of simple words that can be used to unlock fixed beliefs and assumptions that are limiting the other person's possibilities – words such as 'yet', 'maybe', 'and', 'also'. For example:

Sophie: You cannot speak up in our team.
Coach: Yet.
Or:
Michel: Our boss is not open to feedback.
Coach: Maybe.

This third group needs to be used with compassion and without judgment, just a gentle opening of the door which is invitational rather than directive.

Offering a seed phrase

The coach offering a few beginning words of a sentence can provide a spring-board for the coachee to discover their truth, such as 'What is most important for me is . . . . .'.

Philip: I don't know how to get my boss to hear my truth.
Coach: My truth is. . . . .

Echoing key images or phrases from the coachee's story

These can help the other person recognize the power of what they have said and experience having it received by another person. Often, I will pick up on the power in a metaphor that has been used before it is skirted over and lost.

It is important to play it back with the necessary emotional tonality that came with it or even at times slightly amplifying the tone.

Bella: I feel trapped in my role.
Coach: Trapped.
Bella: Caged in.
Coach: Caged in by.

Non-verbal echoes

These are where the coach just echoes a sigh of grief, or an 'O' of awe, so the coachee can witness their expression through its reflection.

Invitations to experiment

There are many different forms of this; here are just a few examples:

- 'Try saying that standing up and louder'.
- 'Can you now change chairs and respond, speaking as your boss?'
- 'Would you like to draw a picture-sculpt of your team on this flipchart?'
- 'Become the wider ecology and comment on the conversation we have just had'.

Rewriting the story

'Now retell me the story the way you would like it to be, or the way that the future requires'.

All of these simple, conversational interventions emerge from metaphorically walking alongside the other, assisting, deepening and broadening the inquiry. In contrast, interrogating or asking about what has been shared breaks the flow of exploratory and collaborative inquiry.

The poiesis of coaching

In Chapter 14, we will explore in depth how coach and coachee, searching for the right language together, can give expression to the ineffable, the not-yet-expressed, the unthought known, the previously un-expressible.

Weaving sentences between us, neither being able to finish alone, each unknotting the knots the other has inadvertently created. Deconstructing our cultural grammar, which imprisons our knowing in propositions, linear causality, subjects acting on objects, things divided, wholes split into parts.

Wondering out loud and inviting the other to step into your half-finished sentences. Giving them an opening phrase to launch into a new statement not previously thought – finding multiple endings, until something new, unexpected and surprising emerges into consciousness.

Coaching with and in the wider ecology

Having taken part in many coaching conferences, webinars, podcasts and courses on ecological and climate conscious coaching, I am struck by how often the focus gets trapped in exploring how we can focus on the ecology or climate in coaching – what questions to ask, how to raise the issue, how to address it. The ecology becomes an 'it', a problem to be addressed, an agenda item, another global challenge we must address, and we end up feeling overwhelmed.

This process is part of a deeper human pattern of consciousness to see situations as challenges to be mastered, as problems to be solved and as difficulties to be overcome. This drive to mastery, over others and the world around us, has been a blessing that has turned into a curse – for it is this very drive to dominance, problem-solving and mastery, that has led humans into a disastrous, exploitive and extractive relationship with the world around them – seeing the natural world as an unlimited resource to be plundered.

Please do not make the ecology the third or fifth item on the coaching agenda, or even the first! Everything we address in coaching and everything we sense is part of the wider ecology, and the wider ecology is a participant in every issue that gets brought to coaching. It is literally the ground of our being, the air we share with every living being, the waters that run through us and comprise the majority of our body mass and the light through which we see.

The 'more-than-human' world is the source of our living and is that which 're-sources' us every moment of our lives. So instead of seeing the ecology as a problem we have to solve and instead of trying to coach from our limited personal perspective and skill, we can turn and ask the ecology to help us coach.

Many professions, from architects to musicians, and from organizational designers to artists, have been influenced by the growing field of biomimicry – how we can learn, as designers, artists, engineers or organizational leaders – from nature and use nature's natural patterns, geometry and design in human work.

It is time that coaching also developed the humility to see that the biosphere has been doing development, learning and evolution longer, more sustainably and with much greater interdependence, than we humans. How can we learn to coach the way nature works? How can we go further and let the ecology do the coaching?

I invite you to give yourself some time to take a discovery walk into nature, be it your garden, a local park, a woodland, coastal path or other part of nature that is important to you. Travel with an open-hearted, wide-eyed and wide-eared curiosity. Try and be as unencumbered as possible – taking very little with you, either in what you carry physically or in the clutter of your mind. Be open to what comes.

Lightly hold the question – 'What can the wider ecology teach me about how to coach?' – and allow yourself to wander and wait for whatever surprising answers may unfold. After a while, the question may change to 'How can I help you, the wider ecology, do most of the coaching?' and 'What do you need me to do differently in order that you have the space to coach?'.

With colleagues, I have been experimenting with ways of letting the ecology coach, and I offer here some of the practices we have found helpful.

The path

Each year, I hold two advanced coaching retreats at Barrow Castle, where I live and teach in the countryside close to the city of Bath. As part of the retreat, people coach each other as they walk through the woodlands close to the house. I invite coaches to use the path to shift between three different time-and-space dimensions: first, to call attention to what is beneath our feet and just in front of us, then to become aware of the path opening up before us, leading us to where we will walk next, and finally, to look up and attend to the far horizon and notice what weather is heading our way.

Without attention to horizon one, we may trip over an unnoticed obstacle right in front of us or tread on an unnoticed form of life. If we ignore horizon two, we will fail to appreciate the co-creation of the journey: how we create the path and how the path creates the journey of our walking. If we do not look up and out to horizon three, we may well get soaked in an 'unexpected' rainstorm. Like the 2020 Coronavirus, the rainstorm was actually expected; we just had not paid attention.

Rhythms of nature

Besides the different spatial horizons mentioned earlier, the wider ecology can also teach us about the natural rhythms that flow through all life on this planet.

I invite you to take another exploratory learning walk into nature. Again, travel with the same openness as in the previous invitation, but this time, alert to as many different time rhythms you detect on your walk.

Some people return having tuned into the diurnal rhythm of the earth's turning, which we experience as the sun travelling across from one horizon to another. Others have tuned into the four-week cycle of the moon as it waxes, wanes and goes dark, changing the tides in the oceans and in our bodies. Others connect to the annual cycle of the seasons, the plants that grow, flower and fruit at different times in the year.

These are certainly the base, background rhythms, but there are also other melodic rhythms playing out within these: the butterfly that may only live for a week but much longer as a caterpillar; the mayfly that may only live a day but longer as a nymph; morning glories, evening primroses and daylilies, whose flowers come fresh and die each day; the hen that lays its eggs almost every day for three or four years; and the steer that becomes enormous on eating just grass over two or three years.

Some have returned with rocks and fossils of geologic time, and one person brought back a jar of air telling how it contains air that has been around and through thousands of generations, before we now breathe it in.

Having completed this exploration, we carry out a coaching session and explore how many rhythms we can discover in the coachee's stories and in the unfolding relationship between us, as well as our joint relationship to the world around us.

Nature as a living system

Like myself, my friends and colleagues – Giles Hutchins, David Jarrett and Sarah McKinnon – all run leadership programmes in woodlands for leaders to have a direct, embodied experience of learning, from the woodland, how living systems work together. Sarah McKinnon writes:

As we walk through the woods, we use the woodland metaphor to explore with genuine curiosity, how these intricate systems are always connected, evolving, challenging and collaborating, as well as fighting for survival. With little effort this segues into the leader's recognition and reflection into their own nested systems – work, societal and physical wellbeing.

People who arrive bent upright at the start of the day, are later happily kneeling in mud, feeling an embodied connection with themselves, the group, their many human communities and the wider ecology.

(McKinnon, quoted in Hawkins and Turner, 2020: 118)

Giles Hutchins (quoted in Hawkins and Turner, 2020: 118) writes about how working in nature helps 'integrate the coachee's different ways of knowing – intuitive, rational, emotional and somatic intelligences'.

Coaching that involves animals takes us out of our neo-cortex, analytic brain and into our limbic brain, the part concerned with non-verbal communication and where we can more directly experience relational inter-connection. David Jarrett (quoted in Hawkins and Turner, 2020: 119) writes about how horses can act as 'a mirror to give us a better sense of how we show up in a given moment in a very inviting and easily accessible way'.

Coaching in nature, with nature and by nature invites us into the beauty of play. As coaches, we can walk alongside the coachee, tease out their latent curiosity and inquire into the connection around us and then within us, as well as the connections between the two.

Evaluating coaching

In Hawkins (2012), I wrote a whole chapter looking at different approaches to evaluating coaching and how the majority of evaluation methods look only at *inputs* – what the coach did, how they were appreciated by the coachee. A few evaluative methods would look at *outputs* (what the coachee learned, discovered and planned) and a few at *outcomes* (what changed in the behaviours, decisions, actions and relationships of the coachee as a result of the coaching).

Hardly any evaluative processes looked at *value creation* – how the coaching enabled the coachee to increase the beneficial value they co-create with, and for, all their stakeholders (their team, employees, organization, customers, suppliers, investors, communities, including their family, and the wider eco-system.)

I have argued that we have to move our focus more strongly along this continuum (Hawkins, 2012; Hawkins and Turner, 2020; Whybrow et al., 2023). However, there is another dimension: evaluating the coaching through the lens of Beauty. Here, we need to evaluate with what Weber (2019: 137–140) terms 'poetic objectivity . . . which is founded in empirical subjectivity . . . which provides not an empirical proof but an embodied proof'. I wrote earlier that if change does not happen in the coaching meeting or the team meeting, it is unlikely to happen afterwards, back at work, and that change is always embodied. Weber (2019: 140) writes:

> Poetic objectivity requires that we can submit any practise to the questions: is this productive of imagination? Is this exchange between self and other? Does it provide grace? Does it enhance aliveness? Does it bring more life? Do I make life fuller?'

We can also ask: Has the coaching or meeting enabled more fertile and productive life, for each of us, for other human individuals involved, for the wider stakeholders, for the eco-system and for the culture as a whole?

These questions can be addressed inter-subjectively, with both coachee and coach or leader, or the team as a whole, exploring them together.

Conclusion

Beautiful coaching is not a set of skills you can learn on a training program – for it is an attitude, a way of being and working. Above all, it comes from loving life, loving the people you coach and, even more, loving their potential and unfolding Beauty – what they can become that will bring more benefit to the world in and around them, their fertility and fecundity. It also comes from loving the Beauty of what we can co-create and give birth to together, the Beauty of the art and craft and always wanting to learn and discover more.

There is a phrase sometimes attributed to Kahlil Gibran, sometimes to Rabindranath Tagore and sometimes the American transcendental poet Ellen Hooper:

> I slept and dreamt that life was joy. I awoke and saw that life was service. I acted, and behold, service was joy.

Chapter 13

Beauty in the space between and the marriage of opposites

Introduction

Through this book, I have been exploring how Beauty is, by its very nature, relational: how it resides neither in the object nor the viewer; neither in the music nor the hearer; neither in the perfume nor the scent inhaled but in the living, relational connection. I have gone further and shown how this relational beauty is not one comprising an object and a subject, where one part is passive and the other active, but a co-creation in the moment of connecting.

In this chapter, we will go further and explore what happens in 'the space between'. This space between exists in many different ways. The space can be an ugly separation between opposing peoples or ideas, or the beautiful, silent space between notes in a piece of music, or between shapes and colours in a great work of art. It can be a space of mutual lovemaking that is giving birth to something new, or the coming-together of opposing ideas, to create a new realization in a 'coincidentia oppositorum'.

We will then discover how this space between can itself be an active participant in the co-creation of Beauty and not just a passive emptiness. This opens up the important concept and practice of 'triangulation'.

Then we will look at how as individuals, teams and organizations, we can so easily get stuck in opposing dualisms, in 'either-or' debates, and I will share the methods I have used to help individuals, teams and organizations transform these stuck polarities into new creativity.

Finally, we will look at the major polarities that are continuing to enclose and imprison our modern consciousness and at ways these, too, can be transcended.

The prison of polarity thinking

In Chapter 2, where we explored the gradual shrinking and imprisoning of human consciousness, we looked at how 'rational, mechanistic and atomistic thinking' and the dominance of the left-hemisphere neo-cortex brain lead us to see parts, not wholes; sense separate things, not relationships and connections;

DOI: 10.4324/9781003349600-17

and become attached to our own fixed perspectives. This shows up in today's organizations, in their leaders and in team meetings in many ways:

- strategic explorations being over-dominated by data analysis of past trends, with little time spent on imaginative explorations of future possibilities, incorporating 'future-back and outside-in' thinking (Hawkins, 2021a)
- attachment to past successful approaches and a failure to see the early-week signals that the context is changing
- conflicts between perspectives, often in the form of 'either-or' debates

After many years of attending executive and management meetings in a wide variety of organizations, I decided the biggest waste of time in such meetings was 'either-or' debates. Every organization seemed to have its own version. For some, it was 'Should we grow organically or by acquisition?' For others, it was 'Should we centralize or decentralize?' or 'Should we structure our organization based on product, geography or customer type?'

Our culture, schooling and the very fabric of our grammar of thinking and talking is fundamentally dualistic. We only understand 'up' by opposing it to 'down', 'light' in contrast to 'dark' and 'good' in relation to 'bad'. This can lead to oppositional thinking and debate, where beliefs are right or wrong and where there are winners and losers. Even the word 'discussion' is like the words 'percussion' and 'concussion', with the sense of bashing each other over the head with our ideas and certainty!

This is not only played out in arguments between people but also in our own internal debates. Often when we are stuck in internal conflict, it is nearly always in dualistic oppositions, such as the following: 'Should I apply for a new job or stay in my current job?' and 'Should I challenge George or just accept his oppressive behaviour?' When these 'either-or' internal conflicts are brought to coaching, the coachee has usually gone round and round their two limiting choices several times already. Therefore, being coached in weighing up these two limiting choices is rarely, if ever, helpful.

Polarity thinking leads to either-or debates and often to competitive opposition. If either pole wins, there is a loser. This may take the form of someone, or some team, feeling resentful, not heard and less cooperative. Or it may lead to 'sub-optimizing' and privileging one part of a larger process or system, at the cost of other necessary parts, and this in turn creates wider systemic degradation. Or it may lead to gaining short-term benefits, while ignoring long-term costs, or 'externalizing' the costs beyond the boundaries of the organization.

Margaret Heffernan (2014) asks us to respond to leaders who say they have cut costs by asking 'Where have you moved the costs to?' In the late 20th century, I worked with many companies who were growing their profits by 'off-shoring' their production, support functions or call centres to countries with lower employment costs and less demanding employment laws, health and safety regulations and ecological safeguards. Even now, we point accusingly at the carbon emissions of China or India, without acknowledging that much of this is created in producing the cheap clothes, toys and manufactured goods that we in the West crave and enjoy.

The four laws of 'either-or'

Through my work with organizations, teams and individuals stuck in 'either-or' debates and conflicts, and inspired by writers such as Hampden-Turner (1990) and Senge (1990, 2008), I created what I call the 'laws of either-or'.

- **Law one:** If you are having the same 'either-or' debate for the third time, you are almost certainly asking the wrong question.
- **Law two:** Both solutions are inadequate and incomplete and likely to sub-optimize one part of the system at the cost of the wider system. Or as Peter Senge (1990) pointed out, simple solutions get us out of one problem but lead back into the next one.
- **Law three:** Each solution represents important systemic needs that must be addressed in order to move forward; but as yet, we have not found a way of connecting, these currently disconnected, needs.
- **Law four:** The way forward is not a compromise between the two opposing 'either-or' solutions, for that would in effect combine two wrong solutions. Rather, what is needed is to collectively find a creative third position that transcends the limited frame of thinking from which the 'either-or' debate emerged.

To do this, we need to listen carefully to the needs represented by both parties and behind each proposed limited solution while at the same time pointing out that both their solutions are inadequate and incomplete. The only way forward is to find a new solution that has not yet been conceived, a new way forward that meets all the needs that are currently disconnected and polarized.

Often to do this, as a leader or a coach, we need to stop the conversation being dominated by the two or more protagonists and mobilize the bystanders, who are sitting as an audience, watching the cerebral wrestlers in the ring. Then we need to reframe the greater collective challenge in a way that contains, but goes beyond, the two or more proposed approaches. Once everyone has bought into the bigger challenge, then a number of methods can be used to engage the whole group in generative dialogue, which we will now explore.

Generative dialogue

Dialogue comes from the Greek words '*logos*' meaning 'knowing' and '*dia*' meaning 'emerging between two places': between two people or two perspectives, creating a third way of knowing and being. Generative dialogue gives birth to new, emergent thinking, beyond the previous thoughts and beliefs of those taking part. Bohm, after a Nobel Prize–winning career in nuclear physics, decided that the most urgent challenge was to shift human consciousness. He decided that to do this, we need a new form of conversational engagement, beyond debate and discussion – a form of 'dialogue' (Bohm, 1994, 1996) where we can take time more fully to empathize and perceive the viewpoint of each other and, from this mutual understanding, interweave new collective thinking. Others (Issacs, 1999; Scharmer, 2007, 2013) and myself (Hawkins, 2001, 2005, 2021a, 2022) have developed Bohm's practices into the worlds of organizations, teams, leadership and coaching.

Facilitating individual internal generative dialogue

Many years ago, when I still worked as a psychotherapist, I was working with a young man who each week would repeatedly explore whether he should stay with his wife or leave her and search for 'the woman of his dreams'. Eventually, with the help of supervision, I realized that this was a classic 'either-or'. To stay with his wife and be constantly dissatisfied and thinking of other women was not going to create contentment or a healthy marriage. To leave and go searching for an ideal relationship, without learning the lessons from this relationship, was likely to lead to repeating the pattern with a new partner. Neither of these opposing options was likely to work for him.

After reflecting this back to him, he started to explore what he had to change about himself, rather than expecting a partner to bring him happiness. He began to have more honest conversations with his wife and listen to what was missing, for them both, in their relationship.

Facilitating team generative dialogue

One of the most effective methods I have developed and used many times with senior leadership teams is what I have named 'collective build' – a method for co-creating a richer way forward than the sum of every individual's ideas (which I describe in detail in Hawkins, 2021a: 114–116; 371–372). In this approach, we ask everyone to do their own individual thinking of how to generate a third option by providing a seed sentence for everyone to complete by themselves, in just 3–5 bullet-points. Then collectively we co-create a new greater possible ways forward by building on individual suggestions and the team fleshing these out and building on them.

For teams and organizations to thrive, the systemic team coaching, whether by a leader or a coach, needs to enable generative dialogues, both within and between teams and between organizations and their key stakeholders, so that we recognize that every stakeholder is not just a competing demand but a potential partner, with whom we can create a 'win-win-win' relationship. We will explore this further later when we explore triangulated thinking.

The curse of dualism

Opposites and polarities are central to creative life and part of bringing different perspectives together to create a richer integrated picture. Blake (1968b) wrote in *The Marriage of Heaven and Hell*, 'Without Contraries no progression'; and Bateson (1972) always emphasized that we need difference – for communication, for relating and for evolution. The poet and writer Octavio Paz (1995: 274) wrote: 'We are the theatre of the embrace of opposites and of their dissolution'.

To embrace the opposites and dissolve them into a richer mixture, we most often try and combine the two opposing poles, as in 'both-and' thinking, or we search for a midpoint between them, which is nearly always a false compromise.

We need to realize that *conflict is a symptom of a connection not yet made – a separation seeking union.* To transcend the opposites, the contraries and polarities, we must embrace them fully and then engage with the tension they create between them. We need to do this in order to find the true, sacred marriage, the '*hieros gamos*' that holds their difference yet also brings them together to give birth to a transcendent third – a third that neither could have produced without each other or their relationship. As McGilchrist (2021: 833) points out, we need to find a transcendent third position that moves beyond both 'either-or' and 'both-and' – a third that moves beyond 'duality and non-duality'.

Our whole collective modernist culture is plagued by the curse of fixed dualisms. As we saw in Chapter 2, our culture, from the time of the scientific revolution, from the 15th to the 17th century, and the writings of Bacon, Descartes, Hobbes and Newton, has taught us to think in oppositional dualities. This book is one of a number of attempts to find our way out of the imprisonment they create.

Andreas Weber (2019) shows the parallels between the English 17th and 18th enclosures of common land and the enclosing of our common sense of experience within the rationalized concepts of the so-called Enlightenment. We will now try and unpick the locks of these mental dualistic chains.

Culture versus nature

The most pernicious of all these dualisms is the separating out of the human and more-than-human world, ascribing consciousness and culture to the human domain and seeing the world of nature as unconscious and 'other'. This leads to seeing nature as a 'resource' for the utility of human consumption, exploitation and a dumping ground for that we no longer need or want. Even today, wellbeing and quality of life, progress and benefit are almost entirely measured within the human domain, and the resulting costs to other life and wider nature are ignored.

Winnicott (1964, 1965), the great child psychoanalyst, said we should not talk about a young baby as a separate entity, but we should talk about the nursing dyad and the triad of Baby, Mother and Father (or other supporting adult) as a baby cannot survive alone. This concept can be expanded to humans as a species, for we, too, cannot survive separate from the wider nature that provides the air we breathe, the fluid we drink and the food we eat. There is no such thing as humanity, only 'eco-humanity', and no such thing as the self, only the 'eco-self'.

Rational thinking versus irrational feeling

In the wake of the scientific revolution, rational thinking became highly prized, and feeling, imagination and intuition became relegated and even despised. Hutchins and Storm (2019: 8) draw a parallel between the scientific revolution and the 'witch trials' that lasted from 1485 for 300 years in Europe and America, torturing and killing thousands (mostly women) and the ethnic cleansing of indigenous peoples during European colonization. Even today, I hear leaders say to team members, 'Don't be so irrational' and 'Where is the evidence?' – wanting to solve the technical problem rather than collectively and imaginatively inquiring into what is needed to create benefit for all parties.

Objective-subjective

Along with the thinking-feeling split came the dualism of the objective and subjective experience. 'Objective' became what can be studied by the empirical scientific method, the material world of objects, the quantifiable, the predictable and testable. Everything else became subjective opinions, feelings and conjecture. But as Weber (2019) points out, everything we know, we know through our subjective experience and our senses; and quantum physics and more recent biology have recognized that even in the most controlled scientific inquiry, the researcher affects what they are researching. Once we recognize this, then this dualism becomes unchained.

This does not need to lead us into an extreme post-modern world of relativism. We can create new criteria for validity (Heron, 1988; Heron and Reason, 2001), including that which has been explored from multiple different perspectives, over time, and which 'rings true' for those beyond our local collective group-think. Indeed, Weber (2019), an academic who has deeply studied both biology and poetry, talks helpfully about 'poetic objectivity' alongside 'scientific subjectivity'.

Parts-wholes

Another imprisoning dualism that has been very prevalent in modern systems thinking is the separation of parts and wholes. We can blithely talk about 'the system' as though it is a fixed, larger object comprised of smaller objects still caught in a Newtonian world of building blocks. In eco-systemic thinking, however, we recognize that every whole is a part of, and nested in, larger systems. We also recognize that the whole only has life through the ever-changing relational dynamics, both within itself and between itself and the systemic levels it is itself, nested within.

The holographic principle also shows how the whole is embedded in the parts. Your 'self' cannot be separated from the physical constituents of your physical being, your actions, your feelings, your thoughts – the ever-changing, entangled meshwork (Ingold, 2011, 2015; Weber, 2019: 4) you are entwined within. The organization does not exist separate from the many functions it fulfils and the dynamic relationships of all its various stakeholders. It is a complex, living, dynamic process, more than it is a thing; and like a river, you can never enter the same organization twice, for it is in constant flux.

There are many more dualisms sewn through our language and ways of perceiving and conceiving the world, many of which I have addressed or touched on in other parts of this book: such as inner and outer (see Chapters 3 and 5), prose and poetry (see next chapter), us and them (chapter 4), theism and atheism, theoretical and practical.

Seeing the relational as primary and objects as secondary

The new leader and the new coach need both to liberate their thinking from the dualistic inheritance that permeated their schooling and development and also to develop a new way of perceiving, thinking and relating in the world. Once again, Beauty can be our guide, for one of the primary disciplines in this new perceiving is to see the Beauty of the 'space between' – the relational spaces out of which relata and objects emerge and are born.

In modernity, we were taught to see objects as primary and relationships as secondary and created by objects. We see relationships as being formed by humans and other animals. To see relationships as primary requires a major shift in our ways of perceiving the world, a metanoia in our epistemology. But as McGilchrist (2021) has shown, our right-hemisphere brain, supported by the heart, can naturally perceive this way if we fully re-embrace it. We need to fall in love with the spaces between, the silence between the notes, the liminal moments between activity, the feel between the words

In 2019, I travelled to teach in Japan but returned having learnt so much more than the teachings I took with me. Japan is a culture where Beauty, rather than being locked away in art galleries and museums, is an integral aspect of everyday life. From the immaculately dressed train ticket collector, wearing white gloves, who bows deeply on entering and leaving every carriage, to the dance of the vegetable cutter, preparing the food they will shortly serve you. From the exquisite garden design, with trees pruned to enhance the beauty of the pattern between the branches – trees that have often been planted near water so that the tree and its reflection are constantly in dialogue one with the other.

I was taken by the Japanese concept of *Ma,* which can be literally translated as 'gap', 'space', 'pause' or 'the space between two structural parts'. The term is used in Japanese gardening, music and dance. It can also be applied to the 'pause' in work created by the coaching session and to the space between the leader and those who they lead, the coach and coachee – a space which, if held appropriately, allows the 'space for grace', attending to the third that is implicit in every dyad.

While sitting in a Buddhist garden in Kyoto, I wrote:

Ma (間)

The space between
Creates the frame,
To see the heavens
Peeping through.
So we can realise
We are three
Not Two.

To see the world relationally, we no longer see the relationship as the product of the relata (those relating) but an active creative force in its own right. A marriage, or life partnership, does not just consist of two people but also the relationship – which is not just the space between them but has a life of its own and changes the partners as much, if not more, than the partners create the relationship.

Triangulated thinking and doing

To move fully beyond dualistic thinking, many spiritual teachers suggest we need to experience the 'oneness of being'; and while recognizing that this may be the core to true enlightenment, for most of us, the way out of dualism is to move from twofold thinking to threefold, or what I term 'triangulated thinking'.

In working with teams, we traditionally view the team as creating itself 'auto-poietically', but in Hawkins (2021a, 2021b), I show how it is the purpose of the team that creates the team, not the team that creates its purpose. The purpose precedes the team and is the 'why' the team has been created.

In counselling couples, I learnt there are always three 'clients' – the two partners and the relationship – and the relationship was core.

Creativity and innovation require 'threes' – three essential aspects or forces to be present. A play requires a minimum of a playwright, an actor and an audience. The playwright creates a text that, when the actors start performing, becomes a script; but it only becomes a play when the audience is also present. Anyone who has ever acted knows that every performance of a play is different every night and emerges from the dynamic interaction of the playwright's imagination, the actors' performance and the audience's response. A work of art requires an artist, a medium – such as paints and a canvas or a block of marble – and a viewer. A great meal involves tasty and nutritious fresh ingredients; a cook who can combine the flavours, aromas and appearance into a whole that is deliciously more than the sum of its parts; and guests who not only savour the food but also bring conviviality, which turns the meal into a memorable communion.

A dance requires dancers, music and choreography. If we just focus on the two people dancing, we see the dancers, not the dance. If we readjust our focus to look at the space they create together, a greater Beauty emerges. Only when we can simultaneously hear, see and feel the dancers, the dancing, the music and the dance narrative can we be fully moved by, and internally move with, the total conjoined, embodied experience.

A business, at a minimum, requires a product or service, a producer or service provider and a customer. It also requires a community and an ecology in which the business can happen. Interestingly, the investors are less essential, and many businesses throughout history have flourished and continue to flourish without investors. It was only with the coming of international colonization and trade, and large-scale, carbon-based industry and railways, that business required up-front capital investment, which grew quickly towards the apotheosis of capitalism in neoliberal market economics that saw the sole purpose of business as being to deliver ever-increasing profits to the investor (Friedman, 1962). The investor is an enabler of large-scale, long-term business but not one of the primary stakeholders.

Threefold Beauty

We need to discover how Beauty is always of a threefold nature – a concept beautifully articulated by the poet and philosopher François Cheng (2009: 105):

> beauty is precisely of a threefold nature . . . true beauty – beauty that occurs and is revealed, that just suddenly appears to touch the soul of the one who perceives it – results from the encounter between two beings or between the human spirit and the living universe. And the work of beauty, is always arising from a 'between', is a third thing that, springing from the interaction of the two, allows the two to surpass themselves. If there is transcendence, it lies in the surpassing.

Threefold Beauty is at the core of giving birth and evolution. Birth, both of a physical organism or a new feeling or meaning, arrives where two elements give birth to the fresh, spontaneous emergence of a third element, which neither could have created without the other or without the unique quality of their relationship.

We are all born out of a relationship, and everything that is, is created from a relationship.

Goodenough (1998: 30), Professor of Cell Biology at Washington University, shows how this 'emergence' is fundamental to evolution and how through emergence, 'life does generate something-more-from-nothing-but, over and over again'. But our grammar reduces creation to a linear cause-and-effect process, where 'a subject' is doing and creating 'an object'. In history, we are mistaught how the great inventors, artists, writers and politicians supposedly gave birth by themselves to something new. In military history and neo-Darwinian evolution, we are taught the dangerous misunderstanding that life is a perpetual battle for survival, with winners and losers: 'a war of all against all' (Hobbes, 2010).

We misread Spencer's phrase that he attributed to Darwin, the 'survival of the fittest', as meaning that the strongest win out and the 'winner takes all'. But Darwin was describing the evolutionary relationship and interplay between a species and its ecological niche and how they 'fit' together and co-evolve in dynamic relationship with each other, together giving birth to the new (see Chapter 6).

All evolution is co-evolution; separate organisms come together not to become a composite of both, 50% of one and 50% of the other, but a totally new and unpredictable being. Goodenough (1998: 121) reminds us how 'Parents give half of their genetic endowment [to their offspring] but end up with a stranger'. Each child is unique, neither a 50-50 compromise of the parents nor a sum of both. The genetic deck of cards is shuffled in every birth, creating a new form that has never before been conceived. Evolution is always through co-creation, evolving new forms, new life, particularizing in new ways, emergence appearing at the threshold.

Eco-systemic perspectives help us understand that Beauty also is co-created not just between organisms of the same or different species but also between different systemic levels. There is a Beauty co-created in the flourishing between a team member and a team, between a family and a family member and between a species and its environmental niche. There are interlacing cycles of co-creation.

In Chapter 9, I described how on my small hobby farm, I watch the sheep in winter as they nibble down the grass to its shortest possible length and how this gives the beautiful display of wild flowers a head start in spring, a rich mixed diet for the cattle in summer and enough hay to be cut for their winter food. The animal excrement feeds the soil, the soil feeds the grassland and the grassland feeds the animals. The geology, the flora and fauna, the insects and animals (including ourselves), the seasons and the wider ecological cycles live in an interlaced meshwork of beautiful interconnection.

All wellbeing is dynamic. Wellbeing cannot be sustained within one bounded system: it requires a healthy interchange and relationship between the system and both the systems within in it and with the wider systems it is nested within. For an individual to thrive, they need a healthy reciprocal relationship with their family. In turn, the family needs a healthy reciprocal relationship with their community and the community with their ecology. But as I indicated earlier, for the ecology to flourish, it needs to be in service of the flourishing of all its biodiverse constituents. The wellbeing lies in the web of connections, not in the parts or the whole.

The wisdom tradition of the law of three

In many religions and philosophies, over millennia, there has been a focus on the three, for whereas two creates opposition and four creates fixed stability, such as in a four-cornered building, three is the basis of all creativity.

It can be found in the Indian *Sankhya* philosophy triad of *Sattvas-Rajas-Tamas*, necessary for overcoming the dualism of matter and soul and *neti-neti*, 'neither this nor that'. It can also be found in the Socratic dialogues of ancient Greece and in Hegelian dialectics. In Taoism, there is the interplay between *yang* (active force), *yin* (receptive force) and *Dao* (the connecting flow). In Egyptian mythology, we are given the family trinity of Father Osiris, Mother Isis and Son Horus. In Christianity, there is the Trinity of God – the transcendent Father, Jesus the incarnate Son and the Holy Spirit – connecting the transcendent and the immanent.

Gurdjieff drew on the perennial philosophical and gnostic teaching, going as far back as Pythagoras and beyond, to teach how the 'law of three' is central to creation and of the trinity of matter, energy and meaning (Ouspensky, 1957; Bennet, 1969; Nicholl, 1984).

> Every manifestation in the Universe is a result of the combination of three forces. . . . The three forces are only creative at the point of their conjunction and, here, a manifestation, a creation, an event takes place, but not otherwise.
> (Nichol, 1984: 108–109)

David Bohm (1987, 1989), the nuclear scientist, philosopher and writer, also suggested that life is created from the interplay of matter, energy and information; and Andreas Weber (2017, 2019), the biologist and philosopher, shows how matter and meaning always co-arise.

Another approach to this transcendence of the dualistic world can be found in Carl Jung, who became fascinated by the concept of '*Coincendentia Oppositorum*' – the coming-together of opposites in a new transcendent form. McGilchrist (2021, Chapter 20) explores this concept at depth, from the Greek philosophers, through great mediaeval mystics such as Nicholas of Cusa, to modern scientists. He quotes Bond (1997: 21):

> the coincidence of opposites provides a method that resolves contradictions without violating the integrity of the contrary elements and without diminishing the reality or the force of their contradiction. It is not a question . . . of forcing harmony by synthesising resistant parties.

But through their creative difference, together, they give birth to the new.

From philosophy to living leadership that can integrate and orchestrate

An increasing number of writers are calling for new types of leadership, from the various pioneers of 'vertical development' (Graves, 1970; Kegan, 1982; Torbert, 2004; Petrie, 2014; Braks, 2021), those arguing for 'regenerative leadership' (Hutchins and Storm, 2019; Hutchins, 2022) and those calling for more ethical leadership and leadership that is more collective and transformative (Curry, 2019; Hawkins, 2017a, 2021a, 2022).

Bill Torbert (2004) has shown that there is an increasing need for leaders who can embrace paradox and work with more than one reality in play at the same time. He and his associates (Rooke and Torbert, 2005; Rooke, 2021), researching the dominant frame of thinking of leaders in organizations in America and Europe, found that only a small percentage come from what Torbert terms the 'redefining' and 'transforming' levels. When individuals have achieved these levels of development, they are much more comfortable with engaging with contradictory truths and realities and understanding each within their own frame of reference. This makes them more able to work with conflict, without taking sides. Instead, they focus on finding a higher-order resolution.

Not all successful managers need to come from this level of development. However, in working with Torbert's framework, I have come to the conclusion that matrixed organizations with complex reporting lines, or organizations that have a complexity of stakeholders, partnerships or alliances, need to have some leaders who can operate from this level. I also conclude that, for an organizational transformation process that shifts not only the strategy but also the culture of an organization, leaders are required who can individually and collectively transcend emerging polarities and co-create new thinking live in the moment.

Watching such leaders in action, we can observe them connect what is being talked about in the future with what is happening in the room right now. We hear them translate one person's world-view to make it understandable to others who come from very different frames of reference. We see them inquiring into and exploring new propositions rather than debating from a fixed, oppositional position. We can observe the leader using paradox, metaphor and humour to make unusual connections and shift people's mindsets and emotions.

Steven Sample (2003) recommends that leaders need to develop 'grey thinking' – the ability to understand the subtle shades of possibility in an issue rather than just the polarized opposites. Others argue for replacing 'either-or' thinking with 'both-and' thinking. Both are partially helpful, but I believe they can still leave us caught in dualistic thinking. To go further, we need to embrace the opposites, holding the creative tension until a new possibility emerges from their relationship, transcending the dualistic frame. Nasrudin, the Sufi wise fool, once pointed out that to understand 'one and one equals two', you need to understand not only the nature of the numbers but also the nature of 'and' (Hawkins, 2005), the space between.

The good or 'righteous' leader we explored in Chapter 7 does not stand rigid at a point of compromise between the opposites. Rather, they embrace both poles and the dance in the space between them and find how the two can be truly integrated at a higher level. They demonstrate the qualities of Torbert's (2004) 'transformative leader' – one able to combine different world-views and arguments and achieve a new synthesis.

On not taking sides

In arguments, we can so easily take the side of our previous belief and, as the argument progresses, become more attached to winning the argument than to discovering some new learning.

When coaching, we can easily be drawn into taking the side of the coachee, as they tell us about their toxic boss, impossible team member, difficult colleague, demanding customer and so on. In doing this, we are not truly taking the side of the coachee but rather, of their current fixed story, which is often holding them back from finding new ways of responding to the world around them. We all become attached to our stories; they become habituated and become the lenses through which we see the world. The lenses can become so thick and opaque that little new light gets through, and we only see the story we are telling ourselves.

As coaches and leaders, we learn to develop empathy for our coachees and our direct reports, which is essential to really understand another person's reality. But it can tip over into seeing the other person's world through the lenses of their fixed stories – seeing the ogre of a boss, the impossible team member and the horrible customer who nobody could possibly deal with!

The role of the wise leader and coach is to develop 'wide-angled empathy and compassion' (Hawkins and Turner, 2020) – that is, for every person they are involved with, directly or indirectly – and as much empathy and compassion for every person, group, system and organization in the stories you are told, as for the storyteller.

Being and non-being giving birth to becoming

In *Tao Te Ching*, it is said that 'being and non-being produce each other'. As we discover more and more of the history of the ever-expanding universe we inhabit, we learn more about the interplay between energy and matter, matter and dark matter, that which is in potential and that which has manifested into perceivable form. With our left-hemisphere, 'scientific' mind, we equate what is living with what has temporarily manifested into some material form, things that can be measured and quantified. The fundamental materialist tells us that these are the only things that exist.

But what we can measure we have to freeze in position in order to measure it. Then the wave becomes a particle; the ever-flowing, changing life-form becomes static. NASA (2023) tells us:

roughly 68% of the universe is dark energy. Dark matter makes up about 27%. The rest – everything on Earth, everything ever observed with all of our instruments, all normal matter – adds up to less than 5% of the universe.

Dark matter is not a vacuum but an essential element, actively creating and affecting that which is manifest, then being and non-being, like *yang* and *yin,* are forever co-creating each other, and one cannot be understood without the other.

If being and non-being, as conceptual entities, give birth, their offspring, their third, is 'becoming'. Before we became incarnate in this world, we were 'potentia', non-being. We became embodied, incarnate beings with flesh and blood, and we will all, at some time in the future, become non-being again, our transient earthly form dissolving back into the elements that will be reabsorbed into the wider Earth and, eventually, the cosmos. But we will we never stop being part of becoming, of the eternal flow of creation and emergence.

Beauty arises in the flow of this dance of perpetual becoming – being emerging out of non-being, the manifest from potential and then dissolving its separateness.

Conclusion

The wise leader and the wise coach play in the 'theatre of opposites'. They become sensitive to the time when the polarized opponents first appear on stage and they avoid taking sides. They listen for the deeper truth that connects them and for the deeper disconnection that creates their separation. Only then do they emerge from the wings of the stage and become the *animateur*, of the '*mise en scène*', the one that helps the new transcendent third emerge.

The work of the coach or leader does not remove the differences; rather, it connects their diversity in a new way. To do this work, we can draw on many of the approaches outlined not only in this chapter but also in the previous two chapters. We need to remember that the transcending of opposites is never completed with the logical, atomizing, left-hemisphere neo-cortex alone. It requires the metaphorical, poetic pattern-recognition of the right hemisphere and a connecting from the heart. In the next chapter, we will discover how to do this work poetically. The leader needs to be more interested in discovering the new that is needed than winning an argument rooted in yesterday's beliefs.

So we arrive at a place where these two sayings of great mystics are both true:

> When opposites exists the Buddha Mind is lost.
> (Zen patriarch Dogen, as quoted by John Crook, personal communication).

And where Mevlana Rumi invites us to meet him in the field that is beyond duality and ideas of wrong and right, good and bad.

Chapter 14

Co-creating Beauty

Inter-poiesis in coaching
and leadership

Introduction

All leadership and coaching take place in and through a discourse between two
or more people. Different discourses require different forms of language. The
language of empirical science is suitable for discourse about the external material world, but for an exploration of the interiority of lived experience, a more
poetic dialogue is required. In discovering new insight or evolving new thinking,
the new rarely, if ever, arrives in fully-formed, constructed sentences, but in felt
awareness, images, analogies, metaphors and half sensings. In such tentative,
generative dialogues, whether they be in one-to-one or team meetings, the 'Difficulty lies not in finding the right words: the difficulty lies in there being no right
words, and so when we use words carefully we must always be both saying and
unsaying' (McGilchrist, 2021: 1226).

We have to search together for the right words and keep remaking them as
the new story and a new truth gradually takes shape, as echoed in the line: 'The
dance of renewal, the dance that made the world, was always danced here at the
edge of things, on the brink, on the foggy coast' (Le Guin, 1989).

I have created the word 'inter-poiesis', as the word 'poesis' means the process
of emergence of something that did not previously exist, and 'inter-poiesis' is,
therefore, the emergence of new thinking, feeling and sensing that emerges in
the space between people – a collective sense-making.

Auto-poiesis, as developed by Maturana and Varela (1980), speaks to how all
organisms, from cells to human beings, are self-creating, the autonomous aspect
of their nature. In contrast, onto-poiesis (Mathews, 2009 and 2021) focusses on
the co-creation between an organism or any living system and its wider ecology,
how the individual is created by its context and the context is changed by the
individuals within it.

Inter-poiesis is speaking to the dance of, and between, these two processes.
Individual development is always entwined with the ever-changing environmental context and the wider ecology. When, with the lens of modernism, we separate
the individual organism and their ecology, we draw a false separation. There is no

DOI: 10.4324/9781003349600-18

individual without an ecological biosphere that sustains them and no ecological biosphere without living organisms. There is no self, other than an eco-self.

My experience is that poetry is a more primary form of communication than prose, more closely connected with lived experience and the interplay of the senses. 'Poetry is not distorted prose. It is the reverse of that: prose is poetry that has been subjected to logic' (Bateson, quoted in Charlton, 2008: 106). Indeed, sometimes the song comes before the lyrics, the gesture before the verbal expression.

Through conversation, we find new responses to the fresh challenges that confront us in our work and lives, through con-versing, not con-speaking. Con-speaking, or serial speechifying, can quickly lead to separate individuals pitching their own contentions in opposition to each other, each asserting their perspective in ways that discount rather than conjoin with the perspectives of others. In conversation, the 'con' means with, and 'versus' comes from the Latin, originally meaning a turn of the plough; so perhaps we can think of conversing as unearthing new meaning together.

The process of leadership is fundamentally rooted in conversation, whether we think of Martin Luther King sharing a dream about civil rights and equality with his followers or a team leader sharing a challenge that they need the team to rally behind. However, very often, conversations can stay at the level of exchanging pre-cooked thoughts. So often in team meetings you tell me what you have been doing and thinking, and I respond by telling you what I have been doing. Next, you tell me your problem, I offer a solution, then you tell me why it will not work. Coaching and leadership are, at heart, a conversation that moves beyond what is currently known, to discover what is possible and new. Effective leadership happens in collective conversations, where all are contributing to the way forward.

We can also become trapped in the stories we tell ourselves and that we repeat to others. Our narratives imprison our ways of thinking, being and doing. Our past culture pervades our language and our stories and inhibits the new emerging.

So often, leadership meetings and coaching become settings for us to further attach ourselves to our frequently repeated narratives. Meetings, conferences and coaching can also become filled up with people 'reporting back' their narrative of what happened, followed by questions from others, which lead the storyteller to provide more layers and detail to the story that is already fixed and framed in their mind.

David Bohm (1996) wrote beautifully about the need for dialogue, where we move from exchanging 'thoughts' to 'thinking together' to where we can discover new meaning between us, which neither of us possessed before we came together. For this, we do not need leaders and consultants who provide answers or coaches who just ask questions, no matter how insightful the answers or questions might be. Instead, we need leaders and coaches who can enter a dialogical conversation as a collaborative inquiry.

We need coaches who help the coachee not to tell well-worn stories about themselves and their life and their problems but rather, coaches who walk with the coachee to the learning edge, where they can discover what is emerging in their life that is new and challenging, and in so doing, they can find a new response. This takes the coachee to the place where neither they nor the leader or coach have an answer, but they are both pregnant with the joint need to find perhaps not an answer but a fresh, spontaneous response.

The work of the coach, mentor or leader is not just to ask questions in order to understand more about the story already constructed nor to know better or to know first and provide answers. This is often done to avoid the pain of staying with the unresolved stuckness. The work, instead, is humbly to walk alongside the other on this foggy shore of unknowing.

All creative change happens at the learning edge 'on the brink of the foggy coast', where the *terra firma* of knowing ends and we face the mists of unknowing. Earlier, the 'learning edge' was defined as where neither coach nor coachee, leader nor followers, have an answer but where we know the question that life is requiring us to address.

The role of coaching is to move beyond words to direct experience, to the place where old words, concepts and narratives fall away – where we abandon our fixed stories and beliefs, and we experience fresh, new life coming into being and into our being. We need to explore our direct experience: according to McGee (1998: 98) that 'which is never adequately communicable in words is the only knowledge we ever fully have. That is our one and only true, unadulterated, direct and immediate form of knowledge of the world, wholly possessed, uniquely ours'. McGee adds, 'People who are rich in that are rich in lived life'.

Direct experience:

is what we know (kennen) better than anything at all, and yet know (Wissen) least of all about. It is therefore difficult to discuss, since neither language nor reason are well adapted to it. Language is already at a remove from direct experience'.

(McGilchrist, 2021: 1918)

The ways we share our direct experience are mainly non-verbal, though our gestures, looks, stance and movement and through the music of our voice – its tempo, pitch, tone, timbre, rhythm. Sometimes we unconsciously communicate our direct experience by doing to the other what has been done to us so they receive an inkling of what it feels like to be in our shoes.

At the borders of the non-verbal and verbal is poiesis: where language is not ordered in conceptual grammar but evocative rather than explanative, a sensing more than a describing. This is where the creative work happens – exploration that leads to co-discovery and co-creation. This work is not done through analytic thinking or problem-solving but through engaging the intuition and imaginal realms, the bodily sensing from the limbic and amygdala parts of the brain and the knowing of the heart and guts. Poetry is the closest language to direct experience, for in its fluidity, its rhythms and sounds, its metaphors and images, it echoes the rich, ever-changing, inter-being life we all partake in.

As a leader or coach, to find the poetic space, we need to see with peripheral vision and with the eyes of the heart. Weber (2017: 199) describes poetic seeing as seeing with the whole body: 'If I look properly, I do not see the outside of beings, but their aliveness and how it is organized around them'. He goes on to describe:

> the poetic space from which all of reality derives its power, a space beyond all division, between the expression of a body and that which exists as an existential gesture in space. The flesh of the world – it is simultaneously body and feeling. It is the breathing skirmish of poetic relations.
>
> (Weber, 2017: 199)

Poetry's purpose, according to Weber (2017: 203), 'is not to describe or analyse but to re-enliven'. He continues by encouraging his readers to 'poetic action', which is achieved by 'letting yourself be inspired to resonance by pure aliveness – not so that you can stockpile pleasing goods, but so you can produce aliveness yourself'.

It is our work as leaders and coaches to sense the aliveness, often buried in the work – to resonate with it, nurture it and let it develop and flourish. The coach also needs to respond from these realms – not sitting and making analytic sense of their coachee's creative imaginings, with their left-hemisphere neo-cortex brain, but responding to image, metaphor and story with image, metaphor and story. Listening not just with their ears but also with the resonance of their whole body and responding from their whole being, with tentative language both from and to the right hemisphere – a language beyond questions and answers, a language of imaginative, collaborative inquiry and conversational inter-poiesis.

Many years ago, my colleagues Peter Reason and Judi Marshall and I explored how to respond to story with story in a way that allowed the deeper patterns and archetypes to emerge from the specific event (Reason and Hawkins, 1988). We were influenced by the writings and trainings of the archetypal and imaginal Jungian psychotherapist James Hillman, who taught us how to follow the images and their connections and trust them more than the storyteller.

By far, the majority of coaching interventions engage the analytical problem-solving brain of the coachee – the left-hemisphere neo-cortex. This is often where the fixed and limiting beliefs of the coachee are located. It is also the part of the human brain that has the narrowest perspective and can often limit creativity and keep the coachee stuck. If we are to engage other parts of the brain, we need different languages.

Poetry bypasses the left-hemisphere neo-cortex and speaks to the other aspects of personal knowing, by engaging the imaginal and intuitive aspects of mind. At the same time, the poetry harmonies of rhythm and sound speak to the limbic brain and the resonances in the heart and gut.

One of my favourite poets, T. S. Eliot (1929), wrote about how poetry can bypass our analytic understanding and our fixed knowing: 'Poetry, like music, should communicate before it is understood'.

The art of inter-poiesis

In Chapters 11 and 12, I described the art of leadership and of coaching when it is informed by Beauty. Here, I will take this further, by looking at how both arts can be further refined by the art of inter-poiesis and by working poetically. To summarize inter-poiesis:

- It is built on a foundation of eco-systemic awareness (see Chapter 4) that every organism is both self-creating (auto-poiesis) and evolving in dynamic relationship to all the systemic levels it is nested within (onto-poiesis), which include their family, team, organization, community, culture, species, eco-logical niche and wider ecology – a multi-level cosmos.
- Inter-poiesis is the relational field between an organism and its ecology, whereby both are co-creating each other in a meshwork of mutual becoming.
- Inter-poiesis is also happening in the relational field between organisms and fellow organisms. We don't just talk to each other; we also co-create each other. People we live with, work with and converse with, all leave a trace within us and in part make us who we are; as simultaneously we make them, in part, who they are.
- These two categories of auto- and onto-poiesis are a useful but, ultimately, a false separation, as both processes flow through and co-create each other. As I have mentioned several times in this book, there is no self, separate from the ecology, only an eco-self. There is also no ecology without self-creating organisms and their relationships within it.
- Evolution is a continual inter-poiesis of unfolding, a birthing of the totally new, birthed out of relationships – a trinity of becoming, where two or more organisms or systemic levels give birth to new creation and all three elements become changed.
- Leadership is a trinity, comprising a leader, follower and shared purpose, which is continually giving birth to a new organization, with new prod-ucts and services, new employees and stakeholders, new relationships and connections. The new is also co-created in the trinity of the organization: self-creating auto-poietically, onto-poietically evolving in relationship to its changing context and inter-poietically through its meshwork of internal and external relationships.

- Coaching, at heart, is an inter-poiesis – where a coach and coachee, or team coach and team, give birth not to what either party wants but to what is necessary, needing to be born, within the wider ecological context. In this process, both or all parties are changed.
- All creative processes are best understood through triangulation, not dualistically (see Chapter 13).
- There is no statis, only a perpetual becoming.
- All change is embodied.
- In the same way that human babies thrive best when born out of a loving relationship, so the new is best birthed from a relational loving in both leadership and coaching.
- The language of loving and co-creation is by its very nature poetic.

So in this chapter, we will look at how to lead and coach more poetically, in ways that further liberate us from the mental prison (Chapter 2).

Starting with the right clue

In Chapter 3, we visited the story of Ariadne holding the clue of wool, which allowed Theseus to find his way out of the labyrinth. But it is important to start with the right type of wool. If our leadership or coaching relationships start by being imprisoned in a left-hemisphere, dualistic language of problems and solutions – right and wrong, linear causality – it is very hard to arrive at the learning edge or find the clues beyond the words.

In coaching others, as a leader or professional coach, this reorientation is simple but powerful. It involves moving away from asking the coachee what they want from coaching today – which immediately creates an answer where 'I want' is the dominant structure – to asking: 'What is the work we most need to focus on together today?' It involves moving away from a world in which 'I' is the centre and where I am driven by wants, personal acquiring, achieving and growing – away from an ego-centric, self-centred, left-hemisphere dominated world, which lies at the base of grasping, consuming and exploiting and builds into colonization, capitalism and the ecological destruction of the Anthropocene.

For some years, I have experimented with opening by asking: 'What is the work that your world needs us to be doing together today?' This begins to put the needs of the wider world more at the centre and see coaching as a collaborative endeavour in service of the wider ecology (see Hawkins in Whybrow et al., 2023). To go further, we might say: 'Let's discover together what needs to emerge in this joint space/time that we are sharing'. Here, discovery and emergence become primary; the invitation is to us both and to our relationship, to become more receptive and wait upon what needs to emerge.

In Chapter 12, we showed more poetic ways of starting a meeting, but we should avoid these becoming formulaic. At a recent international workshop

I was leading, where most participants were meeting for the first time, I thought long and hard about how we should start. I was tired of the ritualized way of going round introducing ourselves, which I had started to call 'creeping death'. I had spent too many years using 'icebreakers' that cut through the delicacy of first meetings. I was in search for something new.

I asked them to work in pairs with the question: 'Tell me about a moment in the last year when your heart was singing'. In the moment, I realized it was the wrong question. I went to the flipchart and crossed out 'tell me about' and wrote: 'Take me to a moment when your heart was singing' – no longer a question but an invitation to share a felt experience.

It creates a profound turning in the dialogue when the other person stops telling me about their life, instead bringing their life alive in the room; and when the other person stops facing me, we find ourselves shoulder-to-shoulder, facing and in service of all that their life and work serve. Now we are not facing each other, talking about the past or what is 'out there', but we are discovering together what is emergent in their life, and we are walking together to face what requires a new, and so far, undiscovered, response.

The challenge is to start every first and subsequent meeting with this open curiosity and a poetic language of the heart, rather than the questioning for understanding. A collaborative inquiry, which follows the clue poetically to where it takes us, means we can travel together and soon arrive at the foggy shoreline of the learning edge and stand side by side on the brink of our knowing and unknowing.

Unravelling the outdated story

However, even if we start out together on this co-discovery and co-inquiry, it is rarely long before we both fall back into old patterns and old stories. The longer we have been living in a habit or a story, the deeper it is engrooved and habituated within us. It starts to have a hold over us. The coachee tells me their much-repeated story, and I fall back into old habits of trying to help.

I remember when I was a psychotherapist and had a client for whom I was their sixth or seventh therapist. Over several sessions, I listened to the story of their past. It sounded like case notes written out and which smelled stale. I asked them how many times they had told this story. 'Oh, many, many times', they replied. I asked, 'In telling me, at the end of this long line of listeners, what do you most need me to hear?' They replied, 'How painful and distressing it has been for me'. 'I really hear and feel that pain and distress buried under this story', I responded, with as much empathy and compassion as I could embody. After a long silence where we held painful eye contact, I looked in front of us both and asked, 'I wonder how you would like to change that story in our time together'.

We need to arrive at the learning edge, unencumbered by our old stories and our old habits, with what Scharmer (Scharmer, 2007; Scharmer and Kaufer,

2013) describes as 'open mind, open heart and open will'. To do this, we need to become adept at catching our own old habits and interrupting them. We need to become skilled at gently helping to unravel the other's old story, so there is the space for something new to emerge.

Recently (Hawkins, 2023c), I have developed this into a deep and challenging practice we can do for ourselves, as well as with and for others.

Practice: from grumble to gratitude

1. Whenever a problem arrives in your life, or in another's story, reframe it not as a problem but as a challenge.
2. Locate the challenge not in a person, or a part or a system, but in a relationship or connection.
3. See the challenge as the latest generous lesson that life has sent you to take your learning and development to the next level.
4. Find the gratitude in your heart for being given this lesson, no matter how awful and shocking it may be at the time.

Liberating our lexicon

Our current languages are fundamentally ones of objectification and atomization. Jem Bendell, in his work on deep adaptation to the ecological and climate catastrophe (Bendell and Read, 2021), shows how this becomes a major block to the radical change needed. We are constrained in our thinking by a grammar and language that is inherently patriarchal, colonial and anthropocentric, inherited frames that pervade our language, mostly out-of-awareness or even out-of-consciousness.

In the practice earlier, I simply reframe 'problems' into 'challenges', which immediately releases a new attitude and feeling. To give another example, the word 'mission' – used so pervasively in leadership discourse – has its roots in military warfare and then grew out into colonization and evangelism. Even when we try and divorce it from its roots, it still carries the sense of what we want to achieve, a concern of how we can succeed, how can we become the number one in our organization or in our sector – the spirit of competition, conquest, conversion and empire.

I also remember working with a chocolate company, where they regularly talked about 'targeting their customers', which conjured up for me a very messy image of customers being shot at with chocolate! I asked them what desires in their customers drew them to buy their products. After some exploration, they realized they were in the 'gift' business and creating 'moments of pleasure'. 'How could you engage your stakeholders in ways that embody those two qualities?' I asked. Needless to say, many of their relationships with key buyers, as well as their marketing, changed from being product-based to featuring the beneficial value their product created in relationships: a grandparent arriving with the gift of chocolates for the grandchildren or the chocolate gift in a romantic liaison.

To create change in ourselves, our relationships and our societies, we need to find a new language of 'poetic activism', finding 'new forms of language and ways of interpreting the world' (Gergen, 2009: 12). As we have painfully discovered, we do not overcome old attitudes of colonialism, racism and sexism just by having more politically correct words. New language is not constructed but tentatively weaved and reweaved through inter-poiesis, in our inter-subjective dialogue. This language needs to be poetic – a language of feeling and sensibility, not of things and rationality. It should communicate through our embodied knowing before it is understood, not processed through our left-hemisphere neo-cortex but rather creating a feeling resonance.

> Anything truly unique cannot be expressed in left hemisphere's tool language. . . . Whatever is profound, personal, or sacred, if it is to be expressed in words, could be so expressed only in poetry, the language of the right hemisphere. In poetry language subverts its normal tendency to precision it becomes rich with ambiguity, with potential meaning again; and through the rifts created in the enclosing veil the light once more streams in.
>
> (McGilchrist, 2021: 867)

Modern quantum physics also points to this need for a tentative, poetic language. Niels Bohr, one of the founders, said in conversation with his fellow pioneer (Heisenberg, 1971):

> We must be clear that when it comes to atoms, language can be used only as in poetry. The poet, too, is not nearly so concerned with describing facts as with creating images and establishing mental connections.

Interweaving

So often, meetings between a leader and one of their team, or between a coach and a coachee, become agenda-driven, with atomized issues being addressed and worked on. Often, the bigger challenge lies not in the separate issues but in the interconnections between them or in an unrecognized pattern or bigger challenge of which they are just the symptoms.

Too many leaders and coaches are trained to believe that all coaching interventions are investigative questions, examining the particular statement and so they have a very limited palate of possible responses. Often in exploring an issue, situation or feeling, we fall back on asking complicated questions, which require the other to leave the flow of their own emerging sensing and thinking to try and understand our question. They stop their exploration and pause to work out what we are asking about and what sort of answer we might require.

What is required is other simple forms of responses that interweave between the coach and the coachee a fuller tapestry that help illuminate the connections both between external experiences and emotional responses, the exterior and internal realities and between different events and issues.

When coachees come to coaching and tell me they are not sure whether to work on issue a, b or c, I suggest we work on issue d, the pattern that connects a, b and c. We have to co-discover issue d.

Privileging the verb

In the white Western world, we have developed a language dominated by nouns and a dualistic Newtonian grammar of subjects acting on objects. Northern European languages have always been more noun-dominated than many other languages of the world. Chinese relies on verb forms more than does English, and in indigenous languages such as Navajo, expression is made more through verbs and gestures (see McGilchrist, 2021: 957).

Our reliance on nouns has become much more accentuated in modern Americanized English, with its tendency to nominalize verbs into nouns. In leadership meetings, we might start with a check-in, we make a plan, we are driven by an agenda, we arrive at a decision, we decide to action an item, and we end by asking, 'Do we have a rap?'

This nominalization of our language is both a symptom and a cause of the growing domination of left-hemisphere perception of the world around us – a world of separate and fixed objects, separated and classified into concepts. Through this way of perceiving, we lose our awareness of 'wholes' and stop realizing how no 'thing' exists alone, and we stop seeing the interconnections that join all that exists. For, as William James (1909: 261) argued, 'When you have broken the reality into concepts you can never reconstruct it in its wholeness'.

Bohm (1980: 29) asked, 'Is it not possible for the syntax and grammatical form of language to be changed, so as to give a basic role to the verb rather than the noun?' For many years, I have been playing with this very endeavour – to reorientate our syntax and grammatical forms so the verb becomes the more dominant. So instead of saying, 'I love the beauty of that tree', I could say, 'Love connects the tree and me in beauty'. Here, we have restored the reciprocal connection and flow between the two subjects – the tree and the I. Love and Beauty are the creative forces, and I am just participating in the process, not the prime subject doing.

To take another example: 'The sea flows in waves on to the beach'. Here, the waves are separate things interacting with a piece of geography, which I have categorized as 'beach'. It is also inaccurate to say the seas flows in waves, as flowing is a perpetual quality of the sea, of which waves are just one of the manifestations of the flowing, as are tides, currents and eddies. Let's reorientate the sentence: 'Flowing shapes the water and the beach'.

This process of privileging the verb can seem at first very overwrought, strange and clumsy. Yet if we continue to practice it, we can start to notice how it moves us from a world of separate things and linear causality to experience participating in inter-being, being part of what is continually in flow and yet emerging fresh in every moment. Gradually, our intelligence moves from IQ to We Q and AQ (collective and aesthetic intelligence) – from left-hemisphere, analytic cleverness, studying objects out there in the material world, to collaborative and participative poetic wisdom.

Theatre of poiesis – bringing in other voices

As coaches and coachees, we can widen the poetic exploration by bringing different voices into the coaching theatre. We can invite the coachee to occupy another space or sit in a different chair where they become their boss, colleague or employee or other significant figure in the narrative that is being explored. We can encourage the coachee deeper into taking the role with such suggestions as 'Show me how you would be sitting and breathing, your gestures and facial expression. Adopt the rhythm and tone of their voice, and express that person's perspective on the issues you have just recounted to me'.

The dramatis personae of this coaching theatre can go beyond significant individuals in the coachee's life. The coach can invite them to step into becoming the collective team and to speak from their collective voice or that of the organization or key groups of stakeholders. We can also invite in the voice and perspective of the wider ecology, the more-than-human world, to move beyond an anthropocentric language and conversation (see Whybrow et al., 2023; Hawkins, 2021a and 2022). Here is an example:

Karl: I have to present our ESG policy to the Board, but I don't think it goes far enough, in addressing our ecological impact.

Peter: Such as.

Karl: Our carbon footprint; pollution and transport impacts in our supply chain; how some of our food products feed obesity and the knock-on health costs.

Peter: (after further exploration of the issues mentioned by Karl): Now we have explored ways of further limiting the negative impacts of your organization, can we move to exploring the positive beneficial impacts, the wider ecology needs you to create?

Karl: Gosh – we haven't addressed those, and I haven't really thought about it.

Peter: Can you go and stand somewhere else in the room and become the ecology your children and grandchildren will inherit. Express as the ecology what you need organization x to do in 2023, to improve your health.

Suddenly, new perspectives, new vistas, opened up for Karl, which led to a very different report. Karl also came back and asked for some coaching on how he could experientially engage the Board, in an embodied and emotional way, that would open up new realization for them.

Changing perspectives

As in the earlier example, our coaching theatre can also space and time travel. In space shifting, we can invite the coachee to view the interaction they have just described from a third-person perspective – as a fly on the wall or as a radio commentator, watching the dance play out between the coachee and the other players (Boston and Ellis, 2019).

In time travel, we can go forward or back in time. One of the most challenging interventions I received when being coached happened when I was justifying what little I was doing to maintain my health by saying I was quite fit and rarely got ill. My coach invited me to step into the shoes of myself at 85 and, when in that role, to ask my 85-year-old self to comment on what they needed Peter to be doing at 65 so he would be relatively healthy at 85. This was a real wake-up call, by a simple shift in time perspective.

I often ask a team I am working with 'What might you regret in two years' time not having explored in this time we have together?' or 'What might come as a shock or surprise to this team in a few years' time, of which you already have an inkling?' These future-back prompts can help a team or an individual develop future foresight (Kryznaric, 2020).

Beyond categorization

Part of our left-hemisphere obsession with categorizing everything we come across has, in the last 100 years, been turned back on ourselves. To discover more about ourselves, we have turned from traditional forms of reflection, self-noticing, mindfulness and meditation to quasi-scientific oracles such as horoscopes, psychological labelling and creating questionnaires that, once they are scored, can allocate us to a box and explain away our idiosyncrasies.

Popular in leadership development and coaching are such frameworks as Hogan, Myers-Briggs and the 'Enneagram'. I had a coachee who told me 'they are' a Myers-Briggs INFP and an Enneagram 2! Psychological profiling, used in the right way, can be very useful and indeed has helped solve many crimes and murders. At best, it is a reflective mirror that can help us see some of the ways we currently show up in certain contexts in the world. However, we must beware of psychometric narcissism, in case we turn ourselves from a flesh-and-blood, constantly changing, living being into a fixture, represented as a number or letters on a page. It is part of the growing compulsion with our own reflection, wanting to turn ourselves and others into fixed and defined objects, to provide ourselves with an illusion of a knowable world and self we can control. We need to focus less on 'who we are' and more on what life is inviting us to 'become'.

Poetry bridging cultures

In 2017, I worked with the Board of a very large pharmaceutical company in Iran, which was still run by multiple members of a family. The Turkish consultants who brought me in asked me to also be one of the key speakers at a leadership event they were planning for the Board and top three levels of executives in Paris. I really liked the leaders in the company and also the consultants, so I readily said yes. Then I discovered that the three-day programme was all taught by white Westerners. I could not agree to being part of bringing very proud and cultured leaders to the West to be taught by people from much younger civilizations; it felt like cultural colonization.

I was told I could not pull out, as the programme was all agreed and published. I struggled through the night with my conflict and next day said to the organizers, 'I will only come if every morning, one-third of the participants stand together at the front on stage and each reads a piece of poetry or writing from their tradition which is close to their hearts, both in Farsi and then translated into English, while the others, and importantly the Western faculty, sit, listen and learn'. This transformed the event and the company's relationships, as Board members and senior- and middle-level executives stood side by side, each speaking poetically from their heart.

I have also encountered psychotherapists who, when working with refugees, would find or invite poems from the refugee's native country, which they would both read aloud. New seams of emotional connection opened up, and together, they would gently co-weave a new language of gestures, sounds and words that belonged neither to the country of origin or the host country.

Poetry inviting a poetic response

Writing poetry to oneself can be a healing process. It helps us find ways to give voice and expression to our embodied half-sensed experience. Sometimes, when someone shares deeply with me at the learning edge, a half-remembered poem will intuitively spring up within me. I was recently supervising and mentoring Johnny, who is the very successful leader of an international consultancy. I could feel, see and hear the weight of what he was carrying. I could see it in his shoulders and feel it in my own.

> 'I am carrying so much', Johnny said. 'I have my clients to hold, my staff to hold and also my family'.
>
> 'Who holds Johnny?' I gently asked.
>
> 'I don't know' was his anxious reply, with a hint of desperation, looking for holding he could not find.

I reached for a poem I had recently written to celebrate the first Sunday in Advent when, in the midst of darkness, we anticipate the coming of the light for which our soul is longing. Here is the poem (Hawkins, 2022):

The Candle of Hope

I saved my bees wax from the summer
knowing I would need light
when the darkness came.
That I might light a candle to remember
'In the midst of darkness cometh light'.
But I only could make one candle.
Then came the choice
Which niche or mihrab should I place it in?
In the political window advocating change,
In temple, mosque, church or synagogue
to worship the Icons of dead teachers,
or in faith in the human spirit,
the spirit that has wrecked carnage on its Mother Earth?

Or should I place my hope
in Nature to heal itself.
or in my heart to burn out all imperfections.
Did I have the courage
to let this small candle, light my life,
so, I could burn more brightly
lighting up hope in dark places?
As I stared into the candle's flame
burning its wax
that others might see,
it helped me see,
I do not have a right to life,
but a life to light.

I asked Johnny what images that awakened in him. Very soon, he was sharing images of staying with his grandparents at their Presbyterian manse in the Northern Irish countryside. There was a stream running through the gardens, and he would escape the dark rooms of the house and go to the trees, which had their roots in the cool, flowing waters of the stream. He started to recall the words of Jeremiah from the Old Testament, which were lodged in his bones, no doubt from his grandfather's sermons:

For he shall be like a tree planted by the waters, which spreads out its roots by the river, and will not fear when heat comes; but its leaf will be green and will not be anxious in the year of drought, nor will cease from yielding fruit.

(Jeremiah 17:7–8)

'I sense you being held by that flowing stream that once nurtured your roots and is still doing so . . . the stream that flows from beyond and through your grandparents' garden and flows through you', I said.
'Yes, I can feel that', he replied. 'Will you send me your poem?'
'I will if you promise me you will write one for me, a poem about this flowing river', I replied.

A few weeks later, I received this beautiful, poetic response.

Beyond This Presbyterianism

The stifling weight of
The Ministerial cloth.
A starched Black Tent
Sheltering hidden doubt and hope.

The deliberate cut of the fabric
Pleated and stitched and
Absent of all colours
Representing only the dualisms.

Stiff and staid and stubborn
Rigid and rote and restrictive.
Yet energy, with its omnipresence
In perpetuity, tests the seams.

For outside of this Tent
And outside of this Manse
And outside of the Patriarchy
And outside of the church

A chaotic life collides
In colours that my eyes
Can't comprehend, for
Their beauty and vastness
Communes with me
In manners beyond
Scripture and sermon and
sacrament and servitude.

Oozing, surging, pressing
Devouring, caressing, biting.
Life! Unharnessed and unleashed
Life! Parables, unpreached
Life! Unqualified and unteached
Life! Imminent and unreached.

My toes in the alluvium
At the river shore.
Trousers rolled up
In anticipation of more.
In the cold shock
Of the Camowen's course,
Beyond this Presbyterianism
I find my source.

(Johnny Parks, Founder of Toward. Poem from personal
communication with Peter Hawkins, December 2022.
Reproduced with permission.)

We were conjoined in poetry's interweaving, both standing in our depth of
mutual feeling and wondering, both standing at the learning edge of the foggy
shore.

Live life poetically

Friedrich Hölderlin, one of the great German romantic poets, intimates in his
poem *In lieblicher Blaue* (*In Lovely Blue*) (Hölderlin, 1984 [1823]) how we
need to inhabit the earth poetically. He shows us how to see with the poet's eye
and how we learn to make our own language beautiful, in a way that reflects the
beauty of creation.

Mevlana Rumi (quoted in Amidon, 2011) writes:

Let the beauty we love be what we do.
There are hundreds of ways to kneel and kiss the ground.

He invites us to join him in responding to the poetic flow of creation, with
our own echoing grace and poetic language. We cannot all be great poets
like Hölderlin or Rumi, and sharing poems in coaching will only occasion-
ally be appropriate. But we can all create more space for tentatively giving shape to our embodied felt experience, learning to co-create a tentative
emergent language between us, an inter-poiesis, a new embodied knowing
that is shared.

With a different coachee, who felt burdened and unheld, I invited not a poem but for them to draw their support system on a large flipchart, placing themselves in the middle and everything that supported them, both close and distant, in relation to themselves, using different thicknesses of different-coloured lines, showing the current state of the connection. This produced a visual, poetic map and opened up clear avenues of relational changes that the coachee could undertake to enrich and enliven her life.

As we end this chapter, I invite you to go outside to a park, a piece of countryside, a wood or a stream, and wander with an 'open heart, open mind and open will'. Discover what speaks to you, what catches you unaware with its Beauty. Stay a while and let a few echoing phrases flow back from you, or perhaps a small drawing, or song, in graceful thanks for what has been given – a small personal creation in response to the never-ending, ever-changing creating we live and breathe within.

These practices can awaken our ears to the latent poetry in the clues of speech of others we are with and enliven our tongue to poetically interweave responses that help a new, richer narrative to unfold in the space between us and the life of another.

We also need to be careful that our lives and our meetings do not become overcrowded with words. When together we arrive at the learning edge beyond our current knowing, there needs first to be the empty silence of unknowing, the humility to be empty, the patience to be waiting for fog and mist to gradually clear and for new inter-poetic Beauty to emerge.

Part 4

Back to one

Chapter 15

Becoming Beauty

There is a lovely story of a Zen Buddhist teacher and his complaining student, who asks why they have to make so much effort. The teacher replies, saying there is no effort in the sun rising each day. 'So why do we need to do all this practice?' asks the student. The teacher replies, 'So you are awake when the sun rises'.

So what does it mean to be truly awake? Beauty is both the awakener and what we awaken to. We can be awakened by Beauty within an operatic duet or a new song that touches our heart; by a great painting or a simple vase; by falling in love with Beauty within another human being or our newborn child or a loving animal companion; by the first snowdrops coming through the snow in early spring or the flaming colours of the dying leaves in autumn. These moments are precious, so precious that we want to hold on to them, capture them, own them. We do not see the picture, as we are so busy capturing it on our camera, nor hear the Beauty of the song, as we want to record it and add it to our collection. We become collectors, and our collections gather dust.

Then Blake's words whisper in our ears, 'He who binds to himself a joy doth the winged life destroy'. Iain McGilchrist gave up his academic studies of literature, as he keenly felt how the analysis of the poetry was dissecting and killing the life force breathing through the words.

Beauty is a call that invites a response. She does not want a collector or an analyser. She will accept nothing less than a response in kind, responding to Beauty with Beauty. You and I may ask, 'What is a kind response?'. In this book, we have explored many different aspects of such a response, from learning to love, serve truth and justice, embrace death and transience and become graceful in the practice of gratitude, not taking sides but seeking the transcendent, more inclusive response and conversing inter-poetically.

Beauty asks that we respond with our whole being but without attachment – that we do not sit passively in the audience watching and listening but let our hearts join the musicians and actors on the stage, embracing all that plays out. This full-hearted participation is not just required in the enclosed theatre, concert hall or gallery, for that is just the school where we practice so later, we

DOI: 10.4324/9781003349600-20

are ready to fully embrace Beauty as it takes us unaware in every moment of life. So we can be awake when the sun rises, we can learn to have our candle burning when the beloved arrives in the dark and have the question from deep within our heart on our lips when the teacher turns up unannounced.

We have explored how a kind response is one that rings true, like the sound from a Tibetan ringing bowl. It is good in the way it creates benefit for all that the response touches, harmonious in the way it is in tune with the context, as well as what is required right now in this particular moment and place and for a beneficial future. It is a response that is graceful and flowing with gratitude and is accepting what is and what ceases to be, how death gives birth to life and embraces the constant flow of transience and impermanence, responding not as a passive bystander but as a full co-creating participant.

The swimmer has no control over the flow of the river they swim within, any more than we chose the parents who brought us into the world or the family, community, place, language and culture we are born into. We do not get to choose the lessons that life delivers to our doorstep every day, but we *do* get to choose how we respond. Victor Frankl (1984) did not choose to be a Jew born in Austria early in the 20th century. He did not choose the holocaust or his concentration camp or to see his family and closest friends die. He was stripped of everything that was dear to him until he discovered the great freedom that cannot be taken from you in life, the freedom of how you respond.

In his great book *Man's Search for Meaning,* Frankl (1984: 135) writes: 'Forces beyond your control can take away everything you possess except one thing, your freedom to choose how you will respond to the situation' and that 'When we are no longer able to change a situation, we are challenged to change ourselves'. Frankl (1984: 131) suggests:

Ultimately, man should not ask what the meaning of his life is, but rather must recognize that it is he who is asked. In a word, each man is questioned by life; and he can only answer to life by answering for his own life; to life he can only respond by being responsible.

Beauty does not reside in objects but in the relational connection – a moment and a response. Beauty is not a thing; it is a practice, a continual practice of more fully awakening and responding to whatever life presents, welcoming every event and unexpected happening, whether seemingly good or bad, as an honoured guest.

As leaders, we need to be awake to the weather that is appearing over the horizon, as well as to the soil that needs preparing, before we plant new strategies or projects. We need to listen deeply to the many conflicting voices in the community of stakeholders that our organization serves. We need to feel the drumbeat that pulses through the organization and whether it is in tune with the changing rhythms of the wider contexts and then to beautifully align the two, like an orchestra conductor does with the elegant gesture of her baton or a potter with his fingers or the sailor with a gentle touch on the tiller. All senses and sensitivities need to be awake at that moment just before the sun rises, just before the child is birthed, not knowing but expecting and accepting whatever comes.

As coaches, we put our awake antennae at the service of the leader, team or organization we are coaching, sensing the emergent pattern beyond the data, listening not just to the story but also to the storyteller and how the story they are telling is limiting their possibilities. We need to sense the embryonic new story that is searching for language and for form and to hear, see and sense the unthought known – what they know but have not yet found the language to express. We do this as we illustrated in Chapter 14, through 'inter-poiesis' and co-poetizing, midwifing the new language into being, rehearsing the new play that needs performing, finding the new music and rhythm needed and co-discovering the third beyond every 'either-or' polarity.

As coaches, we are the openers of the curtains and the windows, letting in the light and the voices that have been left outside in the cold, opening the door to what is knocking and inviting connection to what has been left disconnected.

Rachel Carson, one of the earliest ecological scientists, said, 'Those who dwell, as scientists or layman, among the beauties and mysteries of the earth are never alone or wary of life' (Carson, quoted in Keltner, 2023: 117). For the words 'scientist or layman', we could substitute the words 'leader or coach'. It is the beauties and mysteries that teach us how to be humble and always learning and that school us in Love. Through Beauty, we can experience how we are constantly gifted to – by the cosmos, our sun and moon, the Earth and all we share it with.

In our human-centric ways of thinking, we can easily forget that it is not large companies, banks and governments that produce the true wealth in the world but the natural eco-systems that freely gift us warmth, light, air and food. We have become indigenous orphans (Hawkins, 2017b) and still have much to learn from more indigenous people, who live closer to the earth than us in our technological, locked-in worlds.

To face the challenges of our times, Joanna Macy and Chris Johnstone (2012) argue that we must develop 'active hope'. We need to let go of 'past hope' (Scranton, 2015) which tends to be personalized and specific: 'I hope I do not catch Coronavirus', 'I hope my city is not affected by the sea levels rising or my house burnt down by the forest fires'. These are equivalent to the mediaeval prayers of supplication, praying for one's personal wellbeing and benefit. 'Active hope' comes from service and from partnership with the larger systems that support us and in which we reside, a hope that collective humanity can transform and evolve and find new ways of partnering with, and learning from, the 'more-than-human' world to restore our shared planet to ecological health.

Reecca Solnit (2016) wrote:

> Hope is a gift you don't have to surrender, a power you don't have to throw away. Hope is not prognostication. It is an orientation of the spirit, an orientation of the heart; it transcends the world that is immediately experienced, and is anchored somewhere beyond its horizons.

For me, this book, at one level, has been an inner autobiography, an attempt to integrate my outward life: as a leader who has started, led and chaired the Boards of a number of businesses; a psychotherapist, executive coach, organizational consultant; a teacher, researcher and trainer; with my inner life as a son, father and grandfather; a lover and husband; a gardener and poet; a lifelong spiritual searcher; a Christian, Unitarian Universalist and a Sufi practitioner, influenced by Buddhism, Daoism and many of the world's spiritual traditions.

It is also written as a cry from the heart for a human metanoia, a radical shift in consciousness, which I and many others believe is essential for humanity to have any hope of addressing the great challenges of our time.

It is, I believe, the best gift I can give to my, and the world's, grandchildren; and I give it with a pain in my heart, and a sincere apology, for the great damage I and my generation have done to this beautiful world and how slow we have been to wake up to the dangers we humans have created.

A curriculum that springs from beauty

As we finish this book, let me leave you with a few simple ways we can all partake in becoming Beauty, through our thinking, doing and being.

My good friend and spiritual mentor Pir Elias Amidon (2012) describes three aspects or stages in following the path of Beauty: 'seeing the beautiful', 'doing the beautiful' and 'being the beautiful'. To work in partnership with Beauty, in coaching or in leadership, requires that we first meet with Beauty and get to know her intimately, her many faces, songs and moods. But as Amidon points out, we do not need to go searching for Beauty, or chase Beauty, for Beauty is always reaching out to us, knocking on the door of our heart and calling to us to become fully awake. Like Amidon, I will outline what I see as the different stages on the path of Beauty.

The first is **Awakening to Beauty**, hearing the call, drawing us out of our dark, small, closed internal space, with its constant self-chatter and concerns, to the light, sights and sensuous music of the world beyond. This stage precedes any successful coaching or leadership, and without this, the work of the leader or the coach will be flat, dry and mechanical. It will become work that can be done equally well by a computer or digital app.

The second stage I call **Sensing Beauty**, as it involves all five of our senses, which we need to train so that we begin to see the world as an artist, hear the sounds of nature as a musician or resonant instrument, taste the flavours of food like a connoisseur, savour different smells like a perfumier and feel the vibrations and feelings of the other in a way that 'otherness' melts away. In this stage, the coach or leader can help draw out the sensuous richness lying just beneath the surface in the other's life, helping them rediscover the colour, vibrancy and beauty in their work and living.

The third stage is the journey of **Participative Imagination** – to actively see through the appearance that shows up to the five senses, to what the appearance reveals, the pattern behind the parts, the music behind the sounds, the story behind the apparent. William Blake describes the five human senses as the windows of the soul and describes the dangers of just passively responding to what blows through the windows when he wrote in 'Auguries of Innocence':

> This life's five windows of the soul
> Distorts the Heavens from pole to pole
> And leads you to believe a lie
> When you see with, not thro' the eye
> That was born in a night to perish in a night
> When the soul slept in beams of light.
> (Blake, 1968e: lines 123–128)

The coach or leader who delights in the Beauty of those they work with and the Beauty of their work is helpful but not sufficient. Both leader and coach need to be active participants in bringing forth the deeper Beauty and connection in and with those they are supporting, moving the engagement beyond the utilitarian and surface to greater depth and richer meaning.

The final stage, **Becoming Beauty**, is where experience is no longer punctuated by a sense of 'I'. The leader or coach is no longer 'doing the work', for at this stage, they have surrendered separateness and control to become a vehicle for what is necessary to emerge for life to flourish and Love and Beauty to be the creative forces. They become like a midwife, supporting what is struggling to be born, to become, and assisting whoever and whatever is naturally giving birth.

This is not about making ourselves more beautiful as a separate object or being but about becoming a vehicle for Beauty to flow through you, for the life force that is, at essence, Beauty, born of Love and giving, to shine forth in ever-new ways.

We need to learn how to live and work from source, rather than from effort and goal-driven will. On the advanced retreats I run each summer, we carry out collaborative inquiries into the different experiential phenomena of working from effort and working from source. Working in pairs, I ask one of the pair to adopt the position they are in when working from effort and for two minutes to report out to their partner, 'When I work from effort, I', and to keep discovering new aspects of how this shows up within them.

When both partners have done this, I invite them to find the physical, bodily state they occupy when they work from source and this time to continually repeat and complete the sentence: 'When I work from source, I'. I have found that everyone who has taken part has a deep-felt sense of the difference between these two states and knows them from the inside. Only when these have been deeply accessed do the pair go on to explore how they can let go of 'efforting' and let source flow more fully through their lives.

I have discovered that when I am working from source, I can work a week of long hours and end the week with more energy than I started it. It is as if I am using renewable energy, rather than burning up stored fuel. I am in tune with my biorhythms, rather than working to the clock-time of forced labour.

Since the Industrial Revolution, we have created this life-versus-work split, where we have to use the short time away from work to replenish all the spent energy from being a 'wage-slave' throughout the working week. Even the concept of 'work-life balance' has built into it the notion of work as draining energy and non-work life as replenishing it.

In Chapter 10 on Grace, we explored the whole notion of flow: how we can be in flow in ourselves, our head, heart and body, our thoughts, feelings and actions; how we can be in flow with others in our teams and families, our organizations and communities; and how we can be in flow with our work, our art and our craft and the wider human and more-than-human world with which we are inextricably entwined.

We are born out of Beauty and sustained by Beauty. When we awake and become the Beauty we love, we return home, to the home we have never left.

Beauty practices

There are many ways we can bring our lives into more flow and connection to source. Here, I offer just a few suggestions you can explore further for yourself.

Focussing on the flows in and out of our being

The quickest way I know to sense our constant inter-relatedness with the world around us is to focus on the continual flow of life into and out of our body and being. We can start with breathing practices, first watching the *yin* in-breath enter our body and then sensing its journey through our body in what the Daoists call the 'medium void' between breaths. Then noticing it effortlessly leave our body in the *yang* out-breath and sensing it spread through the world beyond us (see Chapter 11).

We can watch the flow of experience through our senses, becoming more fully aware of the process of sights, sounds, smells, tastes and touch as the sensations enter us and create feelings, reactions and responses.

We can also bring greater reflection to the flow of information and learning, experienced first through the senses, then becoming internal images, sounds and feelings, then forming into thoughts and thoughts forming into beliefs. We can use simple meditation or mindfulness practices to bring a witnessing presence to our thoughts and feelings, to see if we can notice the moment when the thought or feeling first arrives, then watch it, without judgment, travel through us and notice the moment it leaves. As I write this, I am looking out to sea, watching waves build and break and leave, noticing birds, clouds and small fishing boats cross the vista and disappear. Then I close my eyes and watch thoughts and feelings cross my internal cinema, often arriving unbidden and leaving with no effort or seeming action from me.

In Chapter 10 on Grace, I provided some simple practices that can be carried out when we are about to eat a meal to become more conscious of all the living processes that have gone to provide what will soon be part of ourself. In Chapter 9 on death and transience, I included practices around composting our food waste and even adding our own liquid waste.

Practices of moving with flow from the source

There are many movement practices – from *Tai Chi* and *Qi Gong* to yoga, from walking meditations to forms of natural dance – that help us move, without effort, from our *Hara* or *Tan Tien* in the core of our bodies. When I have practiced *Tai Chi* regularly, I have felt all the flows in my body naturally flowing – the flows of blood, oxygen, hormones, lymph, chemicals, digestion and so on. We can develop both listening *to* our bodies and listening *through* our bodies and become attuned with our body's rhythms.

Connecting to the eco-rhythms that flow beyond you and in you

In our post-industrial world, we have lost a sense of the natural rhythms of the day, week, month and season. We have become regulated by the clock, the alerts and alarms on our phones and the switching on and off of lights and appliances. But the inner connection to eco-rhythms is not lost, just buried: going and staying away from electricity and light pollution; rising with the sun and sleeping with the dark of the night; noticing the phases of the moon, its echo in the tides of the sea; and if you are a menstruating woman, noticing how the moon's rhythms flow with your own menstrual cycle.

Many religions have given shape to the natural rhythms of the day and year. Muslims have five daily prayers that match the stages of the day. Christianity has matins and evensong. Druids mark not only the equinoxes and solstices but also the quarter days of Imbolc, Beltane, Lammas and Samhain, and these still echo in May Day celebrations (Beltane) and Halloween (Samhain). I invite you to co-create, with others, your own ways of attuning to and celebrating the beautiful rhythms of the cycles of life.

Connecting to the rhythms of other life-forms

Kimmerer (2020) shares Native American teachings of how 'All life forms give life to others'; and Weber (2019) puts it more bluntly, showing how life is sustainable as we are all edible! Joanna Macy has provided practices such as the 'Council of all Beings', where we can collectively step into the imaginal bodies of many different living beings and listen as others bring alive their perspective (see Whybrow et al., 2023: 86–89). Freya Mathews (2003, 2021, 2023) and Peter Reason (2023a and 2023b) have developed such practices further in their work in 'Panpsychism', listening deeply to other life-forms, from birds, to trees, to rivers. This inter-communing with the non-human world comes naturally to most children, but we are educated out of it. One of my granddaughters, when young, would use phrases such as 'When I see that flower, I am love'.

Gardening

One of the practices that can most heal the disconnection between the human and the more-than-human world is gardening. If you do not have a garden or an allotment to look after, you can garden in a window box or become an 'urban guerilla' gardener, planting seeds on roundabouts or the side of roads, or volunteer through organizations such as Worldwide Opportunities on Organic Farms (https://wwoof.net/).

Wirzba (2021: 212 and 218) describes some of the deep learning and benefits of gardening:

People . . . understand how their lives depend on the fertility of the soil and the health of the plant and animal creatures that nurture them.

How creatures they are with (potentially) create a beautiful, fragrant and delectable world.

[Without gardening people] will not really appreciate the contingency, vulnerability, and grace of life. [or come to] an embodied understanding that they live by gifts that are incomprehensible in their death, and sacred in their origin.

Insofar as people regularly work to procure some of their food, they are also drawn into the world so as to understand better its vulnerability and need.

People do not simply live on the earth. A more accurate description would be to say that they grow out of it and are daily blessed by it.

Gardening . . . places our bodies and centres our imaginations in the context of life's germination, growth and flowering.

A new sacrament

Jonathan Swift, the great 17th- and 18th-century satirist of man's inhumanity to man, wrote: 'We have just enough religion to make us hate, but not enough religion to love one another' (Swift, 1711). We also have enough religion to think we are the chosen of God and that the rest of the Earth, with its rich variety of living beings, is there for our sustenance and pleasure. But we do not have enough religion to really feel in our hearts, bodies and minds that we and the Earth are one indivisible community. We fail to fully comprehend that individuals cannot flourish if their families and communities are not flourishing; that they, in turn, cannot flourish if the whole of humanity is not flourishing; and that humanity can only flourish if the Earth and the whole of living nature is also flourishing.

Wellbeing is always relational and can never be achieved within the boundaries of an individual, an individual community or one nation. So many of our religions have become self-serving, tribal and human-centric, as portrayed by another 18th-century writer, Robert Burns (1786):

And man, whose heav'n-erected face
The smiles of love adorn, –
Man's inhumanity to man
Makes countless thousands mourn!

For eco-humanity to once again be healthy and thrive, we need to find a new universal religion – a religion in which we realize that the one holy book that we all share is the holy book of nature, that is not only spread out in front and around us (that if we open our eyes and senses, we can learn from every day) but that also flows through every cell of our being, for nature is not something just *out there* to be admired and photographed nor just *in here*, inside our solipsistic internal world. Nature knows no boundaries. It flows through us with every breath we breathe, both in and out and through our being; it enters us with every drop of water we drink and every living being we consume throughout our day and our lives.

I stood with a friend on the western edge of the Rocky Mountains, where the terrain gives way to the flat deserts of Arizona, staring at the night sky ablaze with a million burning stars. My friend cupped his hands around his mouth and cried to the heavens, 'IS ANYONE OUT THERE?' The wailing cry of the lonely human. I heard the cry come back from the wide-open distant heavens, 'YES, YOU ARE'. I cupped my hands and echoed it aloud to the bewilderment of my friend.

As it slowly dawned on me, I shared with my friend how we were looking at our history in the universe we could see. When we look to the heavens, we are seeing the moon as it was a couple of seconds ago, Venus and Mars as they were several minutes ago, Jupiter as it was 35–52 minutes ago, but Pluto, on average, five-and-a-half hours prior to our looking. Alpha Centauri, the nearest star system, we see as it was 4.3 years ago and Sirius, the dog star, as it was nine years ago. Through telescopes, we can see stars and galaxies, which are able to look back at us and see every age of humanity, and distant stars which, if they also had telescopes, could see the Earth before humans existed. For those whose light we are seeing today may no longer exist, for that light was sent out into the universe way before human recorded time.

If the planets and stars were looking back at us, everything that has happened on this small living planet of our world would still be able to be seen from somewhere in the universe. Every act we are ashamed or proud of, all of history and pre-history, is still playing out in the light we have all refracted through space.

Time is spread out in space, and space changes through time. Space and time become inseparable twins, which continually dance together. We cannot point to them or see them, but they flow through us and through all that lives, and we flow and move through them.

As I stand here in the 21st century, I feel the pain of how I, and so many of my fellow humans, have lost our felt sense of connection. How the so-called progress of modern man has seen us retreat from a participatory consciousness – first into our separate, individuated bodies and then we have followed Descartes into leaving our bodies and making our homes in our thinking brains. No longer do we experience that life lives through us, but instead, 'I think, therefore, I am'. Gradually, in the so-called 'developed world', the big 'I am' has exponentially grown out of control, until individuals become their inflated cravings – 'I want, therefore, I am. Who will entertain me? Who will feed me? Who will make me feel better?'

Our growth-based economy relies on making each of us into individual, ever-wanting-more consumers, consuming more and more. If the flames of our cravings start to diminish, then the bellows of advertising is there to reawaken new previously unknown needs. Meanwhile, our monstrous needs ravage the world, depleting resources faster than nature can renew; and we consume much more than we can digest or utilize, so we leave uncompostable waste in our wake. Man's inhumanity to man goes beyond our species to become man's inhumanity to all that lives. The 'I am, I want, I need' becomes 'I must control. I must remove that which gets in the way of my needs'.

In the horrors of the gas chambers of Auschwitz and Treblinka, in the desperate conditions of the British concentration camps of Blandfort and Kimberley, in the Siberian labour camps and the Maoist prisons, man's inhumanity to man became industrialized. Human flesh turned to soap, wedding rings melted down and invested in Swiss banks.

In the industrialization of agriculture, pesticides have exterminated uncountable numbers of insects and bees; chemical nutrients have flowed from our fields, killing fish in our once-living streams; and rich life-nurturing topsoil has become depleted into deserts, where nothing now can grow.

Tennyson (1850) wrote in 'In Memorium' about 'Nature red in tooth and claw'; but now it is the tooth of the human axe, cutting down trees for short-term profit and the claw of the combine harvester ripping into the earth that spill the blood of living systems.

McGilchrist (2022) has brilliantly shown how our retreat from participatory, loving life has not stopped by locating ourselves in the house of our brains, for we have retreated even further to the small dark prison of our left-hemisphere neo-cortex, a prison where we look out through iron bars at an atomized, objectified world of separate, measurable and quantifiable things – a world that is other and that we seek to dissect and name, control and consume.

Earlier, I quoted Gus Speth, a senior advisor to US presidents Carter and Clinton, saying, 'The top environmental problems are human selfishness, greed and apathy. And to deal with those we need a spiritual and cultural revolution'. The spiritual and cultural revolution is, I believe, about finding the way out of our self-created prison and discovering the pathway back to being a part of, not apart from, the wider living world.

We cannot do this with the same intelligence that has created the chains of our prison but a *Sophia*, or wisdom, learnt with humility from the larger world of which we are a very recent and small member. The ecological crisis is, at root, an epistemological crisis; and if we cannot evolve our epistemology, we do not have a 'snowball in hell's chance' of surviving the 21st century (Bateson, 1972). Bateson's hope and entreaty was for humans to focus on the 'areas of human action which are not limited by the narrow distortions . . . and where wisdom can obtain'. These, Bateson suggested, included beauty in ritual, aesthetics and nature, but 'Of these the most important is love . . . there is religion' (Bateson, 2000: 452–453).

This is a sentiment only a heartbeat away from Ibn 'Arabi, the great Sufi mystic, poet and metaphysician, who wrote in his poem 'Wonder' (Ibn 'Arabi, n.d.):

My creed is Love;
Wherever its caravan turns along the way,
That is my belief,
My faith.

We can be helped on our path by the great teachers of wisdom, who help us see beyond our own outstretched, grasping hand; but so often we focus on their finger, rather than what their finger is pointing us towards. Our true teacher must be nature, the ecology, the wider world we live within and which lives within us. But our learning must be done not with the left-hemisphere neo-cortex, reducing the external world to mere facts and data, but through deep experiential and participative learning, not reflections *on* nature but reflections *in* nature and as part of nature, learning through deep mutuality and relationship.

This is where Beauty can be our guide, as it was for Lao Tzu and Dante, Mevlana Rumi and Blake, as well as for many indigenous religious teachers across the world. For Beauty draws us back into relationship with the living, beathing world around us: communion that starts in the heart, flows through our body and is felt in the fibres of our being.

Where I live, I care for the garden and the garden cares for me. We are united in a circle of common care. I tickle the pollen of the thousand pink blossoms of the peach and nectarine trees, which come before the bees, so these small stars of beauty will ripen into fruit that will taste sweet upon my tongue. I garner the ghostly deadheads of last year's hydrangea flowers and carry them down to where they will fuel the alchemy of the compost heap, where, married to rotting leaves, sawdust and ashes and last year's banana skins, they magically transform into black gold. I scoop up into my hands this rich, living soil until my hands hold within them more micro living beings than there are people on this Earth. A prayer of thanksgiving wells up in my heart for this nutrient-rich food that will nourish next year's seeds into tender shoots of new green life.

As I add my urine and the chicken's litter to this pyre of metamorphosis, how can I not believe in eternal life? But not as we have been taught it. How can I not sense and celebrate the magical alchemical wedding, the '*hieros gamos*', the '*coincidentia oppositorum*' of Heaven and Earth, or want to be in service of building Blake's 'New Jerusalem', 'in England's green and pleasant land'?

As I stand there, I become aware how I and many of my species so often ask the wrong questions. I find nature saying to me, 'Do not ask: Will I survive death? But rather ask: How can my life and death make the best beneficial contribution to the life that is eternal?' Beauty is now, in the moment when birthing and dying are co-creating life, the life that is forever becoming.

Sean Kelly and Joanna Macy (2021: 207–208) end their beautiful paper, on reconnecting through collapse, with the following words:

> the wisdom, compassion and generosity called for in this time of the Great Turning, answer to a quickening in the heart-mind, the opening of gifts from all our ancestors and a stirring of future life already inhabiting us, waiting and wanting to be born. This new life is not other than the life that lives in us now. The love it summons blesses it in return; it is not conditional upon a guaranteed or even likely tomorrow but knows its **truth and goodness and beauty** in the pulsing mystery of the here and now. This life and love is the only *terra firma* in a time of collapse. It is the only clear path for we people of the passage.

The end and the beginning.

Bibliography

Abram, D. (1996). *The Spell of the Sensuous*. New York: Random House.

Abram, D. (2011). *Becoming Animal: An Earthly Cosmology*. New York: Penguin, Random House.

Alighieri, D. (1301–14a). 'Inferno Canto'. Available at: https://www.danteonline.it/italiano/opere.asp?idope=1&idlang=OR (Accessed 6 November 2023).

Alighieri, D. (1301–14b). 'Inferno Canto' (English translation). Available at: https://poets.org/poem/inferno-canto-i (Accessed 6 November 2023).

Amidon, E. (2011). *Seven Contemplations on Awakening*. Boulder, CO: Open Path Publications.

Amidon, E. (2012). *The Open Path: Recognizing Non-Dual Awareness*. Boulder, CO: Sentient Publications.

Amidon, E. (2021). *The Book of Flashes*. Crestone: The Sufi Way.

Amidon, E. (2023). *Love's Drum: Sufi Views, Practices and Stories*. Boulder, CO: Sentient Publications.

Amidon, E. 'Non-Dual Sufism'. Available at: www.sufiway.org (Accessed 9 January 2023).

Amson-Bradshaw, G. (2019). *Plastic Planet: How Plastic Came to Rule the World (and What You Can Do to Change It)*. London: Franklin Watts.

Armstrong, K. (1993). *A History of God: From Abraham to the Present. The 4000-Year Quest for God*. 1st Edition. London: Heinemann.

Armstrong, K. (2006). *The Great Transformation: The World in the Time of Buddha, Socrates, Confucius and Jeremiah*. London: Atlantic Books.

Armstrong, K. (2022). *Sacred Nature: How We Can Recover Our Bond with the Natural World*. London: Penguin Random House.

Attenborough, D. (2013). Speech given to Royal Geographical Society October 2013.

Baldwin, J. (1963). *The Fire Next Time*. London: Penguin Random House.

Baldwin, J. & Mead, M. (1971). *A Rap on Race*. London: Michael Joseph.

Barfield, O. (1965). *Saving the Appearances: A Study in Idolatry*. New York: Harcourt, Brace & World.

Bateson, G. (1972). *Steps to an Ecology of Mind*. New York: Ballantine Books.

Bateson, G. (1973). *Steps to an Ecology of Mind*. London: Paladin, Granada Publishing.

Bateson, G. (1975). 'What Is Epistemology?' Recording of a talk given at the Esalen Institute, Big Sur, CA.

Bateson, G. (1979). *Mind and Nature: A Necessary Unity*. New York: Dutton.

Bateson, G. (1991). *A Sacred Unity: Further Steps to an Ecology of Mind*. New York: Harper Collins.

Bateson, G. (2000). *Steps to an Ecology of Mind*. New Edition. New York: Ballantine Books.

Bateson, G. & Bateson, M. C. (1987). *Angels Fear: An Investigation into the Meaning of the Sacred*. London: Rider.

Becker, E. (1973). *The Denial of Death*. New York: Free Press.

Bendell, J. (2010). *Evolving Partnerships: A Guide to Working with Business for a Greater Social Change*. Sheffield: Greenleaf Publishing.

Bendell, J. (2021). 'Deeper Implications in Societal Collapse'. In J. Bendell & R. Read (Eds.) *Deep Adaptation: Navigating the Realities of Climate Chaos*. Cambridge, UK: Polity Press.

Bendell, J. & Read, R. (Eds.) (2021). *Deep Adaptation: Navigating the Realities of Climate Chaos*. Cambridge, UK: Polity Press.

Bennet, J. G. (1969). *Gurdjieff: A Very Great Enigma*. Kingston: Coombe Springs.

Bergson, H. (1907). *Creative Evolution (L'Évolution créatrice)*. New York: Henry Holt and Company.

Berman, M. (1981). *The Reenchantment of the World*. New York: Cornell University Press.

Berry, J. W. (1997). 'Immigration, Acculturation, and Adaptation'. *Applied Psychology: An International Review*, 46: 5–34.

Berry, T. (1999). *The Great Work: Our Way into the Future*. New York: Harmony/Bell Tower.

Berry, T. (2006). *Evening Thoughts: Reflecting on Earth as Sacred Community*. San Francisco, CA: Sierra Club Books.

Berry, W. (1983). *Standing by Words*. San Francisco, CA: North Point Press.

Berry, W. (2012). *New Collected Poems*. Berkeley, CA: Counterpoint.

Berry, W. (2015). *Our Only World: Ten Essays*. Berkeley, CA: Counterpoint.

Blake, W. (1799, August 23). 'Letter to Rev Dr John Trussler'. Available at: https://blakearchive.org/copy/letters?descId=lt23aug1799.1.ltr.01 (Accessed 2 January 2024).

Blake, W. (1968a). 'And Did Those Feet in Ancient Time'. In G. Keynes (Ed.) *Poetry and Prose of William Blake*. London: Nonesuch Press.

Blake, W. (1968b). 'The Marriage of Heaven and Hell'. In G. Keynes (Ed.) *Poetry and Prose of William Blake*. London: Nonesuch Press.

Blake, W. (1968c). 'Letter to Thomas Butts, 22 November 1802'. In G. Keynes (Ed.) *Poetry and Prose of William Blake*. London: Nonesuch Press.

Blake, W. (1968d). 'Eternity'. In G. Keynes (Ed.) *Poetry and Prose of William Blake*. London: Nonesuch Press.

Blake, W. (1968e). 'Auguries of Innocence'. In G. Keynes (Ed.) *Poetry and Prose of William Blake*. London: Nonesuch Press.

Blake, W. (1968f). 'Jerusalem'. In G. Keynes (Ed.) *Poetry and Prose of William Blake*. London: Nonesuch Press.

Bohm, D. (1980). *Wholeness and the Implicate Order*. London: Routledge.

Bohm, D. (1987). *Unfolding Meaning: A Weekend of Dialogue*. London: Routledge & Kegan Paul.

Bohm, D. (1989). 'Meaning and Information'. In P. Pylkkanen (Ed.) *The Search for Meaning: The New Spirit in Science and Philosophy*. Wellingborough: Crucible/Thorsons.

Bohm, D. (1994). *Thought as a System*. London: Routledge.

Bohm, D. (1996). *On Dialogue*. London: Routledge.

Bond, H. L. (1997). 'Introduction'. In *Nicholas of Cusa: Selected Spiritual Writings*. New York: Paulist.

Bookchin, M. (1991). *The Ecology of Freedom: The Emergence and Dissolution of Hierarchy*. Montreal and New York: Black Rose Books.

Boston, R. & Ellis, K. (Eds.) (2019). *Upgrade: Building Your Capacity for Complexity*. London: LeaderSpace.

Bragdon, J. (2016). *Companies That Mimic Life*. Austin, TX: Greenleaf Publishing.

Braks, A. (2021). *Executive Coaching in Strategic Holistic Leadership: The Drivers and Dynamics of Vertical Development*. Maidenhead: Open University Press.

Branden, N. (1994). *Six Pillars of Self-Esteem*. New York: Bantam Books.

Brown, B. (2011). 'Conscious Leadership for Sustainability'. Extract from Unpublished Dissertation. Fielding Graduate University, Santa Barbara.

Browning, R. (1883). 'Andrea Del Sarto'. In *Selection of the Poems of Robert Browning*. London: Dodd, Mead & Co.

Bucher, G. (2023). 'Global Inequality Is a Failure of Imagination. Here's Why'. *World Economic Forum*. Available at: weforum.org (Accessed 29 September 2024).

Bullock, A. (2000). *Building Jerusalem: A Portrait of My Father*. London: Allen Lane.

Burke, W. (2002). *Organization Change: Theory and Practice*. London: Sage Publications.

Burns, R. (1786). 'Man Was Made to Mourn'. In *Poems Mostly in the Scottish Dialect*. Kilmarnock: John Wilson.

Camus, A. (1960). *The Rebel: An Essay on Man in Revolt*. New York: Vintage Books.

Capra, C. (1996). *The Web of Life: A New Synthesis of Mind and Matter*. London: Harper Collins.

Capra, F. (1975). *The Tao of Physics*. Boston, MA: Shambala.

Capra, F. (1988). *Uncommon Wisdom: Conversations with Remarkable People*. London: Simon & Schuster.

Capra, F. (2003). *The Hidden Connections: A Science for Sustainable Living*. London: Flamingo.

Capra, F. & Luisi, L. P. (2014). *The Systems View of Life: A Unifying Vision*. Cambridge: Cambridge University Press.

Carlyle, T. (1841). *On Heroes, Hero-Worship, & the Heroic in History: Six Lectures*. London: James Fraser.

Carr, K. & Bendell, J. (2021). 'Facilitating Deep Adaptation'. In J. Bendell & R. Read (Eds.) *Deep Adaptation: Navigating the Realities of Climate Chaos*. Cambridge, UK: Polity Press.

Carson, R. (1962). *Silent Spring*. Boston, MA: Houghton Mifflin.

Cassirer, E. (1977). *The Myth of the State*. New Haven, CT: Yale University Press.

Charlton, N. G. (2008). *Understanding Gregory Bateson: Mind, Beauty and the Sacred Earth*. Albany, NY: State University of New York Press.

Cheng, F. (2009). *The Way of Beauty: Five Meditations for Spiritual Transformation*. Translated by Jody Gladding. Rochester, VT: Inner Traditions.

Cheng, F. (2013). *Five Meditations on Death: In Other Words, on Life*. Translated by Jody Gladding. Rochester, VT: Inner Traditions.

Clynes, M. (1977, second edition 1989). *Sentics: The Touch of the Emotions*. Dorset: Prism Unity.

Coleridge, S. T. (1794). 'The Aeolian Harp'. Available at: https://www.poetryfoundation.org/poems/52301/the-eolian-harp (Accessed January 2024).

Coleridge, S. T. (1798). 'The Rime of the Ancient Mariner'. Available at: https://www.gutenberg.org/files/151/151-h/151-h.htm (Accessed January 2024).

Cosier, S. (2019, May 30). 'The World Needs Topsoil to Grow 95% of Its Food – But It's Rapidly Disappearing'. *The Guardian*. Available at: https://www.theguardian.com/us-news/2019/may/30/topsoil-farming-agriculture-food-toxic-america (Accessed 24 August 2023).

Crick, F. (1994). *The Astonishing Hypothesis: The Scientific Search for the Soul*. New York: Scribner.

Csikszentmihalyi, M. (2000). *Flow: The Psychology of Optimal Experience*. New York: Harper.

Curry, P. (2011). *Ecological Ethics: An Introduction.* 2nd Edition. Cambridge: Polity Press.

Curry, P. (2019). *Enchantment: Wonder in Modern Life.* Edinburgh: Floris Books.

Dalrymple, W. (2019). *The Anarchy: The Relentless Rise of the East India Company.* London: Bloomsbury.

Dante, A. 'Divina Commedia'. Italian: Available at: https://www.danteonline.it/italiano/opere.asp?idope=1&idlang=OR (Accessed 4 November 2023). English version: https://poets.org/poem/inferno-canto-i (Accessed 4 November 2023).

Deakin, R. (2007). *Wildwood: A Journey Through Trees.* London: Hamish Hamilton.

De Bary, W. T., Bloom, I. & Lufrano, R. (1994). *Sources of Chinese Tradition – From Earliest Times to 1600.* New York: Columbia University Press.

Dennett, D. (1991). *Consciousness Explained.* London: Penguin.

Descartes, R. (2001) [1637]. *Discourse on the Method, Optics, Geometry and Meteorology.* Translated by P. J. Olscamp. Revised Edition. Indianapolis, IN: Hackett.

Dewey, J. (1934). *Art as Experience.* New York: Perigee.

Diamandis, P. H. & Kotler, S. (2014). *Abundance: The Future Is Better Than You Think.* New York: Free Press.

Durkheim, E. (1995) [1912]. *The Elementary Forms of the Religious Life.* New English Translation by Karen E. Fields. Cambridge: Free Press.

Earth.Org. (2023). Available at: https://earth.org/the-biggest-environmental-problems-of-our-lifetime/ (Accessed 12 December 2023).

Edelman. (2023). 'Edelman Trust Barometer: Navigating a Polarized World'. Available at: https://www.edelman.com/trust/2023/trust-barometer (Accessed 31 January 2024).

Edmondson, A. C. (2019). *The Fearless Organization.* Hoboken, NJ: Wiley.

Einstein, A. (1930). 'What I Believe: Living Philosophies XIII'. *Forum and Century*, 84: 194–195.

Eisenstadt, S. N. (Ed.) (2017). *Multiple Modernities.* London: Routledge.

Eisenstein, C. (2007). *The Ascent of Humanity. Civilization and the Human Sense of Self.* Oxford: Panenthea Productions.

Eisenstein, C. (2013). *The More Beautiful World Our Hearts Know Is Possible.* Berkeley, CA: North Atlantic Books.

Eliot, T. S. (1929). *Dante.* London: Faber.

Eliot, T. S. (1960). *The Sacred Wood: Essays on Poetry and Criticism.* London: Methuen.

Eliot, T. S. (1963). 'Choruses from "The Rock"'. In *Collected Poems 1909–1962.* London: Faber and Faber.

Featherstone, M., Lash, S. & Robertson, R. (Eds.) (1995). *Global Modernities.* London: Sage.

Ferlinghetti, L. (1975). *Poetry as Insurgent Art.* New York: New Directions.

Ferrucci, P. (2010). *Beauty and the Soul: The Extraordinary Power of Everyday Beauty to Heal Your Life.* Translated by V. R. Ferrucci. New York: Penguin.

Fiaramonti, L. (2017). *Wellbeing Economy: Success in a World Without Growth.* Johannesburg: Pan Macmillan.

Fox, M. (1983). *Original Blessing: A Primer in Creation Spirituality.* Santa Fe, NM: Bear & Company.

Fox, M. (1988). *The Coming of the Cosmic Christ.* San Francisco, CA: Harper.

Fox, M. (1993). *The Reinvention of Work: A New Vision of Livelihood for Our Time.* New York: Harpercollins.

Frankl, V. (1984). *Man's Search for Meaning.* New York: Simon Schuster Pocket Books.

Friedman, M. (1962). *Capitalism and Freedom.* Chicago, IL: University of Chicago Press.

Friedman, T. (2008). *Hot, Flat, and Crowded: Why the World Needs a Green Revolution – and How We Can Renew Our Global Future.* London: Penguin.

Fromm, E. (1964). *The Heart of Man*. New York: Harper & Row.

Fromm, E. (1995) [1956]. *The Art of Loving*. Dublin: Thorsons.

Fukuyama, F. (2020). *The End of History and the Last Man* (Updated with New Afterword). London: Penguin.

Future Markets Leadership. (2022). Available at: https://www.futuremarketinsights.com/reports/leadership-development-program-market (Accessed October 2023).

Gallup Emotions Report. (2023). Available at: https://www.gallup.com/analytics/507719/ (Accessed 20 January 2024).

George, B. (1997). *True North: Discover Your Authentic Leadership*. San Francisco, CA: Jossey-Bass.

George, W. (2003). *Authentic Leadership: Rediscovering the Secrets of Creating Lasting Value*. San Francisco, CA: Jossey-Bass.

Gergen, K. J. (2009). 'Social Construction: Revolution in the Making'. In K. J. Gergen (Ed.) *An Invitation to Social Construction* (pp.1–30). London: Sage.

Gerson, L. (2018). 'Plotinus'. In *Stanford Dictionary of Philosophy*. First published 30 June 2003. Substantive revision 28 June 2018. Available at: https://plato.stanford.edu/entries/plotinus/ (Accessed 13 February 2024).

Ghemawat, P. (2012). 'Developing Global Leaders'. *McKinsey Quarterly*. Available at: www.mckinsey.com/global-themes/leadership/developing-global-leaders (Accessed 13 March 2022).

Global Agriculture. (2022). 'Soil, Fertility and Erosion'. Available at: https://www.globalagriculture.org/report-topics/soil-fertility-and-erosion.html (Accessed January 2024).

Goleman, D. (1995). *Emotional Intelligence: Why It Can Matter More Than IQ*. New York: Bantam Books.

Goleman, D. (2006). *Social Intelligence: The New Science of Social Relationships*. New York: Bantam Books.

Goodenough, U. (1998). *The Sacred Depths of Nature: How Life Has Emerged and Evolved*. Oxford: Oxford University Press.

Gordimer, N. (2010). *Telling Times – Writing and Living, 1954–2008*. London: Bloomsbury.

Graves, C. W. (1970). 'Levels of Existence: An Open System Theory of Values'. *Journal of Humanistic Psychology*, 10 (2): 131–155.

Griffin, J. (2011). *On the Origin of Beauty: Ecophilosphy in the Light of Traditional Wisdom*. Bloomington, IN: World Wisdom Inc.

Gunderson, L. & Holling, C. (2002). *Panarchy: Understanding Transformations in Human and Natural Systems*. Washington, DC: Island Press.

Gupta, I. (2015). 'Sustainable Development: Gandhi Approach'. *OIDA International Journal of Sustainable Development*, 8 (7): 27–32.

Hadot, P. (1998). *Plotinus or the Simplicity of Vision* (Originally in French 1989). Translated by Michael Chase. Chicago, IL: University of Chicago Press.

Hamel, G. & Zanini, L. (2016, March 16). 'The $3 Trillion Prize for Busting Bureaucracy (and How to Claim It)'. Humanistic Management Network, Research Paper Series No. 28/16. Available at SRN: https://ssrn.com/abstract=2748842 or http://dx.doi.org/10.2139/ssrn.2748842

Hampden-Turner, C. (1990). *Charting the Corporate Mind: From Dilemma to Strategy*. Oxford: Blackwell.

Hanh, T. N. (1975). *The Miracle of Mindfulness*. Boston, MA: Beacon Press.

Hanh, T. N. (1987). *Interbeing: Fourteen Guidelines for Engaged Buddhism*. London: Parallax Press.

Harari, Y. N. (2016). *Homo Deus: A Brief History of Tomorrow*. London: Harvill Secker.

Hawkins, P. (1991). 'The Spiritual Dimension of the Learning Organisation'. *Management Education and Development*, 22 (3): 172–187.

Hawkins, P. (2001, August). 'Beyond Opposites'. Five Talks given at the Unitarian Summer School, Nightingale Centre, Derbyshire.

Hawkins, P. (2004). 'Gregory Bateson: His Contribution to Action Research and Organisation Development'. *The Journal of Action Research*, 2 (4): 409–423.

Hawkins, P. (2005). *Wise Fool's Guide to Leadership: Short Spiritual Stories for Organisational and Personal Transformation*. London: O-Books.

Hawkins, P. (2011). *Leadership Team Coaching: Developing Collective Transformational Leadership*. 1st Edition. London: Kogan Page.

Hawkins, P. (2012). *Creating a Coaching Culture*. Maidenhead: Open University Press/McGraw Hill.

Hawkins, P. (2014a). *Leadership Team Coaching: Developing Collective Transformational Leadership*. 2nd Edition. London: Kogan Page.

Hawkins, P. (Ed.) (2014b). *Leadership Team Coaching in Practice*. 1st Edition. London: Kogan Page.

Hawkins, P. (2015). *A Systemic Primer*. Bath: Renewal Associates.

Hawkins, P. (2017a). *Tomorrow's Leadership and the Necessary Revolution in Today's Leadership Development*. Henley: Henley Business School.

Hawkins, P. (2017b). 'The Necessary Revolution in Humanistic Psychology'. In R. House & D. Kalisch (Eds.) *The Future of Humanistic Psychology*. London: Routledge.

Hawkins, P. (2017c). *Leadership Team Coaching: Developing Collective Transformational Leadership*. 3rd Edition. London: Kogan Page.

Hawkins, P. (2018a). *Beyond Authentic Leadership: From Authenticity to Dynamic Congruence*. Bath: Renewal Associates.

Hawkins, P. (Ed.) (2018b). *Leadership Team Coaching in Practice*. 2nd Edition. London: Kogan Page.

Hawkins, P. (2019a). 'Resourcing – The Neglected Third Leg of Supervision'. In E. Turner & S. Palmer (Eds.) *The Heart of Coaching Supervision – Working with Reflection and Self-Care*. Abingdon: Routledge.

Hawkins, P. (2019b). 'Systemic Organizational Learning and the Coevolution of Organizational Culture'. In A. R. Örtenblad (Ed.) *The Oxford Handbook of the Learning Organization*. Oxford: Oxford University Press.

Hawkins, P. (2020). 'Evolving Human Consciousness: Coaching's Great Challenge'. *Perspectives* (The Association for Coaching Global Magazine), (27): 6–7 & 37.

Hawkins, P. (2021a). *Leadership Team Coaching: Developing Collective Transformational Leadership*. 4th Edition. London: Kogan Page.

Hawkins, P. (2021b). 'Beyond the High-Performing Team'. Available at: www.renewalassociates.co.uk/Blogs

Hawkins, P. (2021c). 'Ecology, Mental Health and Eco-Spirituality'. In S. Aris (Ed.) *Spirituality, Mental Health and Wellbeing Handbook* (pp. 299–310). Shoreham-by-Sea: Pavilion.

Hawkins, P. (2021d). 'Evolving Human Consciousness in Coaching'. *Perspectives* (The Association of Coaching Global Magazine), (28): 6–9.

Hawkins, P. (Ed.) (2022). *Leadership Team Coaching in Practice*. 3rd Edition. London: Kogan Page.

Hawkins, P. (2023a). 'How Do I Increase My 'Confidence' as a Team Coach?' Available at: https://www.renewalassociates.co.uk/2023/04/

Hawkins, P. (2023b). 'Is Your Inner Team More Than the Sum of Its Parts?' Available at: https://www.renewalassociates.co.uk/2023/07/is-your-inner-team-more-than-the-sum-of-its-parts/

Hawkins, P. (2023c). 'From Grumble to Gratitude – Four Steps to Align with Life's Agenda'. Available at: https://www.renewalassociates.co.uk/2023/07/

Hawkins, P. & Carr, C. (2023). 'Ethics in Team Coaching'. In W. A. Smith, J. Passmore, E. Turner, Y. L. Lai & D. Clutterbuck (Eds.) *The Ethical Coaches' Handbook: A Guide to Developing Ethical Maturity in Practice*. London: Routledge.

Hawkins, P. & Carr, C. (forthcoming). *Coaching the Team of Teams: Creating a Teaming Culture*. London: Kogan Page.

Hawkins, P. & McMahon, A. (2020). *Supervision in the Helping Professions*. 5th Edition. Maidenhead: Open University Press/McGraw Hill.

Hawkins, P. & Ryde, J. (2020). *Integrative Psychotherapy in Theory and Practice: A Relational, Systemic and Ecological Approach*. London: Jessica Kingsley.

Hawkins, P. & Schwenk, G. (2006). *Coaching Supervision*. London: Chartered Institute of Personnel and Development.

Hawkins, P. & Shohet, R. (1989). *Supervision in the Helping Professions*. 1st Edition. Maidenhead: Open University Press/McGraw Hill.

Hawkins, P. & Shohet, R. (2000). *Supervision in the Helping Professions*. 2nd Edition. Maidenhead: Open University Press/McGraw Hill.

Hawkins, P. & Shohet, R. (2006). *Supervision in the Helping Professions*. 3rd Edition. Maidenhead: Open University Press/McGraw Hill.

Hawkins, P. & Shohet, R. (2012). *Supervision in the Helping Professions*. 4th Edition. Maidenhead: Open University Press/McGraw Hill.

Hawkins, P. & Smith, N. (2006). *Coaching, Mentoring and Organizational Consultancy: Supervision and Development*. 1st Edition. Maidenhead: Open University Press/McGraw Hill.

Hawkins, P. & Smith, N. (2013). *Coaching, Mentoring and Organizational Consultancy: Supervision and Development*. 2nd Edition. Maidenhead: Open University Press/McGraw Hill.

Hawkins, P. & Turner, E. (2020). *Systemic Coaching: Delivering Values Beyond the Individual*. London: Routledge.

Hazlitt, W. (1873). *Essays on the Fine Art*. London: Reeves and Turner.

Heffernan, M. (2014). At her book launch for *A Bigger Prize: Why Competition Isn't Everything and How We Do Better*. Bath, UK: University of Bath.

Heidegger, M. (1962). *Being and Time*. Translated by J. MacQuarrie & E. Robinson. London: SCM Press.

Heisenberg, W. (1958). *Physics and Philosophy*. New York: Harper.

Heisenberg, W. (1971). 'Understanding in Modern Physics'. In *Physics and Beyond: Encounters and Conversations*. New York: Harper & Row.

Helminski, K. (2000). *The Wisdom of the Heart*. Boulder, CO: Shambala.

Heron, J. (1988). 'Validity in Co-operative Inquiry'. In P. Reason (Ed.) *Human Inquiry in Action*. London: Sage.

Heron, J. & Reason, P. (2001). 'The Practice of Co-operative Inquiry: Research with Rather Than on People'. In P. Reason & H. Bradbury (Eds.) *The Sage Handbook of Action Research* (pp. 179–188). London: Sage Publications.

Hillman, J. (1975). *Loose Ends: Primary Papers on Archetypal Psychology*. Zurich: Spring Publications.

Hillman, J. (2001). 'The Practice of Beauty'. In B. Beckley & D. Shapiro (Eds.) *Uncontrollable Beauty* (pp. 261–274). New York: Allworth Press.

Hobbes, T. (2010) [1851]. *Leviathan: Or the Matter, Form, and Power of a Commonwealth Ecclesiastical and Civil*. Edited by I. Shapiro. New Haven, CT: Yale University Press.

Hobson, R. (1985). *Forms of Feeling: The Heart of Psychotherapy*. London: Tavistock Publications.

Hölderlin, F. (1984). *Hymns and Fragments*. Translated by Richard Sieburth. Princeton, NJ: Princeton University Press.

Holliday, M. (2016). *The Age of Thrivability: Vital Perspectives and Practices for a Better World*. Chicago, IL: Cambium.

Holy Bible. Old Testament, Book of Job. London, UK: Collins.

hooks, b. (2001). *All About Love*. New York: Harper Collins.

Hutchins, G. (2012). *The Nature of Business: Redesigning for Resilience*. Totnes: Green Books.

Hutchins, G. (2014). *The Illusion of Separation: Exploring the Cause of Our Current Crises*. Edinburgh: Floris.

Hutchins, G. (2016). *Future-Fit*. Scotts Valley, CA: CreateSpace Independent Publishing Platform.

Hutchins, G. (2022). *Leading by Nature: The Procress of Becoming a Regenerative Leader*. Tunbridge Wells: Wordzworth.

Hutchins, G. & Storm, L. (2019). *Regenerative Leadership: The DNA of Life Affirming 21st Century Organizations*. Tunbridge Wells: Wordzworth.

Huxley, A. (1959). *The Doors of Perception and Heaven and Hell*. Harmondsworth: Penguin.

Ibn 'Arabi, A. (1989). 'On Majesty and Beauty'. Translated by Rabia Terri Harris. *Journal of the Muhyiddin Ibn 'Arabi Society*, 8: 5–32. Available at: https://ibnarabisociety.org/wp-content/uploads/PDFs/Harris_On-majesty-and-beauty.pdf (Accessed 11 April 2023).

Ibn 'Arabi, A. (n.d.). 'Wonder'. Translated by M. Gloton. Available at: https://allpoetry.com/poem/8620729-Wonder-by-Ibn-Arabi (Accessed 8 January 2024).

Inayat Khan, H. (1926). *The Sufi Message*. Volume 1–XII. London: Barrie and Jenkins.

Inayat Khan, H. (1972) [1926]. *The Sufi Message: The Unity of Religious Ideals*. Volume 9. London: Barrie and Jenkins

Ingold, T. (2011). *Being Alive: Essays on Movement; Knowledge and Connection*. London: Routledge.

Ingold, T. (2015). *The Life of Lines*. London: Routledge.

Issacs, W. (1999). *Dialogue and the Art of Thinking Together*. New York: Doubleday.

James, W. (1902). *The Varieties of Religious Experience: A Study of Human Nature*. London: Longmans, Green and Co.

James, W. (1909). *A Pluralistic Universe*. London: Longman.

Jonas, H. (1989). 'Geist, Natur und Schöpfung'. In H.-P. Dürr & W. Zimmerli (Eds.) *Geist and Natur*. Munich: Sherz.

Joyce, J. (1902, February 15). 'James Clarence Mangan'. Essay First Read to the Literary and Historical Society, University College, Dublin. First Published in *St. Stephen's* 1902.

Jullien, F. & Lloyd, J. (2002). 'Did Philosophers Have to Become Fixated on Truth?' *Critical Inquiry*, 28 (4): 803–824.

Jung, C. (1966). *Collected Works*. 2nd Edition. London: Routledge.

Kauffman, S. (2000). *Investigations*. New York: Oxford University Press.

Kegan, R. (1982). *The Evolving Self: Problem and Process in Human Development*. 1st Edition. Cambridge, MA: Harvard University Press.

Kellerman, B. (2008). *Followership: How Followers Are Creating Change and Changing Leaders*. Cambridge, MA: Harvard University Press.

Kellerman, B. (2012). *The End of Leadership*. New York: Harper Business.

Kelly, S. & Macy, J. (2021). 'Reconnecting Through Collapse'. In J. Bendell & R. Read (Eds.) *Deep Adaptation: Navigating the Realities of Climate Chaos*. Cambridge: Polity Press.

Keltner, D. (2023). *Awe: The Transformative Power of Everyday Wonder*. London: Allen Lane.

Kennedy, R. (1968, March 18). 'Campaign Speech at the Phog Allen Fieldhouse'. Kansas State University. Available at: https://en.wikisource.org/wiki/Remarks_at_the_University_of_Kansas. (Accessed 30 January 2024)

Khoza, R. (2006). *Let Africa Lead*. Johannesburg: Vezubuntu.

Kimmerer, R. W. (2020). *Braiding Sweetgrass. Indigenous Wisdom, Scientific Knowledge and the Teachings of Plants*. London: Penguin.

Kiuchi, T. & Shireman, B. (2002). *What We Learned in the Rainforest*. San Francisco, CA: Berrett-Koehler Inc.

Koestler, A. (1967). *The Ghost in the Machine*. London: Hutchinson.

Kolbert, E. (2015). *The Sixth Extinction*. London: Bloomsbury Publishing.

Komjathy, L. (2013). *The Daoist Tradition: An Introduction*. London: A&C Black.

Komjathy, L. (2014). *Daoism: A Guide for the Perplexed*. London: Bloomsbury.

Krishnamurti, J. (1976). *Krishnamurti's Notebooks*. London: Gollancz.

Kryznaric, R. (2020). *The Good Ancestor: How to Think Long Term in a Short-Term World*. London: W. H. Allen.

Kuhn, T. (1970). *The Structure of Scientific Revolutions*. 2nd Edition. Chicago, IL: University of Chicago Press.

Kumar, S. (2013). *Soul, Soil, Society: A New Trinity for Our Time*. London: Leaping Hare Press.

Kumar, S. (2021). 'We Need a London School of Ecology and Economics'. Available at: https://theecologist.org/2021/jan/11/we-need-london-school-ecology-and-economics (Accessed 13 February 2024).

Kumar, S. (2023a). *Radical Love: From Separation to Connection with the Earth, Each Other, and Ourselves*. Berkeley, CA: Parallax Press.

Kumar, S. (2023b). *Resurgence* (pp. 44–46). Hartland, Devon, UK: Resurgence Trust.

Le Guin, U. (1989). *Dancing at the Edge of the World*. New York: Grove Press.

Le Guin, U. (2015). *Late in the Day: Poems 2010–2014*. New York: PM Press.

Lent, J. (2021). *The Web of Meaning*. Gabriola, BC: New Society.

Leopold, A. (1989) [1949]. *A Sand County Almanac with Essays on Conservation from Rouen River*. New York: Oxford University Press.

Lewis, T., Amini, F. & Lannon, R. (2000). *A General Theory of Love*. New York: Random House.

Lovelock, J. (1979). *Gaia*. Oxford: Oxford University Press.

Lucretius, T. (2020). *De Rerum Natura* ['The Way Things Are']. Translated by W. E. Leonard. London: Penguin.

Lushwala, A. (2012). *The Time of the Black Jaguar*. New York: Disruption Books.

Lyotard, J. (1979). *The Postmodern Condition: A Report on Knowledge*. Minneapolis, MN: University of Minnesota Press.

Machado de Oliveira, V. (2021). *Hospicing Modernity: Facing Humanity's Wrongs and the Implications for Social Activism*. Berkeley, CA: North Atlantic Books.

MacLean, P. D. (1990). *The Triune Brain in Evolution. Role in Paleocerebral Functions*. New York: Plenum Press.

Macy, J. & Johnstone, C. (2012). *Active Hope: How to Face the Mess We're in without Going Crazy*. Novato, CA: New World Library.

Margulis, L. (1998). *Symbiotic Planet: A New Look at Evolution*. New York: Basic Books.

Margulis, L. & Sagan, D. (1987). *Microcosmos: Four Billion Years of Evolution from Our Microbial Ancestors*. New York: HarperCollins.

Maslow, A. H. (1962). *Towards a Psychology of Being*. New York: Van Nostrand.

Mathews, F. (2003). *For Love of Matter: A Contemporary Panpsychism*. Albany, NY: SUNY Press.

Mathews, F. (2009). 'Invitation to Ontopoetics'. *PAN Philosophy Activism Nature*, 6.

Mathews, F. (2017). 'Panpsychism'. In G. Oppy & N. Trakakis (Eds.) *Interreligious Philosophical Dialogues*. Volume 1. London: Routledge.

Mathews, F. (2019). 'Living Cosmos Panpsychism'. In W. Seager (Ed.) *The Routledge Handbook of Panpsychism*. London: Routledge.

Mathews, F. (2021). *The Ecological Self*. London: Routledge.

Mathews, F. (2023). *The Dao of Civilization*. London: Anthem Press.

Maturana, H. & Varela, F. (1980). *Autopoiesis and Cognition: Realization of the Living*. 2nd Edition. New York: Springer.

Maturana, H. & Varela, F. (2008). *The Tree of Knowledge*. Boston, MA: Shambhala.

McChrystal, S., Collins, T., Silverman, D. & Fussell, C. (2015). *Team of Teams: New Rules of Engagement for a Complex World*. New York: Penguin.

McGee, B. (1998). *The Story of Thought: The Essential Guide to the History of Western Philosophy*. London: The Quality Paperback Book Club.

McGilchrist, I. (2009). *The Master and the Emissary: The Divided Brain and the Making of the Western World*. New Haven, CT: Yale University Press.

McGilchrist, I. (2021). *The Matter with Things: Our Brains, Our Delusions and the Unmaking of the World*. Volumes I and II. London: Perspectiva Press.

McGilchrist, I. (2022). Available at: https://channelmcgilchrist.com/ (Accessed 29 August 2023).

Meadows, D. (1991). 'Change Is Not Doom'. *ReVision*, 142: 56–60.

Meadows, D. (2008). *Thinking in Systems*. White River Junction, VT: Chelsea Green Publishing.

Mehrabian, A. (1972). *Nonverbal Communication*. New Brunswick: Aldine Transaction.

Mitchell, H., Hamilton, T., Steggerda, R. & Bean, H. (1945). 'The Chemical Composition of the Adult Human Body and Its Bearing on the Biochemistry of Growth'. *Journal of Biological Chemistry*, 158: 625–637.

Montaigne, M. (1893). *The Essays of Montaigne*. Translated by J. Florio. Edited with an Introduction by G. Saintsbury. London: D. Nutt.

Mosquin, T. & Rowe, S. (2004). 'A Manifesto for Earth'. *Biodiversity*, 5 (1): 3–9. Available at: www.ecospherics.net

Murdoch, I. (1970). *The Sovereignty of the Good*. Abingdon: Routledge.

Naess, A. & Sessions, G. (1986). 'The Basic Principles of Deep Ecology'. *The Trumpeter*, 3(4). Available at: https://trumpeter.athabascau.ca/index.php/trumpet/article/view/579 (Accessed January 2024).

Naess, A. (1987). 'Self-realization: An Ecological Approach to Being in the World'. *The Trumpeter*, 4 (3): 35–42.

Naess, A. & Rothenberg, D. (2011). *Ecology, Community and Lifestyle*. Cambridge: Cambridge University Press.

NASA. (2022a). 'Vital Signs of the Planet'. Available at: https://climate.nasa.gov/vital-signs/ (Accessed 23 October 2023).

NASA. (2022b). 'Climate Change: How Do We Know?' Available at: https://climate.nasa.gov/evidence/ (Accessed 20 June 2022).

NASA. (2023). Available at: https://science.nasa.gov/astrophysics/focus-areas/what-is-dark-energy/ (Accessed 19 January 2024).

National Oceanic and Atmospheric Administration (NOAA). (2022). 'What Is Ocean Acidification?' Available at: https://www.pmel.noaa.gov/co2/story/ (Accessed 20 June 2023).

Next Step Solutions (NSS). (2023). Available at: https://www.nssbehavioralhealth.com/nss-blog-the-state-of-mental-health-in-america-2023-adult-prevalence (Accessed 20 January 2024).

Nicholl, M. (1952) [1984]. *Psychological Commentaries on the Teaching of Gurdjieff and Ouspensky*. Volumes 1–3. London: Vincent Stuart Ltd.

O'Donohue, J. (2003). *Beauty the Invisible Embrace: Rediscovering the True Stories of Compassion, Serenity, and Hope*. New York: Bantam Press.

Ouspensky, P. D. (1957). *The Fourth Way: A Record of Talks and Answers to Questions Based on the Teaching of G. I. Gurdjieff*. London: Routledge & Kegan Paul.

Ovid. (1922). *Metamorphoses*. Translated by B. More. Boston, MA: Cornhill Publishing Co.

Palmer, P. J. (2004). *A Hidden Wholeness: The Journey Toward an Undivided Life*. San Francisco, CA: Jossey Bass.

Palmer, P. J. (2018). *On the Brink of Everything: Grace, Gravity & Getting Old*. San Francisco, CA: Berrett-Koehler Inc.

Parks, J. (2022). 'Poem' from Personal Correspondence with Peter Hawkins.

Parlett, M. (2015). *Future Sense: Five Explorations of Whole Intelligence for a World That's Waking Up*. Leicester: Matador.

Parlett, M. & Hawkins, P. (2023). 'In Conversation on the Five Capacities'. Available at: https://www.renewalassociates.co.uk/renewal-foundation/scholars-in-residence/

Paz, O. (1995). *The Double Flame: Love and Eroticism*. Translated by H. Lane. New York: Harcourt Bruce & Company.

Petrie, N. (2014). *The How-To of Vertical Leadership Development–Part 2*. Retrieved September 29, 2024, from https://static1.squarespace.com/static/660c6c79cf17854ea0682aee/t/6618995386b32742e1c42795/1712888166080/Vertical+Development+Part+II.pdf.

Plato. (1970a). 'Phaedrus'. In *Dialogues of Plato* (pp. 239–299). Translated by B. Jowett. London: Sphere Books.

Plato. (1970b). 'The Symposium'. In *Dialogues of Plato* (pp. 179–239). Translated by B. Jowett. London: Sphere Books.

Plotinus (1966–1988). *The Enneads*. 7 Volumes. Translated by A. Armstrong. London: Heinemann.

Plumwood, V. (2006). 'The Concept of a Cultural Landscape: Nature, Culture and Agency of the Land'. *Ethics and the Environment*, 11 (2):115–150. DOI:10.1353/een.2007.0005.

Polman, P. & Winston, A. (2021). *Net Positive: How Companies Can Thrive by Giving More Than They Take*. Cambridge, MA: Harvard Business Review Press.

Popper, K. (1959) [1934]. *The Logic of Scientific Discovery*. Translation of the *Logik der Forschung*. London: Routledge.

Prigogine, I. & Stengers, E. (1984). *Order Out of Chaos*. New York: Bantam Books.

Puett, M. & Gross-Loh, C. (2016). *The Path: A New Way to Think About Everything*. New York: Simon and Schuster.

Pulman, P. (2018). *His Dark Materials: A Trilogy*. London: Scholastic.

Ravindra, R. (2014). *The Pilgrim Soul: A Path to the Sacred*. Wheaton, IL: Quest Books.

Raworth, K. (2017). *Doughnut Economics: Seven Ways to Think Like a 21st-Century Economist*. London: Penguin.

Reason, P. (1994). *Participation in Human Inquiry*. London: Sage.

Reason, P. (2017). *Search of Grace: An Ecological Pilgrimage*. Winchester: John Hunt Publishing.

Reason, P. (2023a). 'The Sacred as Immanent in a Sentient World'. *Pari Perspectives*, 15: 42–51.

Reason, P. (2023b). 'Extending Co-operative Inquiry Beyond the Human: Ontopoetic Inquiry with Rivers'. *Action Research*: 1–21.

Reason, P. & Bradbury, H. (Eds.) (2001). *Handbook of Action Research*. London: Sage.

Reason, P. & Bradbury, H. (2004). 'Action Research: Purpose Vision and Mission'. *Action Research*, 2 (1).

Reason, P. & Hawkins, P. (1988). 'Storytelling as Inquiry'. In P. Reason (Ed.) *Human Inquiry in Action.* London: Sage.

Rennaker, M. A. (2022). *Essentials of Followership: Rethinking the Leadership Paradigm with Purpose.* Dubuque, IA: Kendall Hunt Publishing Company.

Rifkin, J. (2009). *The Empathic Civilization.* New York: Tarcher Perigee.

Rifkin, J. (2022). *The Age of Resilience: Reimagining Existence on a Rewilding Earth.* London: Swift Press.

Rohr, R. (2009). *The Naked Now: Learning to See as the Mystics.* New York: Crossroad Publishing Company.

Rooke, D. & Torbert, W. R. (2005). 'Seven Transformations of Leadership'. *Harvard Business Review*, 83 (4): 66–76.

Rooke, D., et al. (2021). 'Harthill Leadership Development Framework'. Unpublished Research Compiled from Leadership Surveys with Senior Leaders Across Mainly Europe. Monmouth, Wales: Harthill Consulting.

Rose, D. B. (1992). *Dingo Make Us Human.* Cambridge: Cambridge University Press.

Rovelli, C. (2017). *Reality Is Not What It Seems: The Journey to Quantum Gravity.* London: Penguin.

Rowe, S. (2006). *Earth Alive: Essays on Ecology.* Edmonton: New West Press.

Roy, A. (2002). *The Algebra of Infinite Justice.* London: Flamingo/Harper Collins.

Rumi, J. (1977). *The Mathnawi.* Translated by R. Nicholson. London: Luzac & Co.

Rumi, J. (1995). *The Essential Rumi.* Translated from Persian by C. Barks and J. Moyne. London: HarperCollins.

Rumi, J. (2003). *The Book of Love: Poems of Ecstasy and Longing.* Translated by C. Barks. New York: Harper Collins.

Rumi, J. (2004). *Selected Poems.* Translated by C. Barks with J. Moyne, A. Arberry & R. Nicholson. London: Penguin.

Ruskin, J. (1894). *Modern Painters: Vol II. Of Ideas of Beauty.* Orpington: George Allen.

Ryle, G. (1967). *The Concept of Mind.* Chicago, IL: University of Chicago Press.

Sacks, J. (2018). *Morality in the 21st Century Podcasts.* London: BBC Sounds.

Salami, M. (2020). *Sensuous Knowledge: A Black Feminist Approach for Everyone.* London: Bloomsbury.

Sample, S. (2003). *The Contrarian's Guide to Leadership.* San Francisco, CA: Jossey-Bass.

Sanchez, A. (2017). *The Four Sacred Gifts: Indigenous Wisdom for Modern Times.* New York: Simon & Schuster.

Sardello, R. (2012). *The Power of Soul.* London: Goldenstone Press.

Scharmer, C. (2007). *Theory U: Leading from the Future as It Emerges: The Social Technology of Presencing.* Cambridge: Society for Organisational Learning.

Scharmer, O. & Kaufer, K. (2013). *Leading from the Emerging Future – From Ego-System to Eco-System Economies.* San Francisco, CA: Berrett-Koehler Inc.

Schon, D. (1983). *The Reflective Practitioner.* New York: Basic Books.

Schrödinger, E. (1951). *Science and Humanism, Physics in Our Time.* Cambridge: Cambridge University Press.

Schwab, K. (2016). *The Fourth Industrial Revolution.* Surrey Hills, NSW: Currency Press.

Schweitzer, A. (1987). *The Philosophy of Civilization.* New York: Prometheus Books.

Schweitzer, A. (2009). *Out of My Life and Thought: An Autobiography [Aus meinem Leben und Denken].* Translated by Antje Bultmann Lemke. Baltimore, MD: Johns Hopkins University Press.

Scranton, R. (2015). *Learning to Die in the Anthropocene: Reflections on the End of Civilization.* San Francisco, CA: City Light Books.

Scruton, R. (2011). *Beauty: A Very Short Introduction.* Oxford: Oxford University Press.

Seligman, M. (2011). *Flourish.* Boston, MA: Nicholas Brearley Publishing.

Seligman, M. & Csikszentmihalyi, M. (2000). 'Positive Psychology: An Introduction'. *American Psychologist*, 55 (1): 5–14.

Senge, P. (1990). *The Fifth Discipline: The Art and Practice of the Learning Organization.* New York: Doubleday.

Senge, P. (2008). *The Necessary Revolution: How Individuals and Organizations Are Working Together to Create a Sustainable World.* New York: Doubleday.

Senge, P., Flowers, B., Scharmer, O. & Jaworski, J. (2005). *Presence: An Exploration of Profound Change in People, Organizations, and Society.* New York: Doubleday Publishing.

Shakespeare, W. (1609). 'Sonnet 18, "Shall I Compare Thee to a Summer's Day"'. Available at: https://www.poetryfoundation.org/poems/45087/sonnet-18-shall-i-compare-thee-to-a-summers-day (Accessed 5 November 2023).

Sharpe, B. (2013). *Three Horizons: The Patterning of Hope.* Axminster: Triarchy Press.

Shotter, J. (1993). *Cultural Politics of Everyday Life: Social Constructionism, Rhetoric and Knowing of the Third Kind.* Toronto: University of Toronto Press.

Siegel, D. (2010). *Mindsight.* London: Oneworld Publications.

Sloman, S. & Fernbach, P. (2017). *The Knowledge Illusion: Why We Never Think Alone.* New York: Penguin.

Smuts, J. (1927). *Holism and Evolution.* Moscow: Рипол Классик.

Snyder, G. (1995). *Place in Space: Ethics, Aesthetics and Watersheds.* Washington, DC: Counterpoint.

Solnit, R. (2016) [2004]. *Hope in the Dark.* London: Haymarket Books.

Speth, G. (2023). 'Interview'. Available at: https://earthcharter.org/podcasts/gus-speth/ (Accessed 13 February 2024).

Spinoza, B. (1954). *Ethics.* Edited with an Introduction by J. Gutmann. New York: Hafner Publishing Company.

Stevens, W. (1967). 'Sunday Morning'. In *The Making of Harmonium.* Princeton, NJ: Princeton University Press.

Stevenson, R. (1883). *The Silverado Squatters.* London: Chatto and Windus.

Stolorow, R. & Atwood, G. (1992). *Context of Being: The Intersubjective Foundations of Psychological Life.* Hilldale, NJ: The Analytic Press.

Swift, J. (1711). 'Thoughts on Various Subjects, Moral and Diverting'. Available at: https://www.gutenberg.org/files/623/623-h/623-h.htm

Sylvan, R. & Bennet, D. (1994). *The Greening of Ethics: From Human Chauvinism to Deep-Green Theory.* Cambridge: White Horse Press.

Tagore, R. (1997). *Rabindranath Tagore: An Anthology.* Edited by A. Robinson. London: Saint Martin's Press.

Tarnas, R. (1991). *The Passion of the Western Mind: Understanding the Ideas That Have Shaped Our World View.* New York: Ballantine.

Taylor, F. W. (1911). *The Principles of Scientific Management.* New York: Harper Brothers.

Tennyson, A. (1850). *In Memoriam.* London: Edward Moxon.

Tillich, P. (1958). 'The Lost Dimension in Religion'. *Saturday Evening Post*, 230 (50): 28–29 & 76–79.

Tirthankar, R. (2012). *The East India Company: The World's Most Powerful Corporation.* London: Penguin.

Tolstoy, L. (1922–23) [1869]. *War and Peace.* Translated by A. Maude & L. Maude. Oxford: Oxford University Press (Revised by A. Mandelker (2010). Oxford University Press).

Torbert, B. (2004). *Action Inquiry: The Secret of Timely and Transforming Leadership.* San Francisco, CA: Berrett-Koehler Inc.

Toulmin, S. (1990). *Cosmopolis: The Hidden Agenda of Modernity.* Chicago, IL: University of Chicago Press.

Toynbee, A. (1961) [1934]. *A Study of History. Volume 12 – Reconsiderations.* Oxford: Oxford University Press.

Traherne, T. (1908). 'Centuries of Meditations'. Available at: https://ccel.org/ccel/traherne/centuries (Accessed 11 January 2024).

Turner, E. & Hawkins, P. (2016). 'Multi-stakeholder Contracting in Executive/Business Coaching: An Analysis of Practice and Recommendations for Gaining Maximum Value'. *International Journal of Evidence Based Coaching and Mentoring,* 14 (2): 48–65.

United Nations. (2019). 'Blog on UN Report: Nature's Dangerous Decline "Unprecedented"; Species Extinction Rates "Accelerating"'. Available at: https://www.un.org/sustainabledevelopment/blog/2019/05/nature-decline-unprecedented-report/ (Accessed 25 June 2023).

United Nations Declaration on Human Rights. (1948). Available at: https://www.un.org/en/about-us/universal-declaration-of-human-rights (Accessed 25 June 2023).

United Nations Sustainable Development Goals. (2015). Available at: https://sdgs.un.org/

Ury, W. (2007). *The Power of a Positive No: How to Say No and Still Get to Yes.* New York: Random House.

Van Gennep, A. (1977) [1909]. *Les Rites de Passage (in French).* Paris: Émile Nourry. [*The Rites of Passage.* Translated by M. Vizedom & G. Caffee. Hove: Psychology Press].

Van Gogh, V. (1997). *The Letters of Vincent Van Gogh.* Edited by R. de Leauw. London: Penguin.

Varela, F. (1991). 'Organism – "A Meshwork of Selfless Selves"'. In A. Tauber (Ed.) *Organism and the Origin of Self.* New York: Springer.

Varela, F. (1999). *Ethical Know-How: Action, Wisdom and Cognition.* Stanford, CA: Stanford University Press.

Vaughan-Lee, L. (2021). *Seasons of the Sacred: Reconnecting to the Wisdom within Nature and the Soul.* Point Reyes, CA: The Golden Sufi Center.

Vaughan-Lee, L. & Hart, H. (2017). *Spiritual Ecology. 10 Practices to Reawaken the Sacred in Everyday Life.* Point Reyes, CA: The Golden Sufi Center.

Waldock, T. (2017). *To Plant a Walnut Tree: How to Create a Fruitful Legacy by Using Your Experience.* London: Nicholas Brearly.

Waldock, T. (2021). *Becoming Mandela: Be Your legacy.* London: Neilsen.

Watts, A. (1975). *Tao: The Watercourse Way.* New York: Pantheon Books.

Weber, A. (2016). *The Biology of Wonder. Aliveness, Feeling, and the Metamorphosis of Science.* Gabriola Island, BC: New Society Press.

Weber, A. (2017). *Matter and Desire: An Erotic Ecology.* Chelsea Vermont: Chelsea Green.

Weber, A. (2019). *Enlivenment: Toward a Poetics of the Anthropocene.* Cambridge, MA: Massachusetts Institute of Technology.

Weil, S. (2005). 'Human Personality'. In *Simone Weil: An Anthology.* London: Penguin Classics.

Weller, F. (2015). *The Wild Edge of Sorrow: Rituals of Renewal and the Sacred Work of Grief.* Berkeley, CA: North Atlantic Books.

Whybrow, A., Turner, E., McLean, J. & Hawkins, P. (2023). *Ecological and Climate-Conscious Coaching: A Companion Guide to Evolving Coaching Practice.* London: Routledge.

Williams, T. (2009). *Finding Beauty in a Broken World*. New York: Vintage Books.

Wilson, E. (1984). *Biophilia*. Cambridge, MA: Harvard University Press.

Wilson, M. (2018, March 30). 'How a Handful of Soil Holds More Than 50 Billion Life Forms'. *Financial Times*. Available at: https://www.ft.com/content/2833fdee-2dbe-11e8-97ec-4bd3494d5f14 (Accessed 29 September 2024).

Winnicott, D. (1964). *The Child, the Family and the Outside World*. London: Penguin.

Winnicott, D. (1965). *Maturational Processes and the Facilitating Environment*. London: Hogarth Press.

Wirzba, N. (2021). *This Sacred Life: Humanity's Place in a Wounded World*. Cambridge: Cambridge University Press.

Wordsworth, W. (1798, July 13). 'Lines, Composed a Few Miles Above Tintern Abbey, on Revisiting the Banks of the Wye During a Tour'. Available at: https://www.gutenberg.org/files/12145/12145-h/12145-h.htm (Accessed 11 January 2024).

Wordsworth, W. (1850). 'The Prelude' (Published Posthumously). Available at: https://www.gutenberg.org/files/12383/12383-h/12383-h.htm (Accessed 11 January 2024).

World Bank. (2023). Available at: https://www.worldbank.org/en/topic/urbandevelopment/overview (Accessed 22 August 2023).

World Health Organization (WHO). (2023). Available at: https://www.who.int/teams/mental-health-and-substance-use/world-mental-health-report (Accessed 20 January 2024).

WWF. (2022). 'Threats: Soil Erosion and Degradation: Overview'. Available at: https://www.worldwildlife.org/threats/soil-erosion-and-degradation (Accessed 25 January 2023).

Young, E. (2018). 'Lifting the Lid on the Unconscious'. *New Scientist*. Available at: https://www.newscientist.com/article/mg23931880-400-lifting-the-lid-on-the-unconscious/ (Accessed 12 June 2023).

Zeldin, T. (1998). *Conversation: How Talk Can Change Your Life*. London: Harvill Press.

Index

Printed in the United States
by Baker & Taylor Publisher Services

Printed in the United States
by Baker & Taylor Publisher Services